HETCH HETCHY

THE **BROADVIEW**
SOURCES SERIES

Hetch Hetchy

A HISTORY IN DOCUMENTS

edited by CHAR MILLER

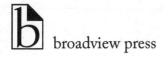

broadview press

BROADVIEW PRESS – www.broadviewpress.com
Peterborough, Ontario, Canada

Founded in 1985, Broadview Press remains a wholly independent publishing house. Broadview's focus is on academic publishing; our titles are accessible to university and college students as well as scholars and general readers. With 800 titles in print, Broadview has become a leading international publisher in the humanities, with world-wide distribution. Broadview is committed to environmentally responsible publishing and fair business practices.

Library and Archives Canada Cataloguing in Publication

Title: Hetch Hetchy : a history in documents / edited by Char Miller.
Names: Miller, Char, 1951- editor.
Series: Broadview sources series.
Description: Series statement: The Broadview sources series | Includes bibliographical references.
Identifiers: Canadiana (print) 20190233222 | Canadiana (ebook) 20190233257 | ISBN 9781554814404 (softcover) | ISBN 9781770487321 (PDF) | ISBN 9781460406885 (HTML)
Subjects: LCSH: Water-supply—California—San Francisco—Sources. | LCSH: Hetch Hetchy Reservoir (Calif.)—Sources. | LCSH: Hetch Hetchy Valley (Calif.)—Sources. | LCSH: Yosemite National Park (Calif.)—Sources. | LCSH: Reservoir drawdown—California—Hetch Hetchy Valley—Sources.
Classification: LCC TD225.S25 H48 2020 | DDC 363.6/10979447—dc23

Broadview Press handles its own distribution in North America:
PO Box 1243, Peterborough, Ontario K9J 7H5, Canada
555 Riverwalk Parkway, Tonawanda, NY 14150, USA
Tel: (705) 743-8990; Fax: (705) 743-8353
email: customerservice@broadviewpress.com

For all territories outside of North America, distribution is handled by Eurospan Group.

Canadä Broadview Press acknowledges the financial support of the Government of Canada for our publishing activities.

Copy-edited by Juliet Sutcliffe
Book design by Em Dash Design

PRINTED IN CANADA

CONTENTS

ACKNOWLEDGEMENTS

Historians never work alone, and this project is one more demonstration of that reality. I am indebted most of all to this volume's many contributors, living and dead, whose insights and arguments have framed the evolution of the Hetch Hetchy controversy. I am grateful as well to the remarkable archivists and librarians who have made many relevant collections accessible and online: the National Archives, the Library of Congress, YosemiteOnline, and many other repositories, public and private, have digitized reams of material that have sustained this project. My colleagues in Special Collections at the Claremont Colleges Library—Ayat Agah, Lisa Crane, and Carrie Marsh—once again have been indispensable. Leslie Dema, Stephen Latta, and the editorial team at Broadview Press, along with the anonymous external reviewers, have sharpened my ideas and expanded my understanding of this book's many possibilities. I owe considerable thanks to Pomona College for a sabbatical during which I conducted the bulk of research for this project, and to its David L. Hirsch III and Susan H. Hirsch Research Initiation Grant for its generous support. At the college's Humanities Studio, Director Kevin Dettmar and Program Coordinator Gretchen Rognlien provided a rich and collegial environment in which to write (and drink coffee). Joseph Lent, Tribal Historic Preservation Officer of the Bridgeport Indian Colony, was especially helpful at key moments in this project, as was University of Colorado historian Patricia Limerick. I am grateful to my wife Judi Lipsett for letting me babble about Hetch Hetchy every now and again. This project is dedicated to my students in EA 199: Native American and Environmental Histories, who taught me to think much more carefully about how past injustices are thickly woven into the foundations of the US environmental movement.

INTRODUCTION

Some environmental issues appear unending, driven by a kind of self-perpetuating energy. One of these is the enduring controversy that has surrounded the Hetch Hetchy Reservoir and O'Shaughnessy Dam complex since its construction in Yosemite National Park was first debated in the early years of the twentieth century. As evidence, consider these two related events that occurred in the second decade of the twenty-first century.

In March 2014, the San Francisco Board of Supervisors unanimously passed a law banning the sale and distribution of plastic water bottles on public property, legislation that would apply to all events on city-owned land—including streets—beginning in January 2018. One key motivation for the legislation was the massive carbon footprint of bottled water; its production, distribution, and disposal consumes upwards of 2,000 times more energy than tap water. Once in effect, the ban would also slow the flow of an estimated 10–15 million bottles a year into local landfills. These significant savings dovetailed with the claims of San Francisco Public Utilities Commission President David Chiu that tap water also is "much healthier and cheaper," and that the city's waterworks provided the "the best-tasting tap water in the nation."[1]

Validating these assertions, the ban's proponents believed, was the remarkable single source of the municipal water that the Public Utility Commission (PUC) pumps to the community's faucets, fountains, and sprinklers: Sierran snowmelt that the O'Shaughnessy Dam impounds in the Hetch Hetchy reservoir. The pristine quality of this High Sierra resource was touted boldly on the reusable water bottles and jugs that the PUC distributed as part of its environmental-education campaign in support of the water-bottle ban: "Hetch Hetchy Tap Water: It's Delicious."[2]

The self-congratulatory character of this 2014 campaign might have been toned down had a November 2012 local initiative, Proposition F, prevailed at the polls. Although the proposition's formal name was innocuous enough, the "Water Sustainability and Environmental Restoration Act" was anything but. Supported by a number of environmental groups, notably the grassroots organization Restore Hetch Hetchy,[3] Proposition F would have required San

1   Bay City News Service, "San Francisco Bans Selling Plastic Water Bottles on City Property," *Mercury News*, 5 March 2014.

2   "How to Comply with the Bottled Water Ban," San Francisco Water, Power, and Sewer.

3   Restore Hetch Hetchy was established in 1999 as a spin off from the Sierra Club's Hetch Hetchy Restoration Task Force. The mission of Restore Hetch Hetchy is "to return the Hetch Hetchy Valley in Yosemite National Park to its natural splendor—while continuing to meet the water and power needs of all communities that depend on the Tuolumne River."

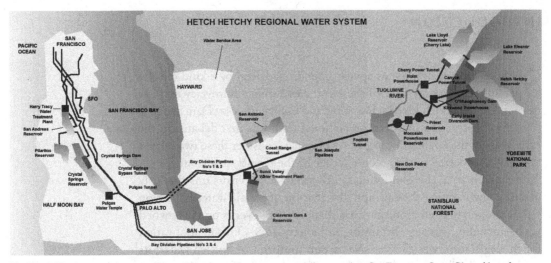

HETCH HETCHY REGIONAL WATER SYSTEM

The Hetch Hetchy regional system of water delivery provides water to 2.4 million people in San Francisco, Santa Clara, Alameda and San Mateo counties. Eighty-five percent of the water comes from Sierra Nevada snowmelt stored in the Hetch Hetchy reservoir situated on the Tuolumne River in Yosemite National Park. The system consists of over 280 miles of pipelines, over 60 miles of tunnels, 11 reservoirs, 5 pump stations, and 2 water treatment plants and delivers approximately 260 million gallons of water per day.
Bay Area Water Supply and Conservation Agency, http://bawsca.org/water/supply/hetchhetchy

Francisco, which receives 100 per cent of its potable water supplies from the reservoir, to develop a two-phase plan to evaluate how to drain the Hetch Hetchy Reservoir and identify replacement water and power sources. Given the community's dependence on this sole source of water, the outcome was never in doubt; Proposition F garnered 23 per cent of the vote.[4]

Yet the fact that the reservoir is still making headlines illustrates just how intertwined the past and present can be. Those contending over Proposition F, for example, drew heavily on the pro-and-con arguments that their predecessors had developed in the initial fight over the dam and reservoir. That they borrowed from the past to make their contemporary case is a testament to how well their predecessors spoke to the future of the nation, its wealth and welfare. On the one hand, the O'Shaughnessy Dam has been crucial to the growth and development of San Francisco and the larger Bay Area, just as its early-twentieth-century advocates had envisioned it would be. To them, the dam's construction was emblematic of Progressive-Era reforms that provided essential—and publicly owned—resources to an urbanizing society, and did so efficiently, effectively, and equitably. On the other hand, the idea of a dam built inside a national park designed to protect and preserve iconic landscapes sparked a potent pushback from such legendary conservationists as John Muir, founding president of the Sierra Club (est. 1892). For Muir and his allies across the country, many of whom also thought

---

4   San Francisco Hetch Hetchy Reservoir Initiative, Proposition F (November 2012), Ballotpedia.

of themselves as progressives, the destruction of what they believed was a wild and sacred Hetch Hetchy Valley was far too high a cost to pay for San Francisco's economic gain and public health.

Despite their differences, each group believed that their vociferous debate was a pitched battle between Good and Evil (they just disagreed on who was blessed and who was damned). What neither side admitted, however, was that their respective arguments also depended on a shared perception of Hetch Hetchy—that no one lived there, that it was empty. Its emptiness, for those supporting the dam's construction, would be turned to good use as a reservoir. Its emptiness, for those like Muir who pressed for the valley's preservation, was a mark of its higher utility as *wilderness*, as pristine nature. Yet to conceive of this central Sierran landscape as devoid of people and untouched by human hands required two forms of erasure.

The first occurred in the mid-nineteenth century, when California and the United States governments sanctioned the violent expulsion of the Indigenous nations from the Sierras, its flanking valleys, and foothills. The brutal dispossession of the Miwok, Numu (Paiute), Newe (Shoshone), and others from their ancestral territories was an act of genocide, historian Benjamin Madley argues. Noting that the "pressures of demographics (the migration of hundreds of thousands of immigrants), economics (the largest gold rush in US history), and profound racial hatred all made the genocide possible, it also took sustained political will—at both the federal and state levels—to create the laws, policies, and well-funded killing machine that carried it out and ensured its continuation over decades."[5]

The second erasure is embedded in the disquieting silence ever since about the interlocking connection between the ruthless uprooting of Indigenous people from the Yosemite region, the establishment of the national park, and the subsequent Hetch Hetchy controversy. Until that silence is broken, our understanding of the ongoing debate about the dam and reservoir will remain incomplete. This accounting is especially necessary because scholars and activists assert that the original battle over Hetch Hetchy marked the birth of the modern environmental movement in the United States.[6] What that assertion reveals is a troubled and troubling origin story that ignores those with ancestral ties to the valley (and elsewhere) whose lived experience has been largely expunged from the historical record. This innovative collection of documents attempts to rewrite and reengage with this more complicated history by probing the dynamic interplay between land, people, and politics.

---

5   Benjamin Madley, *An American Genocide: The United States and the California Indian Catastrophe, 1846–1873* (New Haven: Yale UP, 2016), 13.

6   Robert W. Richter, *The Battle Over Hetch Hetchy: America's Most Controversial Dam and the Birth of Modern Environmentalism* (New York: Oxford UP, 2005); Roderick Frazier Nash, *Wilderness and the American Mind*, 5th ed. (New Haven: Yale UP, 2014), 161–81.

Hetch Hetchy Valley, Sierra Nevada Mts., California, c. 1911.
Library of Congress, https://www.loc.gov/item/2007660474/

PLACE AND PEOPLE

Start with the physical world itself. The Sierra Nevada range, which extends more than 250 miles from the Mojave Desert northward to the Cascades, is asymmetrical. Its eastern side is a short, steep escarpment that rises above the Owens River valley. The western front offers a longer and gentler descent into the Central Valley. Structurally, the Sierras are a massive granite block, and are the product of millions of years of geologic evolution. Once buried deep beneath the earth's surface, the range's granite core became exposed towards the close of the Cretaceous period, roughly 65 million years ago. Then low in elevation, the landscape began to be uplifted and tilted 25 million years ago, a slow process that created the jagged and rough terrain that would result in some of the highest elevations in what would become the United States. The uplift also increased stream gradients, which sped up the flow of water across the exposed granite and accelerated its capacity to cut deep into the rock formation: the Merced River, for example, created a 3,000-foot-deep canyon that is the predecessor of present-day Yosemite Valley; the ancestral Tuolumne River carved out a canyon subsequently known as the Hetch Hetchy Valley. Fifteen million years later, these canyons were filled in by mudflows and volcanic lava, and once again the region's rivers and streams began to carve through this material, an erosive force that has continued ever since. Just as powerful were the Ice-Age glaciers that formed in the Sierra upwards of two to three million years ago. Their grinding energy scoured the still rising and tilting range, and, when the ice started to melt about 12,000 years ago, left behind were u-shaped canyons, valleys, and alpine lakes, and tons of glacial till and sediment; now-swift rivers swept much of the rocky debris downstream and into the Central Valley.[7]

Over these eons emerged the spectacular outcroppings and domes, water-falls, rivers, and verdant valleys in the Yosemite region that have sustained and inspired Indigenous people for millennia. The ancestors of contemporary Indigenous people in California arrived in the region ~12,000 years ago. Across that long stretch of time, each and every day the "indigenous people of California interacted with the native plants and animals that surrounded them," observes ethnobotanist M. Kat Anderson. These intentional interac-tions were transformative: Indigenous people turned "roots, berries, shoots, bones, shells and feathers into medicines, meals, bows, and baskets." They burned, tilled, and weeded; seeded, tended, and harvested, an annual and precise management that produced dependable results: "California Indians were able to harvest the foods and basketry and construction materials they needed each year while conserving—and sometimes increasing—the plant populations from which they came." Theirs was, Anderson notes, a "tempered use of nature," a deliberate stewardship that made them "active agents of environmental change."[8]

This long-practiced management held true for those who made their homes in and learned to reap and enhance the rich biota along the Pacific coast, around bays, rivers, and estuaries, or the broad interior valleys, as well as for those who inhabited the high country of the Sierra. There, the Miwok, Numu/Paiute, and Newe/Shoshone fished and hunted, fabricated clothing, and constructed housing and other structures. They built grana-ries and ovens, harvested pine needles, pitch, branches, and roots for toys, bedding, basketry, and necklaces and clothing. They used fire to maintain meadows and inhibit the growth of some plants and select for those they prized, including deergrass (for baskets), California black oak (for acorns), and Pinyon (for seeds). Other flora were planted, irrigated, and reaped each year, a rate of annual production and processing, for example, that is signaled in the 600 granite mortar holes that archeologists have located in and around Yosemite's Big Meadows, holes that Indigenous people used to grind acorns and other food products.[9] Similar management occurred in the Hetch Hetchy Valley, and its inhabitants, the Numu/Paiute, are also

---

7 N. King Huber, "The Geologic Story of Yosemite National Park," Bulletin 1595 (Washington, DC: US Geological Survey and US National Park Service, 1987), 10–57.

8 M. Kat Anderson, *Tending the Wild: Native American Knowledge and the Management of California's Natural Resources* (Berkeley: U of California P, 2005), 1–2.

9 Anderson, *Tending the Wild*, 42, 130, 156, 171–74, 218–26, 281–86.

credited with successfully transplanting pinyon to this higher altitude, testified by relict groves.[10]

The Indigenous people's insight and labor, tested, and repeated over the centuries, produced an intimate understanding of the land and its resources that is also reflected in their creation stories, naming practices, cosmology and ritual, as well as oral histories. Some of these, notes Anderson, "place the origins of plants, animals, and people, and the earth in the very heart of the respective tribal territory." And should a community forget this binding together, this life-affirming mutuality, other stories detailed the dire consequences. According to the Miwok, when one of its ancient chiefs did not pray for sufficient rain to water the earth, the angered Creator split Yosemite's Half Dome, arguably the most iconic geological structure in the valley.[11]

By word and deed, Indigenous people had so thoroughly woven themselves into the Sierra that to outsiders the results of their multi-millennia management seemed natural, that is, was *Nature*. John Muir was among those who mistook the rich biota for an unspoiled Eden. When he first visited Hetch Hetchy in 1871–72, he found that it was "a wonderfully exact counterpart of the great Yosemite, not only in its crystal river and sublime rocks and waterfalls, but in the gardens, groves, and meadows of its flower park-like floor." Awed by its magnificent groves, and struck by a plethora of "shrubs forming conspicuous flowery clumps and tangles," he cataloged their abundance—"manzanita, azalea, spiraea, brier-rose, ceanothus, calycanthus, philadelphus, wild cherry, etc." He reveled in the thick carpet of lilies, tulips, and orchids, iris, columbine, goldenrods, sunflowers, and mints, and the many species of fern that fringed rock and ledge and rose up beneath oak and pine. This rapturous listing was an important component of Muir's denunciation of those who wished to inundate the valley for a reservoir. If they succeeded, they would destroy Hetch Hetchy's purity, its holiness; this "grand landscape garden," he asserted, is "one of Nature's rarest and most precious mountain mansions."[12] Where Muir saw the hand of God, M. Kat

10 Joseph Lent, "Bridgeport Yosemite Paiutes: Who We Are," in *Voices of the People by the Traditionally Associated Tribes of Yosemite National Park* (Yosemite Conservancy, 2019), 101–03.

11 Anderson, *Tending the Wild*, 37, 57; Frank R. LaPena, Craig D. Bates, and Steven P. Medley, *The Legends of the Yosemite Miwok* (Yosemite: The Yosemite Association, 1993), vii–xii; Gaylen D. Lee, *Walking Where We Lived: Memoirs of a Mono Indian Family* (Norman: U of Oklahoma P, 1998), 6–7, 16.

12 John Muir, "The Hetch Hetchy Valley," *Sierra Club Bulletin* 6, 4 (January 1908): 211–20. That Muir's perspective has dominated the management ethos of Yosemite National Park is illustrated by the agency's longstanding disregard of the Indigenous populations in the Yosemite region. Mark David Spence, *Dispossessing the Wilderness: Indian Removal and the Making of the National Parks* (New York: Oxford UP, 1999), 101–32; Marguerite S. Shaffer, "Performing Bears and Packaged Wilderness: Reframing the History of National Parks," in Char Miller, ed., *Cities and Nature in the American West* (Reno: U of Nevada P, 2010), 137–53; it took the Miwok more than 40 years of negotiations with park management to secure the right to rebuild a traditional village that the National Park Service bulldozed in 1969: Carmen George, "Decades after Destruction, Yosemite Welcomes Home Native Americans," *Fresno Bee*, 2 June 2018.

Carleton Watkins's (1829–1916) stereograph of Tutocanula or El Capitan is among the many images that captured the imagination of Americans about Yosemite's stunning landscapes.
Library of Congress, https://www.loc.gov/item/2005696761/

Anderson sees the human imprint: "Muir was eyeing what was really the fertile seed, bulb, and greens gathering grounds" of local Indigenous people, "kept open and productive by centuries of carefully planned indigenous burning, harvesting, and seed gathering."[13]

CHANGE AGENTS

Actually, Muir bore witness to a diminishing remnant of Indigenous peoples' careful cultivation and sustained stewardship. He had arrived in the central Sierra in 1868, two decades after invading miners and ranchers had begun disrupting the capacity of Indigenous peoples to continuously manage these Indigenous landscapes. By then, too, photographers and artists had unpacked their cameras and paint and brushes to capture Yosemite's iconic scenery, its views and vistas, images that drew awed visitors to museums and galleries in San Francisco and eastern cities. Carleton Watkins's stunning 1861 photographs of El Capitan not only were displayed in the Paris and Philadelphia World's Fairs, but their framing strongly influenced other artistic impressions of the massive granite formation, including Albert Bierstadt's 1870s paintings.[14] Some enchanted viewers then made the arduous journey to see the rugged landscape for themselves, lured to the valley as well by the writings of James Mason Hutchings, who hired Muir to work at his Yosemite hotel. A relentless promoter, Hutchings drew a swelling number of artists,

13 Anderson, *Tending the Wild*, 3.
14 Tyler Green, *Carleton Watkins: Making the West American* (Berkeley: U of California P, 2018), 97–98.

scientists, and tourists to the remote location through his publication of tour guides, lithographs, and magazine articles about Yosemite's wonders and curiosities.[15] Late on the scene, Muir, who spent his first summer in the Sierra as a shepherd, initially added to Yosemite's cultural cachet by his pioneering ideas about the region's unique geology. His tramps into the highest elevations led him to speculate that glaciers had been the driving force in the creation of upcountry lakes, polished rock walls, and level valley floors. These early investigations and novel conclusions contributed to the scientific explanation of the Yosemite region's physical evolution, later a key factor in the 1890 designation of Yosemite National Park.

Yet although this pursuit of scientific knowledge seems neutral, the history of how geologists came to explore and explain the Sierra is not. Their arrival on the ground came paired with Manifest Destiny, the popular nineteenth-century conceit that God ordained the westward expansion of the United States. In this view, which many Americans—its scientists not least—fervently embraced, the nation's cross-continental imperial surge was justified and inevitable. The California State Geological Survey, whose origins lay in Gold Rush surveys that the state financed, announced that its expansive mission was to "trace out all the steps by which our planet passed from chaotic desolation up to order, life and beauty as at present exhibited on its surface."[16] To organize, catalog, and name brought structure and control, making geology a handmaiden of empire.

This framing has continued to shape discussions of the emergence of central Sierran geology, such as N. Frank Huber's 1989 report, "The Geologic Story of Yosemite National Park." Some of its first words uncritically reinforce the close relationship between Manifest Destiny and geological investigations. "From the earliest days, the Sierra Nevada ... was a formidable barrier to western exploration," exploration, that is, by Euro-Americans. In 1833, however, Joseph Walker pierced the mountainous barrier, Huber writes, leading "a party up the east escarpment and westward across the range through the Yosemite country"; the explorers followed, although Huber does not say so, well-beaten Indigenous trails across the Sierra. Unable to reach Yosemite Valley, Walker described the vista as seen from above, Yosemite's sheer chasms and towering precipices, a depiction that made him "probably the first of European descent to view Yosemite Valley and the Big Trees."[17]

---

15 Jen A. Huntley, *The Making of Yosemite: James Mason Hutchings and the Origin of America's Most Popular National Park* (Lawrence: UP of Kansas, 2011).

16 Quoted in Donald Worster, *A Passion for Nature: A Life of John Muir* (New York: Oxford UP, 2008), 190; Michael L. Smith, *Pacific Visions: California Scientists and the Environment, 1850–1915* (New Haven: Yale UP, 1988).

17 Huber, "The Geologic Story of Yosemite National Park," Bulletin 1595 (Washington, DC: US Geological Survey and US National Park Service, 1987), 1–3.

Discovery would open the way for destruction. Huber would amplify this argument when he introduces the putative second "discovery" of the valley. "Yosemite Valley and the giant sequoias remained unknown to the world at large for nearly 20 years after the Walker party's discovery, until Maj. James Savage and the Mariposa Battalion of militia entered the valley in pursuit of Indians in 1851." The 500-man battalion, responding to reports that members of the Ahwahnechee Nation had attacked white settlements, did more than just pursue the Ahwahnechee—they killed 30 or more, burned their valley villages and torched their supplies, making survival difficult for those who managed to escape into the high country. Among those the marauding Americans captured was Chief Tenaya, who subsequently signed a treaty under duress and protest that sanctioned the Ahwahnechee's forced removal to the tiny, poorly supplied, and corruptly managed Fresno Reservation in the Central Valley.[18]

The Mariposa Battalion's onslaught was part of a well-funded campaign to eradicate the Indigenous peoples of California. With support from the federal government, the state spent $1.7 million on military operations that decimated the total population of Indigenous people, cutting it from an estimated 150,000 in 1846 to 30,000 in 1873. Extermination also entailed erasure of another kind. One member of the Mariposa Battalion, Dr. Lafayette Bunnell, was, in Huber's words, "overwhelmed by the majesty of the valley ... and remarked that it needed an appropriate name. He suggested Yo-sem-ity, the name of the Indian tribe that inhabited it, and also the Indian word for grizzly bear." Bunnell was wrong on both counts: Yosemite was neither the people's name nor the term they used for *Ursus arctos californicus*; other tribes called them Yosemite (those who kill); they called themselves Ahwahnechee (those who live in Ahwahnee). But Bunnell's linguistic presumption and passive construction of his rationale for naming the valley Yo-sem-ity remains revelatory: by adopting the term Yosemite, he wrote, "the name of the tribe of Indians which we met leaving their homes in this valley, perhaps never to return, would be perpetuated." With that, the Ahwahnechee were doubly vanquished—they did not voluntarily depart their homeland, the invaders forcefully drove them from their ancestral territory; and then they stripped them of their real name.[19]

Such expropriation has been paradoxical, writes geologist Lauret Savoy. "To become oriented, to find their way and fill their maps," settler-colonists

---

18   Huber, "The Geologic Story," 1–3; Benjamin Madley, *An American Genocide: The United States and the California Indian Catastrophe, 1846–1873* (New Haven: Yale UP, 2016), 186–94; Brendan C. Lindsay, *Murder State: California's Native American Genocide, 1846–1873* (Lincoln: U of Nebraska P, 2012), 171, 240–43. The US Senate never ratified the treaty with the Ahwahnechee.

19   Madley, *An American Genocide*, 192–94; Huber, "The Geologic Story," 1–3; a fuller version of Bunnell's discussion is included in this volume on p. 000.

The O'Shaughnessy Dam is a 430-foot (131 m) high concrete arch-gravity dam that impounds the Tuolumne River, forming the Hetch Hetchy Reservoir Yosemite National Park. Named for engineer Michael O'Shaughnessy, who oversaw its construction, the dam remains a symbol of the intense debate over the inundation of the Hetch Hetchy Valley.
[source line to come]

like Bunnell—and generations before him—"needed Native people's knowledge of the land. Maps and then names would obscure that knowledge from its context, as Indigenous people themselves were removed from the land." As the United States expanded westward across the nineteenth century, and its genocidal assaults on Indigenous nations intensified, the "use of Native or native-sounding place names grew ever more popular among Anglo Americans." The poet Walt Whitman understood the reason why such terminology was re-deployed. "All the greatness of any land, at any time, lies folded in its names" because names "are the turning point of who shall be master."[20]

Such mastery was not just linguistic. The work of early photographers like Carleton Watkins, arriving in the east at the start of the Civil War, helped integrate California into the wider culture; as his biographer Tyler Green observes, Watkins's Yosemite images made the west American.[21] Geologists did their part, too, contributing to the subjugation of the Sierra. Within a

---

20 Lauret Savoy, *Trace: Memory, History, Race, and the American Landscape* (Berkeley: Counterpoint, 2015), 76, 79, 87. Savoy contextualizes Whitman's enthusiasm for Indigenous toponyms on 79–80, and 87.

21 Green, *Carleton Watkins*, 116–50.

decade of the Mariposa Battalion's genocidal cleansing of Yosemite, scientists had conducted fieldwork in and mapped the Hetch Hetchy and Yosemite valleys along with the headwaters of the Tuolumne and Merced rivers. Later geoscientists would draw on this knowledge when the city of San Francisco enlisted their technocratic expertise to determine how best to blast and drill the O'Shaughnessy Dam into bedrock and rock wall. When its construction was complete in 1923, conquest was cast in concrete.

DAM BATTLE

The O'Shaughnessy Dam is a 430-foot arch-gravity dam that backs up the waters of the Tuolumne River. The Hetch Hetchy reservoir then feeds this captured flow into a highly engineered system of tunnels and aqueducts. This network carries the stored water 167 miles west to the outskirts of San Francisco, where it is pooled in local reservoirs before being distributed to the residents of San Francisco and the counties of Alameda, San Mateo, and Santa Clara. Upwards of 2.4 million people quench their thirst with Hetch Hetchy's waters, which annually amounts to 265,000 acre-feet. The cost is unbeatable: San Francisco leases the Hetch Hetchy reservoir from the federal government for a mere $30,000 a year. Unbeatable, too, is the water's quality. San Francisco is one of only six cities in the nation that the US Environmental Protection Agency does not require to filter its tap water. It is no surprise, then, that the city was so resolute in fighting to secure this bounteous water supply in the early twentieth century, or that it still does so into the twenty-first century.

The idea of capturing the flow of the thunderous Tuolumne River had been floated as early as 1850s, when Central Valley farmers conceived of damming the Tuolumne River at the mouth of the Hetch Hetchy Valley to sustain and expand their irrigation operations. Although they did not follow through, instead continuing to make use of the river's annual natural flow, these downstream irrigators held senior rights to the river's streamflow. Their legal claim would complicate San Francisco's ambition to channel the Tuolumne's waters to the Bay Area (and it remains a source of considerable political tension between the two sets of interests). This early complication of water rights is one reason why San Francisco scuttled a series of its own nineteenth-century dam-building plans, but its efforts took on urgency in the immediate aftermath of the 1906 temblor and firestorm that devastated San Francisco. To secure permission to build the dam, however, required an act of Congress because the land and water in question were located inside

Yosemite National Park, and were thus federally owned. Securing congressional approval took seven tumultuous years.

Between 1906 and 1913, the US House of Representatives and the US Senate held a series of separate and highly charged public hearings. The national media, especially the major magazines and newspaper chains, picked sides and filed story after story, and wrote countless editorials for and against the dam. Local civic and conservation organizations, women's clubs, unions, university faculty and students, and countless individuals buttonholed their representatives and petitioned Congress. Three presidents—Theodore Roosevelt, William Howard Taft, and Woodrow Wilson—were deeply engaged in the political brawl. Roosevelt was the only one to have visited Yosemite, touring it in 1903 with a special guide—John Muir; the famed naturalist would use whatever political capital he gained from their encounter to urge Roosevelt to protect Hetch Hetchy. Equally engaged were each administration's Secretaries of the Interior, who oversaw this and other public lands. So were notable conservationists, among them Muir, who opposed the dam, and Gifford Pinchot, founding chief of the US Forest Service, who testified in support of its construction. These two men had been good friends, yet their friendship frayed as the controversy exploded. They were not alone in experiencing the rough consequences of having to choose sides. The Sierra Club, which Muir founded and which was headquartered in San Francisco, did not fully support its progenitor's furious efforts to stop the dam. And different sections of the country responded with varying degrees of intensity. Quipped Democratic Senator James Reed[22] from Missouri: "The degree of opposition increases in direct proportion with the distance the objector lives from the ground to be taken. When we get as far east as New England the opposition has become a frenzy."[23] The uproar could not have been more dramatic, unsettling, or consequential. The battle over Hetch Hetchy was the first time in US history, historian Roderick Nash argues, that the "principle of preserving wilderness was put to the test."[24]

The initial test finally came to a vote on 3 September 1913, when the US House of Representatives passed the Raker Act by a wide margin of 183–43.[25] The US Senate passed the bill three months later by a vote of 43–35, and on 19 December President Woodrow Wilson signed it into law. These legislative and executive decisions brought to a close this most raucous debate, but this would not be the last such brawl. Until the Big Dam Era ended

---

22 James Reed (1861–1944) was mayor of Kansas City, MO, before serving three terms in the US Senate, from 1911 to 1929.

23 Richter, *The Battle Over Hetch Hetchy*, 129–30.

24 Roderick Frazier Nash, 5th ed., *Wilderness and the American Mind* (New Haven: Yale UP, 2014), 162.

25 The Raker Act was named for its congressional sponsor, California Representative John E. Raker (1863–1926).

in the United States in the early 1970s, for each new dam that the federal government proposed to bottle up portions of the Colorado, Columbia, or Missouri river basins, environmentalists, tribes, and concerned communities rose up in opposition. Similar opposition surfaced every time the California state government planned to slot additional structures into its river systems, streamflow that it would funnel into the State Water Project.[26] One of the most effective rallying cries that dam opponents utilized was to equate these later projects to Hetch Hetchy. Remembering Hetch Hetchy, then, became an effective shorthand for the enduring and ever-pressing need to protect some of the nation's most wild and scenic rivers.

Yet framing the original debate, and its subsequent iterations, in such black and white terms misses the complexity of these struggles. John Muir and his peers could only argue for the protection of wilderness—which they defined as a place devoid of people—after the original inhabitants of Yosemite had been violently removed. That bloody struggle also casts an uncomfortable light on the subsequent conversion of Yosemite into a white tourist enclave. These related developments in turn raise important questions about the longstanding, if flawed, argument that Muir and Pinchot serve as stand-ins for a larger debate over the conflicting values of preservationism and utilitarianism; neither man's principles cannot be so easily pigeonholed.[27] Equally complicated has been the odd assortment of people who over the years have advocated for the restoration of the Hetch Hetchy Valley. Some, but not all, environmental organizations have been staunch proponents of the restoration project—the most significant being Restore Hetch Hetchy. Conservative Republicans have joined with them in an uneasy alliance, among them President Ronald Reagan's Secretary of the Interior, Donald P. Hodel; in 1987, he made a much-publicized pitch for tearing down the O'Shaughnessy Dam.[28] Since then, several congressional representatives from California's Central Valley, home to some of the nation's largest agricultural and industrial livestock operations, have joined the cause, eager to divert water away from San Francisco and to their districts' water-intensive industries. And in 2016 Restore Hetch Hetchy, devoted to keeping the valley's restoration in the forefront of public opinion, filed suit against San Francisco alleging that the O'Shaughnessy Dam and the Hetch Hetchy Reservoir violated a provision in the California state constitution

26 Mark W.T. Harvey, "The Changing Fortunes of the Big Dam Era in the American West," in Char Miller, ed., *Fluid Arguments: Five Centuries of Western Water Conflict* (Tucson: U of Arizona P, 2015), 276–302; Mark W.T. Harvey, *A Symbol of Wilderness: Echo Park and the American Conservation Movement* (Seattle: U of Washington P, 2000).

27 Char Miller, *Gifford Pinchot and the Making of Modern Environmentalism* (Washington, DC: Island Press, 2001), 138–41.

28 Dan Morain and Paul Houston, "Hodel Would Tear Down Dam in Hetch Hetchy," *Los Angeles Times*, 7 August 1987.

that requires water to be diverted in a "reasonable way." Two years later, in July 2018, an appeals court unanimously upheld a lower court's rejection of the lawsuit. All was not lost: 12 days later President Donald Trump's interior secretary, Ryan Zinke, met with Restore Hetch Hetchy, subsequently tweeting: "Good meeting with Restore Hetch Hetchy. Taking a fresh look at different opportunities and options to restore public access and recreation to the valley."[29] One critic likened Zinke's visit to "poking environmentalists in San Francisco in the eye," but it is also a reminder that Hetch Hetchy remains a cultural touchstone and a political lightning rod.[30] As a place and an idea, it continues to evoke and embody a broad range of environmental perspectives and social concerns that have changed over time and repeatedly have roiled modern American culture.

That tumult's evolution is the focus of this unique collection of documents, including public records, newspapers, magazines, illustrations, and other sources. It is broken up into four sections, and within each the relevant documents are chronologically organized. Part One, Indigenous Grounds, is framed around two sets of materials. The first set, Origin Stories, involves a series of oral histories that describe the close understanding and intimate weave of people and place in the central Sierra, the Yosemite region especially. The second, Expulsion, details the punitive steps that the State of California took to expel the Miwok, Numu/Paiute, and Newe/Shoshone from the Sierras, reproduces the scathing petition that Indigenous people submitted to Congress critiquing these actions, and concludes with John Muir's assertion of the primacy of wilderness as a landscape absent of an Indigenous presence. Part Two, Tourist Sanctuary, explores the development of a visitor economy in Yosemite and does so through the eyes of those who made the arduous journey into the remote mountain site and the relevant legislative initiatives that created what would become the national park. The tourists' growing presence, and the services created to serve their needs, had a political impact: the federal government transferred the valley to the state to operate as a pleasure ground. Part Three, Battle for Wilderness, builds off the consequences of the preceding documents. Only when the Indigenous people were cleared away, to be replaced by white tourists, could Yosemite be said to be "wild." Preserving its wildness, and especially that of the little-visited Hetch Hetchy Valley, then becomes the basis for the long, very public, and ultimately unsuccessful, struggle to block the construction of the O'Shaughnessy Dam. The title of Part Four, Hetch Hetchy Restored?,

---

29 Alissa Greenberg, "Is Zinke Trolling San Francisco with Plan to Dismantle City's Reservoir?" *Guardian*, 22 July 2018.

30 Paul Rogers, "Court Rejects Environmentalists' Lawsuit to Drain Hetch Hetchy Reservoir," *San Jose Mercury News*, 10 July 2018.

is deliberately open-ended. At the time of this writing, more than a century after the US Congress granted San Francisco the authority to build the dam-and-reservoir complex that inundated the Hetch Hetchy Valley, the fight to decommission the dam and restore the long-submerged terrain persists. And there is no end in sight.

CHRONOLOGY

~8000 BCE	The ancestors of the modern Paiute, Miwok, and Shoshone Nations began to inhabit, manage, and steward the Yosemite and Hetch Hetchy valleys.
1846–73	Gold Rush miners and ranchers invade the central Sierra, provoking hostilities with Indigenous peoples in California and precipitating a rapid decline in Indigenous populations.
1850	Joseph Screech is reportedly the first European-American to enter Hetch Hetchy Valley and witnesses the Paiute managing the valley's resources.
1851	The State of California funds militias to attack Indigenous nations, effectively launching a genocidal war of extermination.
1851	The Mariposa Battalion attacks Ahwahnechee settlements in Yosemite Valley; survivors are force-marched to reservation on the Fresno River in the Central Valley.
1850–60s	Hoteliers like James M. Hutchings, and artists, photographers, journalists, and visitors turn Yosemite into a "must see" destination for those with the money and time to journey there. Their reports also locate Yosemite's grandeur as a mark of divine beneficence and integral to the American culture.
1864	President Lincoln signs legislation granting Yosemite to the State of California "to be held for public use, resort and recreation."
1868	California Geological Survey publishes the first assessment of the Hetch Hetchy Valley.
1872	John Muir first visits Hetch Hetchy and publishes an article about his impressions in March 1873.
1882	San Francisco begins searching for water to serve its growing population and considers Hetch Hetchy Valley as possible reservoir site.
1890	President Harrison signs the law creating Yosemite National Park, which includes the Hetch Hetchy Valley.
1892	The Sierra Club is established, with John Muir as its first president.

| 1902 | As a citizen and with his own money, San Francisco Mayor James Phelan files for water rights on the Tuolumne River. |

| 1903 | Mayor Phelan applies to the Department of the Interior for rights to Hetch Hetchy's water. Secretary of the Interior Ethan Hitchcock denies the city's request. |

| 1903 | President Theodore Roosevelt visits Yosemite with John Muir, heads into the backcountry to escape the crowds, and urges preservation of the valley. |

| 1905 | Mayor Phelan again applies to the Department of the Interior for water rights to Hetch Hetchy, and the permit is once again denied. |

| 1905–06 | The State of California regrants the Yosemite Valley and Mariposa Grove to the federal Government; the US Congress accepts the return of the land. |

| 1906 | A powerful earthquake and fire devastates San Francisco and energizes the campaign to enlarge the city's public water supply and break the Spring Valley Water Company's monopoly. |

| 1907–13 | The battle over Hetch Hetchy becomes a national controversy. Congressional hearings are held, petitions from civic and conservation groups are sent to Washington, DC, politicians and public officials make their respective cases, and newspapers and magazines closely monitor and comment on the growing debate. |

| 1908 | Secretary of the Interior James Garfield approves San Francisco's permit to build a dam in Hetch Hetchy. The Hetch Hetchy project goes before the city's electorate, who vote overwhelmingly in support of spending $600,000 to purchase the "lands, rights, and claims" of Hetch Hetchy. To dam Hetch Hetchy, John Muir counters, one "may as well dam for water-tanks the people's cathedrals and churches, for no holier temple has ever been consecrated by the heart of man." |

| 1909 | The Taft administration takes office in March 1909, and the new secretary of the interior, Richard Ballinger, suspends the Roosevelt administration's approval of the city's Hetch Hetchy right of way. |

| 1912 | Woodrow Wilson is elected president, and appoints former San Francisco City Attorney Franklin Lane as secretary of the interior. |

1913 ● California Rep. John Edward Raker, whose district includes Yosemite, is lead sponsor of the Raker Act (HR-7207). This legislation would allow San Francisco to build its dam and reservoir complex in Hetch Hetchy, but the structure must also generate electric power that would be sold directly to the citizens through a municipal power agency. This latter stipulation would result in a series of subsequent investigations into the city's failure to comply—and as of 2019 is still a matter of legal contention.

1913 ● After another round of congressional hearings and public debate, Congress passes the Raker Bill, granting San Francisco permission to construct the O'Shaughnessy Dam. President Woodrow Wilson signs the bill on December 19.

1923 ● Construction of O'Shaughnessy Dam is completed, at a cost of $100 million and the lives of 68 people. The project transports water 160 miles via a gravity-fed system of tunnels and pipes to customers in San Francisco and 32 other Bay Area communities.

1924 ● San Francisco voters approve a bond proposition for $10 million to pay for a series of tunnels that would deliver water through the Sierra and Coast Range mountains.

1928 ● San Francisco voters approve $24 million in bonds to help further the Hetch Hetchy Dam Project.

1934 ● Completion of the Hetch Hetchy water and power system.

1947 ● San Francisco voters approve $25 million for a second pipeline for the system.

1961 ● San Francisco voters approve $115 million in bonds to expand the existing Hetch Hetchy system.

1970 ● Sierra Club board of directors recommends removal, rather than an expensive restoration or reconstruction, of the O'Shaughnessy Dam and Lake Eleanor Dam.

1987 ● President Reagan's interior secretary, Donald Hodel, proposes removing the dam and restoring the Hetch Hetchy Valley. The Sierra Club responds by creating the Hetch Hetchy Restoration Task Force to promote the restoration of the valley.

1999 ● The non-profit advocacy group, Restore Hetch Hetchy, is established as a spin off from but independent of the Sierra Club. Its mission is "to restore the Hetch Hetchy Valley in Yosemite National Park to its original condition."

2004 ● Environmental Defense Fund publishes study concluding the valley can be restored without impacting Bay Area water supplies.

2005 ● Restore Hetch Hetchy publishes a feasibility study on the options and costs for how the valley could be restored.

2006 ● A California Resources Agency report indicates that before restoration could occur, considerably more research and public input—particularly from Indigenous nations in California—would be necessary.

2012 ● San Francisco voters defeat Proposition F. Had the measure succeeded, the city would have been compelled to "to evaluate how to drain the Hetch Hetchy Reservoir and identify replacement water and power sources."

2014 ● The San Francisco Board of Supervisors unanimously passed a law banning the sale and distribution of plastic water bottles on public property. The law took effect in 2018.

QUESTIONS TO CONSIDER

1. How have the Indigenous nations in the Yosemite region understood their relationship to the mountains and valleys in which they have lived for millennia? How do their oral traditions (Documents 1–6) explain their varied connections to these landscapes?

2. What were Indigenous people's management strategies for sustaining themselves? And what are the implications of their centuries-long stewardship for the landscapes and subsequent settler-colonials' understanding of their "pristine" nature?

3. What impact did the Gold Rush and the westward expansion of the United States have on the Indigenous nations that called the central Sierra home?

4. When California governor Peter Burnett declared in his 1851 State of the State Address (Document 7) "that a war of extermination will continue to be waged between the races until the Indian race becomes extinct must be expected," what did he mean? What were some of the ramifications of his declaration?

5. On what grounds did the Indigenous people of the Yosemite region challenge their forced removal from the ancestral territory? What arguments did they deploy to make their case about their rights to and in their homeland? (Documents 8 and 10)

6. What did it mean to "discover" and rename what has become called Yosemite?

7. John Muir described the members of the Mono Nation he met while hiking in the Sierra (Document 11) as "a drove of gray hairy beings ... lumbering toward me with a kind of boneless, wallowing motion like bears." How does his comment relate to Governor Burnett's declaration of war on Indigenous populations in California? To the concept of Manifest Destiny?

8. What links the attempt to extirpate Indigenous nations in California and the formulation of Yosemite as wilderness and as a scenic tourist destination?

9. Who was James Mason Hutchings and what role did he play in making Yosemite Valley a must-see landscape for artists, photographers, and wealthy visitors?

10. How did nineteenth-century tourists respond to Yosemite—by what means did they reach the remote site, what did they see along their route to it and within the valley, and how did they describe their experiences?

11. In what ways did tourists and other visitors contribute to subsequent generations' understanding of Yosemite and Hetch Hetchy, and these landscapes' significance to American culture?

12. What was the legislative process by which Yosemite and Hetch Hetchy Valleys became part of Yosemite National Park? How was this park defined *as* a park?

13. Based on the documents in the Battle for Wilderness section, what did conservationists of the late nineteenth and early twentieth centuries value? Who and what were some of the conservation movement's key figures and terms?

14. What sense do these documents give for the different ways that conservation could be defined in the context of the Hetch Hetchy controversy?

15. How did some conservationists—often called preservationists—argue in opposition to the Hetch Hetchy dam? How did other conservationists—those usually called utilitarians—argue in support of the dam's construction? (Documents 22–36)

16. Do the testimonies at congressional hearings and petitions sent to Congress identify any gender, occupational, and/or regional differences of opinion about the value of the dam and reservoir? Did particular interest groups voice specific concerns about its construction?

17. Although the O'Shaughnessy Dam was approved in 1913, completed in 1923, and a decade later the reservoir's water reached San Francisco, why has the battle over Hetch Hetchy continued well into the twenty-first century?

18. What are some of the reasons that Interior Secretary Donald Hodel gave in 1987–88 for why he proposed restoring the Hetch Hetchy Valley? (Documents 37 and 38)

19. What arguments do some environmentalists advance in support of decommissioning/destroying the O'Shaughnessy Dam? How do they discuss the restoration of the Hetch Hetchy Valley?

20. How have San Francisco and some of its supporters argued in favor of keeping the dam?

21. If the dam and reservoir are an "occupation" of Yosemite National Park (Document 42), why and how might contemporary Indigenous people use that same term to describe the park itself?

22. Based on the documents, are you able to identify particular connections between the historic debates over Hetch Hetchy and the continuing arguments about it?

PART 1

Indigenous Grounds

ORIGIN STORIES

The nineteenth-century ethnographers who fanned across the westward-expanding United States to capture the oral histories and traditions of Indigenous people did so in the firm belief that they were on rescue missions. They assumed—falsely, as it turned out—that if they did not interview tribal elders about their cultural heritage, transcribe their reflections and stories, and annotate the final texts, these traditions, like the people themselves, would be lost to history. This conviction was of a piece with the US Army's operations in, and occupation of, what would become the western territories of the United States, and with the larger thrust of settler-colonialism: to eliminate the Indigenous people, as was the purpose underlying California's genocidal war against Indigenous nations; to replace the defeated peoples with migrants whose burgeoning presence depended on the new society's judicial authority and imported conception of property rights; to legitimize this new system by arguing that these invading outsiders in fact represented "civilization" in contrast to the putative "savagery" of those they attacked and dispossessed. This oppressive binary not only justified forcing the Indigenous survivors to live out their days in small reservations with few resources, but laid the foundation for the idea of "wilderness" as a place devoid of people.

Into this disrupted world came ethnographers whose mission to record and relay the stories they heard reinforced the imperial conceit that winners write history. But it is also clear that these transliterations, as is evident in the selections included here, offer important insights into the deep knowledge that the ancestral Yosemite nations had developed about the central Sierra. Read with care and sensitivity, these oral histories reveal their intense connections with this rugged terrain, the manifold lessons its geology and ecology offered them, and the resources, whether spiritual or material, that they daily drew from their home ground. These insights continued to motivate, inspiring late-nineteenth-century Indigenous protests against their forced marginalization and in defense of Yosemite itself, an enduring counter-narrative that continues to thrive well into the twenty-first century.

DOCUMENT 1:

How the World Grew[1]

Part of what makes this and the following origin stories of the Indigenous people living in and around the Yosemite region so compelling is the intimate knowledge they convey of how generations of narrators communicated their close relationship with the sustaining natural world. Clear too is that these oral histories helped these human communities inscribe themselves into the land itself.

In the beginning the world was rock. Every year the rains came and fell on the rock and washed off a little; this made earth. By and by plants grew on the earth and their leaves fell and made more earth. Then pine trees grew and their needles and cones fell every year and with the other leaves and bark made more earth and covered more of the rock.

If you look closely at the ground in the woods you will see how the top is leaves and bark and pine needles and cones, and how a little below the top these are matted together, and a little deeper are rotting and breaking up into earth. This is the way the world grew—and it is growing still.

---

1   C. Hart Merriam, *The Dawn of the World: Myths and Weird Tales Told by the Mewan [Miwok] Indians of California* (Cleveland: The Arthur H. Clarke Co., 1910), 226. Merriam (1855–1942), an ethnographer, ornithologist, and naturalist, collected this and other stories between 1890 and 1910. They are based on interviews with Indigenous people in California, and as Indigenous scholar Frank LaPena observes, Merriam's is a "key source book, and the most complete treatment of southern Miwok legends ever written." Frank LaPena, et al., comp., *Legends of the Yosemite Miwok* (Yosemite: Yosemite Association, 1993), 83. LaPena's collection, which was published with the imprimatur of the local Indigenous people, itself is a brilliant retelling of these stories, and I followed his lead wherever possible.

DOCUMENT 2:

Origin of the Mountains[2]

Stephen Powers (1840–1904) was a journalist, ethnographer, and historian, and between 1871 and 1876, traveled throughout California studying Indigenous peoples, their lives, and livelihoods. This story, like others in his book, was originally published as part of a series of articles appearing in *Overland Monthly*; he later collected them into this volume, published as part of the US Geological Survey's *Geographical and Geological Survey of the Rocky Mountain Region*. In the 1870s, Powers traveled throughout California to capture what he thought would be the memories of the last generation of Indigenous people. After relating this origin story about the formation of the Sierra, Powers appended the following note: "This legend is of value in showing the aboriginal notions of geography. In explaining the story, the Indian drew in the sand a long ellipse, representing quite accurately the shape of the two ranges; and he had never traveled away from King's River."

Once there was a time when there was nothing in the world but water. About the place where **Tulare Lake** is now, there was a pole far out of the water, and on this pole perched a hawk and crow. First one of them would sit on the pole for a while, then the other would knock him off and sit on it himself. Thus they sat on top of the pole above the waters for many ages. At length they wearied of the lonesomeness, and they created the birds which prey on fish such as the kingfisher, eagle, pelican, and others. Among them was a very small duck, which dived down to the bottom of the water, picked its beak full of mud, came up, dried, and lay floating on the water. The hawk and crow then fell to work and gathered from the duck's beak the earth which it had brought up, and commenced making the mountains. They began at the place now known as **Ta-hí-cha-pa Pass**, and the hawk made the east range, while the crow made the west one. Little by little, as they dropped in the earth, these great mountains grew athwart the face of the waters, pushing north. It was a work of many years, but they finally met together at Mount Shasta, and their labors were ended. But, behold, when they compared their mountains, it was found that the crow's was a great deal larger. Then the hawk said to the crow, "How did this happen, you rascal? I warrant that you have been stealing some of the earth from my bill, and that is why your mountains are the biggest." It was a fact, and the crow laughed

Tulare Lake: Once located in the southern end of the San Joaquin Valley, Tulare Lake in the nineteenth century was the largest freshwater lake west of the Mississippi River. Its rich biota sustained the Yokut people for millennia, but by the late nineteenth century settler-colonists were rapidly draining it for agricultural lands and irrigation. The lake is now dry.

Ta-hí-cha-pa Pass: Tehachapi Pass links the San Joaquin Valley to the north with the Mojave desert to the south. It is considered the dividing line between the southern end of the Sierras and the Tehachapi Mountains in Kern County.

---

2   Stephen Powers, *The Tribes of California* (Washington, DC: Government Printing Office, 1877), 383–84.

in his claws. The hawk went and got some Indian tobacco and chewed it, and it made him exceedingly wise. So he took hold of the mountains and turned them round in a full circle, putting his range in place of the crow's; and that is why the Sierra Nevada is larger than the Coast Range.

DOCUMENT 3:

The Legend of Tu-tok-a-nu'-la[3]

> Stephen Powers relates this origin story in his *Tribes of California*, and adds a concluding comment that it presents a clear depiction of the "Indian idea of the formation of Yosemite, and that they must have arrived in the valley after it had assumed its present form. It should be remarked that the word *tutakana* means both the measuring-worm and its way of creeping."

❧

There were once two little boys who went down to the valley [Ah-wah'-nee] to swim. After paddling and splashing about to their hearts' content they went on shore and crept up on to a huge boulder that stood beside the water, on which they lay down on the warm sunshine to dry themselves. Very soon they fell asleep, and slept so soundly that they never waked more.

Through sleeps, moons, and snows, winter and summer, they slumbered on. Meantime the great rock whereupon they slept was treacherously rising day and night, little by little, until it soon lifted them up beyond the sight of their friends, who sought them everywhere weeping. Thus they were borne up at last beyond all human help or reach of human voice, lifted up into the blue heavens, far up, far up, until they scraped their faces against the moon; and still they slumbered and slept year after year safe amid the clouds.

Then all the animals [of Ah-wah'-nee] assembled together to bring down the little boys from the top of the great rock. Every animal made a spring up the face of the wall as far as he could leap. The little mouse could only jump up a handbreadth; the rat, two handbreadths; the raccoon little further, and so on, the grizzly bear making a mighty leap far up the wall, but falling back in vain, like all the others. Last of all the lion tried, but he too soon fell flat on his back.

Then along came Tul-tak-a-na, an insignificant **measuring worm**, which even the mouse could have crushed by treading on it, and began to creep up the rock. Step by step, a little at a time, he measured his way up until he was presently above the lion's jump, then pretty soon out of sight. So he crawled up and up through many sleeps for about one whole snow, and at last he reached the top. Then he took the little boys and came down the same way he went up and brought them safely down to the ground. So the rock was called after the measuring worm **Tu-tok-a-nu'-la**, in honor of Tul-tak-a-na, the measuring worm.

measuring worm: Inch worm.

Tu-tok-a-nu'-la: El Capitan.

---

3 Stephen Powers, *The Tribes of California*, 367.

DOCUMENT 4:

Ah-wah'-nee: Yosemite.

The Origins of the Present Floor of the Ah-wah'-nee Valley[4]

℮

great rock: Tu-tok-a-nu'-la; El Capitan.

Measuring worm again ascended to the top of the **great rock** and then leaned out and finally stretched across to the opposite side of the canyon, so that his head was on the one side while his tail was on the other. He then crossed over to the south rim of the canyon. Later he recrossed to [Tu-tok-a-nu'-la] and again descended to the floor of the valley.

The walls of the canyon then began to cave in and all the people were obliged to flee down the river. The [Ah-wah'-nee] valley was, in those days, much deeper than now and somewhat narrower. The caving-in of its walls partly filled the valley and made all of the earth and the piles of rocks now in the floor of the valley.

---

4   "The Origins of the Present Floor of the Yosemite Valley," in A.L. Kroeber, ed., *University of California Publications in American Archaeology and Ethnology*, vol. XVI (1919–20), 22.

DOCUMENT 5:
The Legend of Tis-se'-yak[5]

Tis-se'-yak and her husband journeyed from a country very far off, and entered the Ah-wah'-nee valley foot-sore and weary. She came in advance, bowing far forward under the heavy burden of her great conical basket, which was strapped across her forehead, while he followed easily after, with a rude staff in his hand and a roll of skin-blankets flung over his back.

After their long journey across the mountains they were exceedingly thirsty, and they now hastened forward to drink of the cool waters. But the woman was still in front and thus she first reached the lake called A-wai'-a. Then she dipped up the water of the lake in her basket and drank long and deep. She drank up all the water and drained the lake dry before her husband arrived.

Because the woman had drunk all the water, there came a grievous drought in that land, and the earth was dried up so that it yielded neither herb nor grass.

But the woman's husband was displeased, and in his wrath he beat the woman with his staff. She fled from before him, but he pursued her and beat her some more. And the woman wept, and in her anger she turned about and reviled the man and flung her basket at him.

So happened that, even while they were in this attitude, one standing over against the other, they were turned into stone for their wickedness, and there they have remained to this day. The basket lies upturned beside the husband, while the woman's face is tear-stained with long dark lines trailing down.

---

5   Powers, *Tribes of California*, 367; LaPena, et al., comp., *Legends of the Yosemite Miwok*, 41–42. Powers comments that the woman is South Dome and the man North Dome, while the basket represents a lower dome.

DOCUMENT 6:

The Spirits of Po-ho-no[6]

A short distance above Bridal Veil Falls is a lake somewhat like Mirror Lake. Here live certain beautiful maidens whose tresses hang down to their feet. They have a very sharp sense of smell and can detect easily the approach of a human being. They cause a violent wind in an endeavor to blow the victim into the lake and drown him. These maidens then devour him. The victim's spirit remains forever in the depths of the lake. Very little is known of the personal appearance of these women except that they are very beautiful, are pure white, with blue eyes, and have very long hair. That so little is known of them is due to the fact that they are greatly feared and anyone who is so unfortunate as to come in sight of one of them takes no time for observations but makes off if possible at top speed.

Another class of these supernatural beings once lived in the pool at the foot of Po-ho-no [Bridal Veil Falls]. Little is known about these beings but that they were harmless except in that they always caused the water of the fall to blow out and wet anyone who approached too close to its foot.

---

6   S.A. Barrett, "Myths of the Southern Sierra Miwok," *University of California Publications in American Archaeology and Ethnology*, vol. 16, part 1 (1919), 23; and LaPena, *Legends of the Yosemite Miwok*, 49–50.

EXPULSION

DOCUMENT 7:

Extract from Governor Peter Burnett, "State of the State Address" (speech, 6 January 1851)[7]

Peter Hardeman Burnett (1807–95) was one of thousands of white settler-colonists to migrate to the Pacific coast of the US, first traveling west to Oregon, where he served in its provisional legislature, and then in 1848, during the Gold Rush, to California. Within a year, he ran for, and won, the first gubernatorial election in California, a year before official statehood. In his two years in office, Burnett argued for the exclusion of all African Americans, whether free or enslaved; imposed a heavy tax on foreign miners; opposed the publication of laws and legislation in Spanish; supported refusing Indigenous people the right to vote, sit on juries, or give evidence in trials against whites; and blocked what he considered to the too-generous land grants that the federal government had negotiated with various nations in the state.

Since the adjournment of the Legislature repeated calls have been made upon the Executive for the aid of the Militia, to resist and punish the attacks of the Indians upon our frontier. With a wild and mountainous frontier of more than eight hundred miles in extent, affording the most inaccessible retreats to our Indian foe, so well accustomed to these mountain fastnesses, California is peculiarly exposed to depredations from this quarter. The various small towns upon the confines of California have no political organization, and no regular government among them. The influence their chiefs have over them arises from that personal popularity gained by superior prowess in war, or wisdom in council; there is, therefore, no reason to suppose that there has been any regular or well-understood combination among them to make war upon the whites. They are all, however, urged on by the same causes of enmity, and the result has been, that at almost all points upon our widely extended and exposed frontier, hostilities, more or less formidable, have occurred at intervals, and many valuable lives have been lost.

Among the more immediate causes that have precipitated this state of things, may be mentioned the neglect of the General Government to make treaties with them for their lands. We have suddenly spread ourselves over the country in every direction, and appropriated whatever portion of it

---

7   Archived at Governors' Gallery website, California State Library, accessed 19 September 2019.

we pleased to ourselves, without their consent and without compensation. Although these small and scattered tribes have among them no regular government, they have some ideas of existence as a separate and independent people, and some conception of their right to the country acquired by long, uninterrupted, and exclusive possession. They have not only seen their country taken from them, but they see their ranks rapidly thinning from the effects of our diseases. They instinctively consider themselves a doomed race; and this idea leads to despair; and despair prevents them from providing the usual and necessary supply of provisions. This produces starvation, which knows but one law, that of gratification; and the natural result is, that these people kill the first stray animal they find. This leads to war between them and the whites; and war creates a hatred against the white man that never ceases to exist in the Indian bosom.

This state of things, though produced at an earlier period by the exciting causes mentioned, would still have followed in due course of time. Our American experience has demonstrated the fact that the two races cannot live in the same vicinity in peace.

The love of fame, as well as the love of property, are common to all men; and war and theft are established customs among the Indian races generally, as they are among all poor and savage tribes of men, as a means to attain the one, and to procure a supply of the other. When brought into contact with a civilized race of men, they readily learn the use of their implements and manufactures, but they do not readily learn the art of *making* them. To learn the use of new comforts and conveniences, which are vastly superior to the old, is but the work of a day; but to acquire a knowledge of the arts and sciences, is the work of generations. Like the people of all thinly populated but fertile countries, who are enabled to supply the simplest wants of Nature from the spontaneous productions of the earth, they are, from habit and prejudice, exceedingly averse to manual labor. While the white man attaches but little value to small articles, and consequently exposes them the more carelessly, he throws in the way of the Indian that which is esteemed by him a great temptation and a great prize; and as he cannot make the article himself, and thinks he must have it, he finds theft the most ready and certain mode to obtain it. Success in trifles but leads to attempts of greater importance. The white man, to whom time is money, and who labors hard all day to create the comforts of life, cannot sit up all night to watch his property; and after being robbed a few times, he becomes desperate, and resolves upon a war of extermination. This is the common feeling of our people who have lived upon the Indian frontier. The two races are kept asunder by so many causes, and having no ties of marriage or consanguinity to unite them, they must ever remain at enmity.

That a war of extermination will continue to be waged between the races until the Indian race becomes extinct must be expected. While we cannot anticipate this result but with painful regret, the inevitable destiny of the race is beyond the power or wisdom of man to avert....

DOCUMENT 8:

Extracts from James Mason Hutchings, "The Yo-Ham-i-te Valley," *Hutchings' California Magazine* 1, 1 (July 1856): 2–8

James M. Hutchings (1820–1902) authored this unsigned article that appeared in *Hutchings' California Magazine* in July 1856. This extract deals with the actions of the Mariposa Battalion, a state-funded and -sanctioned militia that was charged with clearing out the Miwok and other Indigenous nations in the Sierra and the Central Valley. Its violent actions also opened the way for tourism to flourish in the now "empty" Yosemite—which Hutchings, who ran a hotel in the valley, was eager to expand.

ev

... [Yosemite Valley] is situated on the middle fork of the river Merced, Mariposa County, about fifty miles from the town of Mariposa, and about the same distance from Coultersville.

Until the last year this remarkable valley has been comparatively unknown, altho' Major **James D. Savage** visited it as early as 1848, and was perhaps the first white man that ever entered it.

It appears that Major S., while living with a tribe of Indians inhabiting the lower valleys of the Merced and Tuolumne rivers, accompanied them on an expedition to the Yo-Ham-i-te country for the purpose of making war with them. A large party met them near the summit of a mountain, now crossed by visitors on their way to the valley, where a desperate fight ensued, and the Major with his party, finding the Yo-Ham-i-tes too much for them, had to make a hasty retreat in the best way they could without the much prized trophies of Indian warfare—the Indian women—and which is almost invariably the only case of warfare among themselves, and with the whites.

Women are considered the most valuable property the Indian can possess; and, for the sole purpose of capturing this desirable property, they invade each other's territory and make war, that the young men of the victorious party may take them home in triumph, to support their new and lazy husband.

Nothing in particular occurred from that time until the winter of 1850, as they seldom came down among the miners, except at night, to steal horses, mules, and cattle; nor could they be induced to adopt our manners, dress, or customs, as did most of the other tribes. In that winter the Yo-Ham-i-tes declared war against the whites, and were joined by most of the surrounding tribes.

A volunteer battalion [the Mariposa Battalion] was soon raised for the protection of the mining settlements, and Major Savage was chosen

James D. Savage: James D. Savage (1817–52) served in John Fremont's California Battalion during the Mexican American War (1846–48), and subsequently lived with, married into, and fought for the Yokuts, a dominant group in the Central Sierra foothills. With the discovery of gold in 1849, Savage established trading posts along three key Sierra rivers. His military expertise led Governor John McDougall in 1851 to appoint him to the rank of major and to head the so-called Mariposa Battalion to suppress Indigenous nations believed responsible for a series of raids on white miners and settler-colonists. William Abrams, who visited Savage's trading post in 1849 before his journey into Yosemite, was little impressed with Savage, calling him "a blasphemous fellow who has five squaws for wives for which he takes his authority from the Scriptures."

commander. After a short but vigorous campaign, and by the influence of Major S., the Indians were induced to make treaties of peace, enter the **reservation**, and learn the invigorating art of agriculture. Contrary to expectations, they were dissatisfied, and began committing depredations almost daily. From the intimate knowledge of Indian character, the Major was not long in tracing out the aggressors. He immediately fitted out an expedition; and, accompanied by Capt. **John Boling**'s command, and a few friendly Indians, paid the Yo-Ham-i-tes another visit, in March, 1851. After swimming the south fork of the Merced and passing through snow two to eight feet deep, and encountering all the hardships and privations incident to a winter campaign in the mountains of California, [they] finally succeeded in reaching the Yo-Ham-i-te Valley, where they found about six hundred of the Indians encamped; who would have fled, could they have ascended the almost perpendicular mountain walls that hedged them in on every side. There are narrow ledges of rock, that look very small from below, but, are nevertheless large enough for an Indian to walk upon, carefully, when not excited; but would present destruction to himself and his valuable property—his wives—to attempt in haste, as one slight slip would precipitate them thousands of feet below, and thus hasten their departure to the Spirit Land before they might desire to take such a journey.

Finding that they were caught, their discretion taught them that "the better part of valor" would be to surrender with a good grace, which they did; when they were taken as prisoners to the Reservation farm on the Fresno river.

After a week's residence on the farm, they agreed to enter a treaty of peace, on the condition that they were allowed to return to their mountain home on a short visit, to gather up the remaining portion of their tribe, and the plunder they were so unceremoniously required to leave behind, which, appearing to be very reasonable, they were allowed to go for that purpose.

Soon after their departure, the whole country around the Reservation was thrown into excitement by the constant reports of robberies and murders, committed by the Yo-Ham-i-tes. Major S. then fitted out another expedition against them, composed of about twenty volunteers, and an equal number of friendly Indians, taken from the farm. This party reached the valley on the 15th of May, (1851) and, after erecting their encampment, they sent out small scouting parties in different directions. The Indians, however, having seen them, had moved *their* encampment to the shores of a **beautiful lake**, some thirty miles above, lying in a northeast direction from the valley, and near the headwaters of the middle and main fork of the Merced.

The information was immediately taken to camp, by one of the small scouting parties that had discovered them, and the whole command marched against them; and by stratagem, surrounded the Indians, before they became

reservation: The short-lived Fresno River Reservation (1851–60), created as a result of the 1851 treaties, operated as a series of small farms located in the immediate vicinity of the present-day City of Madera. Many Northfork Mono and other Sierran nations were compelled to relinquish their ancestral lands and the hunting and foraging that had sustained their lives in the past, were forced to live and work on the reservation. These "first farmers of the San Joaquin Valley" had endured harsh farming conditions, neglectful and corrupt administrators, and the unrelenting, white settler-colonists' encroachment on official reservation lands. To survive, the Mono and other resident Indigenous peoples supplemented their meager agricultural yields with traditional subsistence activities in the surrounding foothills and river systems. By 1860, the federal government abandoned the reservation and farms, leaving their one-time residents, who a decade earlier had rights to millions of acres, landless. Most returned to Yosemite and the surrounding areas. See www.sierranevadageotourism.org/content/historical-fresno-river-farm-reservation/sieaaa792a6d1a8b2b66.

John Boling: Boling (1821–64) later became the sheriff of Mariposa County.

beautiful lake: Tenaya Lake, named after the leader of the Ahwahnechee (or Awahnichi) people of the valley, is located between Yosemite Valley and Tuolumne Meadows at an elevation of 8150 feet (2484m).

aware of their presence. After killing a few, the whole party of Indians begged for mercy, and surrendered. They were again moved down to the farm, and there kept as prisoners until the crops were all gathered in.

Their great chief, **Je-ne-a-eh**, was among the prisoners. He was a man of about sixty-five or seventy years of age; and, as he cast a lingering look around the home of his childhood—perhaps for the last time—to spend his days among strangers—apparently his enemies—his rage knew no bounds; and drawing his manly form to its full height, his eyes seemed flashing with fire; and his nostrils distended, and his chest heaving, through his interpreter he gave, in substance, the following address:—

Je-ne-a-eh: This appears to be a reference to Tenaya's father. In other contexts, whites in the region recast his name as that of the group itself, Ahwahnechee.

> White men, you are a bad people. You have invaded my country. You have killed my people, my own dear son, simply because we have stolen a few horses—a privilege granted to us by the Great Spirit—to steal all we want, wherever we can find it. We steal that we may live—every tribe does it. I know very well that you all steal. You steal among yourselves, that you may be rich: we steal something to eat. You come and steal my country. You steal me and my people from my hunting-grounds. These were given to me and my people exclusively, by the Great Spirit, that we might hunt and eat; we have lived here undisturbed for many hundred moons. Yes: when these mountains, now so high, were but little hills, this was our country; and now you come and take us away, that we may look upon them no more. I am astonished at your impudence and presumption.

Mr. John D. Hunt: John Hunt was a member of the Mariposa Battalion.

"When we arrived at the spot," writes **Mr. John D. Hunt**, late partner of Major Savage, and who accompanied the expedition,—"from whence we saw the valley for the last time, on our way home, his passion arose to its greatest height; and walking up to Captain Boling, in a voice almost choked his rage, he begged that he might be shot, saying, 'I had rather leave my ashes here, in the hunting-ground of my fathers, than to be a slave to the white man, who has ever been the mortal foe of me and mine.' Then, laying his hand upon his breast, he exclaimed, 'Shoot me! kill me! murder me! and the echo of my voice shall be heard resounding among the mountains of my native home, for many years afterwards; and my spirit—which you cannot tame—instead of taking its flight to the spirit-land, shall linger around these old gray granite hills, and haunt you and your posterity, as long as there is one of you or your tribe remaining.' Finding that his pleadings were of no avail, he bade the hunting-ground of his fathers an affecting adieu; and in moody silence, marched on, with a heavy heart, to spend, as he supposed and felt, the remnant of his days among his and his people's enemies.

"We arrived in safety at the Reservation, where he, with the others, were kept as prisoners.

"The canker-worm of grief was busy at the old man's heart, and his fast declining health, along with his constant entreaties, aroused the sympathies of the Commissioners; and he was allowed once more to go free, when he immediately returned to his favored valley, and joined the remnant of his tribe, that had been left behind.

"The poor Indian soon found a grave, and his ashes were placed at the side of his fathers. Degraded in his own estimation, the shock was too much for him; and he died broken-hearted."

Nothing in particular occurred after poor Je-ne-a-eh's death, until the middle of May, 1852, when a party of miners from the Coarse Gold Gulch—a tributary of the Fresno—started for the upper Sierras on a prospecting trip. They had scarcely entered the valley, when a large party of Indians, that had been lying in ambush, came suddenly upon them and killed two of their number—one named Rose, the other Shurbon—and wounding a third, named Tudor.

As this was altogether unexpected, and being overpowered by numbers, they sought refuge in flight. The Indians hotly pursued them, when luckily, on ascending the mountains, they came upon a large overhanging rock, from which they could receive protection, and see and fire upon their assailants. Nothing could have been more providential, nor any place better adapted for defense.

Bravely did this little party struggle for their lives, and one by one did their savage assailants bite the dust, from the unerring aim of the rifle and revolver. Finding they were losing many of their number, among them their best chief, without even wounding the defenders, they changed their plan of assault; and climbing the mountain above, commenced rolling down huge rocks, trying to drive them from their secure retreat; but in vain. When night was advancing, black and heavily charged clouds began to roll among the mountain-tops; and before darkness had set in, the Indians seemed disposed to postpone any further struggle until the morning. Under cover of the darkness, that brave little band crept stealthily out, and set their face towards the settlements, where they arrived in safety, but nearly famished with hunger, having been five days without a thing to eat.

Their tale was soon told, and every able miner in camp shouldered his rifle willingly; and a company of forty men were soon upon the way.

Arriving in the valley, they found the dead bodies of their companions, and gave them burial, the Indians meanwhile giving taunts of defiance.

This being the season when the melting snows swell every mountain stream, the waters of the Merced river were very difficult to cross; and before the party could reach the opposite side, the Indians had escaped.

After several ineffectual attempts, they abandoned, for the present, their pursuit, and returned to their homes.

About the middle of June, Lieut. Moore, with a company of United States Infantry, left Fort Miller on the San Joaquin; and, accompanied by Major Savage, in command of a company of volunteers, started for the scene of the recent murders, to establish a military post in the Yo-Ham-i-te valley, and chastise the Indians. The Yo-Ham-i-tes have always been the most hostile of any of the Indians in this section; and have always refused to treat with the Commissioners; but stampeded and returned to their mountain fastnesses.

On the arrival of Lieut. Moore and Major Savage in the Yo-Ham-i-te valley, with their command, they found the Indians, with their redoubtable chief '**Ptompkit**,' had crossed the mountains and were wandering about on the Eastern side of the Sierras. They immediately started in pursuit. Discovering a new pass at the head of the Merced, they named it Mono Pass, after the Indians of that name. Although several bands of Indians were seen wandering about, little or nothing was accomplished for their chastisement, and the command returned.

Ptompkit: This refers to Chief Tenaya.

Fearing an attack from the whites, the Yo-Ham-i-tes had remained like guests with the Monos; until the great depth of snow which fell during the winter of 1852, prevented their return to their native valley. Early in the spring of 1853, they left their hospitable entertainers, the Monos; but, before doing so, appropriated a large amount of their property for their own use.

Whether this was in accordance with the teachings of the Great Spirit, we do not know; but the Monos, demurring to such an interpretation, thought their savage brethren had violated the rules of hospitality; they immediately raised a large war party, and pursued their thieving guests, even into their own mountain fastnesses,—nearly exterminating the whole tribe. The few that remained, for protection, either mingled with other tribes, or lived upon anything they could get in the mining camps of their so-called enemies, the whites.

By the kindness of Mr. Hunt, on the Frezno, we were provided with Indian guides, which took us speedily into the valley; and when we arrived there, scarcely an Indian could be seen. The trails were overgrown with grasses, and nothing remained but the whitened bones of animals, and an old acorn-post or two, to tell of the once flourishing settlement, and numerous tribe of the Yo-Ham-i-tes....

DOCUMENT 9:

Extract from L.H. Bunnell, "How the Yo-Semite Valley Was Discovered and Named," *Hutchings' California Magazine* (May 1859): 498–505[8]

Lafayette Houghton Bunnell, MD (1824–1903) was a member of the Mariposa Battalion, credited himself with the naming of Yosemite, and later served as a surgeon for the Union army during the Civil War. By claiming rights of "discovery" and thus the right to rename the valley, Bunnell contributed to the rapid conversion of Yosemite from an Indigenous landscape to an "American" one. Thirty-three years later, Bunnell would say more about why he chose to name the valley Yosemite: "As I did not take a fancy to any of the names proposed, I remarked that 'an American name would be the most appropriate;' that 'I could not see any necessity for going to a foreign country for a name for American scenery—the grandest that had ever yet been looked upon. That it would be better to give it an Indian name than to import a strange and inexpressive one; that the name of the tribe who had occupied it, would be more appropriate than any I had heard suggested.' I then proposed 'that we give the valley the name of Yo-sem-i-ty, as it was suggestive, euphonious, and certainly *American*; that by so doing, the name of the tribe of Indians which we met leaving their homes in this valley, perhaps never to return, would be perpetuated.'"[9]

ev

... It is proper to say, what I have before stated, that the Yo-sem-i-te Indians were a composite race, consisting of the disaffected of the various tribes from the Tuolumne to King's River, and hence the difficulty in our understanding of the name, Yo-sem-i-te; but that name, upon the writer's suggestion, was finally approved and applied to the valley, by vote of the volunteers[10] who visited it. Whether it was a compromise among the Indians, as well as with us, it will now be difficult to ascertain. The name is now well established, and it is that by which the few remaining Indians below the valley call it.

One of them—in the presence of Col. Ripley, U.S.A.; Mr. Forbes, P.M.S.S. Co.; Mr. Easton, Mr. Holliday, and **Mr. Ayres**, who first sketched the valley for this magazine—said that Yo-sem-i-te was the name by which they had called it. It is not denied that it is called Yo-hem-i-te, (not Yo-sem-i-te,) by the Indians living on the Fresno; but it is denied most emphatically that it is so called by any of the original Yo-sem-i-te tribe, or that any of

Mr. Ayres: Thomas Almond Ayres (1816–58) arrived in California in 1849 seeking gold but made his mark several years later, in 1855, when he traveled to Yosemite in the company of James Hutchings, produced the first, now iconic, renderings of the valley that Hutchings then promoted through his magazine. Ayres made several more trips to the valley; the last was in 1857–58, but these images were lost with Ayres when the steamer on which he was traveling between Los Angeles and San Francisco, sank.

---

8   L.H. Bunnell, *Hutchings' California Magazine* (May 1859): 498–505.

9   L.H. Bunnell, *Discovery of the Yosemite*, 3rd ed. (New York: Fleming H. Revell Company, 1892), 62.

10 Bunnell is referring to the volunteers who made up the Mariposa Battalion.

them are now living on the Fresno, or have been since 1852. Having been in every expedition to the valley made by volunteers, and since that time assisted George H. Peterson (Fremont's engineer,) in his surveys, the writer, at the risk of appearing egotistical, claims that he had superior advantages for obtaining correct information, more especially as in the first two expeditions, Ten-ie-ya was placed under his special charge, and he acted as interpreter to Capt. Boling.

It is acknowledged that Ah-wah-ne is the Indian name for the valley, and that Ah-wah-ne-ehee is the name of its original occupants; but as this was discovered by the writer long after he had named the valley, and as it was the wish of every volunteer with whom he conversed that the name Yo-sem-i-te be retained, he said very little about it. He will only say, in conclusion, that the principal facts are now before the public, and that it is for them to decide whether they will retain the name Yo-sem-i-te, or have some other.

—L.H. Bunnell

We, the undersigned, having been members of the same company, and through most of the scenes depicted by Dr. Bunnell, having no hesitation in saying that the article above is correct.

—James M. Roane
—Geo. H. Crenshaw

"Petition to the Senators and Representatives of the Congress of the United States in the Behalf of the Remnants of the former Tribes of the Yosemite Indians Praying for Aid and Assistance," *1891 Report of the Acting Superintendent* (Washington, DC: Government Printing Office, 1891)

> Because few Yosemite Indians were fully literate in English, this document may well have been written by a Euro-American. But, as Ed Castillo has argued, the text offers a powerful analysis and "an incredible description of the political, military, and ecological factors driving remaining tribesmen from their valley" that only local Indigenous people could have articulated.[11]

TO HIS EXCELLENCY, THE PRESIDENT OF THE UNITED STATES AND TO THE CONGRESS OF THE UNITED STATES

Your Honors:

We, the undersigned chiefs and head men of the existing remnants of the tribes of the Yo-Semite, the Mono and the Piute Indians, who hold claims upon that gorge in the Sierra Nevada Mountains known as the Yosemite Valley, and the lands around and about it, by virtue of direct descent from the aforenamed tribes, who were inhabitants of that valley and said territory at the time when it was so unjustifiably conquered and taken from our fathers by the whites, do utter, petition and pray your Excellency and your honorable bodies in Congress assembled to hear, deliberate upon, and give us relief, for the following reasons to wit:

1st. In all of the difficulties, disagreements, quarrels, and violences which sprang up between our fathers and the whites of their days, the first causes can invariably be traced to the overbearing tyranny and oppression of the white gold hunters, who had and who were continually usurping our territory. Those causes were briefly as follows: The white gold hunters brought among us drunkenness, lying, murder, forcible violation of our women, cheating, gambling, and wrongful appropriation of our lands for their own selfish uses. We have been made aware that at this period there was no harmonious system of laws or bonds of restraint operating to check the lawlessness or violence of these bands of adventurous and desperate white men, who had

---

11   Ed Castillo, "Petition to Congress on Behalf of the Yosemite Indians," *The Journal of California Anthropology* 5, 2 (Winter 1978): 271–77 offers the best analysis of the petition and its insights.

sought our shores in search of gold, and little or nothing could be expected of them as remuneration for our lands; nor could punishment be inflicted upon them by laws which, if existing, remained in the main unenforced: yet in after years, when the long list of oppressions and outrages to which our fathers were forced to submit at the hands of the whites had long ended by the slaughter and dispersal of our tribes, no notice was taken of the few who remained, and who from then until now have continued to travel to and fro, poorly-clad paupers and unwelcome guests, silently the objects of curiosity or contemptuous pity to the throngs of strangers who yearly gather in this our own land and heritage. We are compelled to daily and hourly witness the further and continual encroachments of a few white men in this our valley. The gradual destruction of its trees, the occupancy of every foot of its territory by bands of grazing horses and cattle, the decimation of the fish in the river, the destruction of every means of support for ourselves and families by the rapacious acts of the whites, in the building of their hotels and operating of their stage lines, which must shortly result in the total exclusion of the remaining remnants of our tribes from this our beloved valley, which has been ours from time beyond our faintest traditions, and which we still claim. Therefore, in support of our petition, we beg leave to offer the following reasons for our prayer:

We, as Indians and survivors of the aforenamed tribes, declare that we were unfairly and unjustly deprived of our possessions in land, made to labor in the interest of the whites for no recompense, subjected to continual brutality, wrong, and outrage at the hands of the whites, and were gradually driven from our homes into strange localities by their action, and that our few retaliatory acts were feeble and deserving of no notice, in comparison to the gross injustices and outrages that we were continually subjected to. And we respectfully call your attention to the official report of Maj. Gen. Thomas J. Green to Gov. Peter H. Burnett, dated May 25, 1850, (page 769, Journals of the Legis. of Cal. for 1851); Brig. Gen. Thomas B. Eastland's report to Gov. Burnett, June 15th, 1850, (page 770, Ibid); letters of Gen. Eastland to Gov. McDougal (page 770, Ibid), and various others. If we were in the wrong the punishment we have suffered and the war indemnity which our fathers were forced to pay—their all and their lives besides—is in monstrous disproportion to the damage they inflicted, however just they may have deemed the provocation.

2d. The action of the Mariposa Battalion towards our chief at that time, Tenaya, and his tribe was wantonly unjust and outrageous. Our only quarrel with the whites then was owing to our determination not to go upon a reservation being established on the Fresno, and give up to the whites this magnificent valley, which was to us reservation and all that we desired and that for a few paltry blankets, gewgaws and indifferent supplies of rations, that might be furnished us or not, at the discretion of any appointed Indian Agent. Our fathers had the sorrow to see their tribe conquered, their dignified and honored chief Tenaya led out by a halter, like a beast, into a green field to eat grass, amid the wonder and laughter of our pursuers; and his youngest son shot dead for no other reason than that he had tried to escape the unjust thralldom of our persecutors. For proof of these statements, you are referred to Dr. Bunnell's History of the Discovery of the Yosemite. He was himself attached to this battalion, and was an eye witness to all the facts related. Those who were left of our fathers were taken with their chief, however, to the reservation on the Fresno, from which place hunger and destitution finally forced them to run away; after which, we have been informed, the reservation was broken up, having shed disgrace upon all connected with its management.

3d. From that time up to the present the remnants of the various bands formerly in possession of the valley have earned a scanty livelihood by hunting, fishing, etc. There has never been a cause of complaint against the descendants of the old Yo-Semites, neither have they broken the peace or indulged in warfares of any kind; they have silently been witness to the usurpation of their lands and valley; they have never been provided for in any way by the Government of either the State or the United States. The wisdom of their action in quietly escaping from the Fresno reservation was justified by the bad management of that reservation, which finally led to its being abolished by the United States Government. Now we, the last remnant of the once great Yosemite tribe, and also those from the Mono and Piutes tribes who have claims here, see that the time is fast approaching when we must all abandon this, our valley, together, for the following reasons. White men have come into this valley to make money only. They have continually disobeyed the laws which were made for the government of this valley by the Washington Government. Those laws declared that this valley should be kept as a reservation and park for the white people forever but the head men appointed to govern this valley by the State Government do not obey those laws; instead, they have given control of the lands of the entire valley into the hands of a few whites, who only wish to make money here, and care neither for the laws nor the Indians. Those white men have fenced the valley all up with wire fences, with sharp barbs all along the wire, close together; it is divided off into fields, many of which are ploughed up by the white men to raise grain and hay to feed their own horses upon, and the Indians are forbidden to walk across their own fields by reason of this farming; the other fields are filled with the horses and cattle of these white men, as many as 125 horses, and sometimes 40 head or more of cattle being at large in these fields; all of the tender roots, berries and the few nuts that formed the sustenance of the Indians are trampled down and torn up by the roots, or eaten and broken off in this way by these few white men's horses and cattle. If the Indians have two or three horses they must starve, for there are no fields left for them to run in, neither can the strange whites, who came in wagons to look at the great rocks in the valley, find food for their horses, by reason of these wire fences of these few white men. Where there are no fences, the valley is cut up completely by dusty, sandy roads, leading from the hotels of whites in every direction. The head men of the whites also order their workmen to cut away the trees in every direction, and destroy the shade and beauty of the valley, so that they may have more room to plough and raise hay to sell to strangers, and to plant in gardens and build their houses upon.

Every once in a while the State Government changes its head men, and every new lot turn away from their homes more and more of the old resident whites, whom we have known so long, and young, strong and hungry looking new faces come in their places. All seem to come only to hunt money. Why the old ones are turned away we do not know, but when they are sent away their houses are torn down, and new ones are built for these new men to live in. This does not seem to us to be right, neither do we believe the great Washington Government wants this wonderful valley to be ploughed up into a hay farm, or its fine forest trees to be cut down and destroyed for the pleasure of those whites who seem to be afraid of and to hate trees. This is not the way in which we treated this park when we had it; and we know that these white headmen often say that the Indians were the only ones who knew how to take care of Yosemite. We have heard that the white men in the valley intend to plough up nearly all of the open and level portion of the valley, to raise hay upon, and it will only be a short time before they will tell the Indians that they must go away and not come back any more. Now, in this valley grow all the things that we can rely upon for our winter supplies, and we cannot go away from here to gather acorns and nuts, or to hunt game, without trespassing upon some other Indians' ground and causing trouble; besides, we do not wish to leave this valley if we can help it, though as it is governed now in the interest of only a few white people, and for them to make money in, we do not see that we can possibly stay here much longer, for every year these few whites reach out for more, more, and drive us slowly further back. We have already been told by the former chief of the whites in this valley, that we must go away from here and stay away; but we say this valley was not given to us by our fathers for a day, or a year, but for all time. The whites are too numerous and powerful for us. We willingly keep the peace, we have no desire to do otherwise, but it is with an uneasiness that we see the time approaching when we must leave this spot which has been the home of our people from time immemorial. Therefore we pray our head white father at Washington and his Great Council to consider the following things, viz:

First. Soon after this valley was taken away from us by the whites, the great Washington Council gave it to all the white American people for a pleasure ground, a park, where they might come and see the great rocks and waterfalls, and enjoy themselves.

Now it seems to us that the laws imposed upon the head men of this valley by the Washington Government are being willfully disregarded, and that Yosemite is no longer a State or National Park, but merely a hay-farm and cattle range.

Second. The valley is almost entirely fenced in, mostly with barbed wire. There are no walks for pleasure. There are horses and cattle in every field. There are nine fenced-off fields within a space of two miles or less, at this upper end of the valley, and consequently the People's Park is a thing of the past. It has now resolved itself into a private institution, making only a show and pretense of being a public benefit and is supported by the State in this condition. Consequently, as we have been wronged and robbed of this valley in the first place by the whites, and has been turned by them into a place for their own benefit, and has been withheld from us for **37 years** and we have received not one iota of remuneration for our natural rights and interests therein at any time and as we see we must relinquish all our possessions here soon, and go among strange tribes and in strange places to live, and as we are sufficiently civilized to understand the ways of the whites, and conform in a measure to their habits and customs, we pray you, our great White Chief, and you, the great Washington Council, to give us for our just claims upon this Yosemite Valley, and our surrounding claims so violently and wrongfully wrested from us without either cause or provocation, out of the abundance of your great wealth, for the future support of ourselves and our descendants, one million of dollars, United States gold coin; for which consideration we will forever bargain and convey all our natural right and title to Yosemite Valley and our surrounding claims.

37 Years: The text is referring to the 1864 Yosemite Grant Act transferring the valley to the state of California. See Document 14, p. 000.

We know that Indians far away in your country have received indemnities in this way for lands forcibly taken from them and other wrongs inflicted upon them by whites in former times; and also that the whites constantly receive such indemnifications for losses sustained at the hands of Indians.

Therefore, we hope in justice that you, the Great White Chief, and you of the Great White Council of this Nation, at Washington, may hear with wide open ears, and grant our prayer; also, in case that you declare justly and favorably for us in our great need, suffering under this condition of great wrong and poverty, we desire to be heard, and have a voice in the Council which shall appoint the men who are to receive the indemnity money for us, as we do not wish to part with our last remnant of territory for merely the enrichment of a few adventurous white men. Here we place our marks as opposite our names, the Chiefs and head men of the petitioning remnants of the former Yosemite tribes with our principal women and children.

YOSEMITE INDIANS
Te-he-he or Capt. Henry.
Cha-muk or Lancisco.
Sung-ok or John.
Capt. Di Chich-k or John Lawrence.
Hick-ah or Peter Hilliard.
Wit-ta-ra-bee or Tom Hutchings.
Low-a or "Bill."
Bu-lok or "Bullock."
Chor-cha or "Austin."
Chre-cra or "Mike."
Hul-i-na or "Capt. Reuben."
Una-moy-na or "Capt. John."
"Scipio."
"Cary."
Su-pan-chee or "Capt. Paul."
Car ra-nee or "Pedro."
Chee-tee or "Jim."
"Wilson."
"Willie Wilson."
Meme-lem or "Melquita."
Pancho or "Jack."
Cha-muk or "Louie."
Ha-tam-e-we-ah or "Nancey."
"Billy Stanley."

MONO-YOSEMITES.
Shi-ban-nah or "Capt. John." (Head Chief of the Mono Piutes)
Bos-seek.
"Johnny Brown."
"Charley Bill."
Chen-na-pee.
Tor-tah-hock-a-mah.
Pah-aw-zack or "Jim."

YOSEMITE INDIANS: WOMEN
Pa-ma-ha or "Callipene."
Y-mu-sa or "Betsey."
Yo-ne-pa or "Mary Ann."
Chen-na-chu or "Susey Lawrence."
Shu-wi-o-nee or "Jenny."
Why-to-ne.
To-nee-pa or "Mary."
Awl-kim.
"Dulcy."
"Caledonia."
"Julia Ann."

DOCUMENT 11:

DOCUMENT 11:

Extract from John Muir, *The Mountains of California* (New York: The Century Co., 1894), 90–94

This is an excerpt from John Muir, *The Mountains of California*, a passage that is itself extracted from Muir's journals. For Muir (1838–1913), wilderness was defined by the absence of people—most especially of Indigenous people. His troubling depiction of them in this passage—"Somehow they seemed to have no right place in the landscape, and I was glad to see them fading out of sight down the pass"—is part of the larger cultural argument that westward expansion of white civilization marked the end of Indigenous society, and the start of a new, presumably better, appreciation of nature. As part of this wiping out of Indigenous people, note Muir's contention that Mono Pass, which for millennia the Miwok, Paiute, and other Indigenous peoples had blazed, was rather a product of the Gold Rush. It is, he writes, "the best known and most extensively traveled of all that exist in the High Sierra. A trail was made through it about the time of the Mono gold excitement, in the year 1858, by adventurous miners and prospectors—men who would build a trail down the throat of darkest **Erebus** on the way to gold. Though more than a thousand feet lower than the Kearsarge, it is scarcely less sublime in rock-scenery, while in snowy, falling water it far surpasses it. Being so favorably situated for the stream of Yosemite travel, the more adventurous tourists cross over through this glorious gateway to the volcanic region around Mono Lake. It has therefore gained a name and fame above every other pass in the range."[12]

Erebus: In Greek mythology, Erebus, born of Chaos, personified darkness and the Underworld.

ev

... My first visit to **Bloody Cañon** was made in the summer of 1869, under circumstances well calculated to heighten the impressions that are the peculiar offspring of mountains. I came from the blooming tangles of Florida, and waded out into the plant-gold of the great valley of California, when its flora was as yet untrodden. Never before had I beheld congregations of social flowers half so extensive or half so glorious. Golden **compositæ** covered all the ground from the Coast Range to the Sierra like a stratum of curdled sunshine, in which I reveled for weeks, watching the rising and setting of their innumerable suns; then I gave myself up to be borne forward on the

Bloody Cañon: Bloody Cañon, Muir observes, forms the main section of Mono Pass, beginning at the summit of the Sierra and running in an east-northeasterly direction to the edge of the Mono Plain.

compositae: Goldenrod.

---

12 John Muir, *The Mountains of California* (London: Penguin Random House, 2008), chap. 5. See also Ross Wakefield, "Muir's Early Indian Views: Another Look at *My First Summer in the Sierra*," *The John Muir Newsletter* 5, 1 (Winter 1994–95).

crest of the summer wave that sweeps annually up the Sierra and spends itself on the snowy summits.

At the Big Tuolumne Meadows I remained more than a month, sketching, botanizing, and climbing among the surrounding mountains. The mountaineer with whom I then happened to be camping was one of those remarkable men one so frequently meets in California, the hard angles and bosses of whose characters have been brought into relief by the grinding excitements of the gold period, until they resemble glacial landscapes. But at this late day, my friend's activities had subsided, and his craving for rest caused him to become a gentle shepherd and literally to lie down with the lamb.

Recognizing the unsatisfiable longings of my Scotch Highland instincts, he threw out some hints concerning Bloody Cañon, and advised me to explore it. "I have never seen it myself," he said, "for I never was so unfortunate as to pass that way. But I have heard many a strange story about it, and I warrant you will at least find it wild enough."

Then of course I made haste to see it. Early next morning I made up a bundle of bread, tied my note-book to my belt, and strode away in the bracing air, full of eager, indefinite hope. The plushy lawns that lay in my path served to soothe my morning haste. The sod in many places was starred with daisies and blue gentians, over which I lingered. I traced the paths of the ancient glaciers over many a shining pavement, and marked the gaps in the upper forests that told the power of the winter avalanches. Climbing higher, I saw for the first time the gradual dwarfing of the pines in compliance with climate, and on the summit discovered creeping mats of the arctic willow overgrown with silky catkins, and patches of the dwarf vaccinium with its round flowers sprinkled in the grass like purple hail; while in every direction the landscape stretched sublimely away in fresh wildness—a manuscript written by the hand of Nature alone.

At length, as I entered the pass, the huge rocks began to close around in all their wild, mysterious impressiveness, when suddenly, as I was gazing eagerly about me, a drove of gray hairy beings came in sight, lumbering toward me with a kind of boneless, wallowing motion like bears.

I never turn back, though often so inclined, and in this particular instance, amid such surroundings, everything seemed singularly unfavorable for the calm acceptance of so grim a company. Suppressing my fears, I soon discovered that although as hairy as bears and as crooked as summit pines, the strange creatures were sufficiently erect to belong to our own species. They proved to be nothing more formidable than Mono Indians dressed in the skins of sage-rabbits. Both the men and the women begged persistently for whisky and tobacco, and seemed so accustomed to denials that I found it impossible to convince them that I had none to give. Excepting the names of these two products of civilization, they seemed to understand not a word of English; but I afterward learned that they were on their way to Yosemite Valley to feast awhile on trout and procure a load of acorns to carry back through the pass to their huts on the shore of Mono Lake.

Occasionally a good countenance may be seen among the Mono Indians, but these, the first specimens I had seen, were mostly ugly, and some of them altogether hideous. The dirt on their faces was fairly stratified, and seemed so ancient and so undisturbed it might almost possess a geological significance. The older faces were, moreover, strangely blurred and divided into sections by furrows that looked like the cleavage-joints of rocks, suggesting exposure on the mountains in a cast-away condition for ages. Somehow they seemed to have no right place in the landscape, and I was glad to see them fading out of sight down the pass.

Then came evening, and the somber cliffs were inspired with the ineffable beauty of the alpenglow. A solemn calm fell upon everything. All the lower portion of the cañon was in gloaming shadow, and I crept into a hollow near one of the upper lakelets to smooth the ground in a sheltered nook for a bed. When the short twilight faded, I kindled a sunny fire, made a cup of tea, and lay down to rest and look at the stars. Soon the night-wind began to flow and pour in torrents among the jagged peaks, mingling strange tones with those of the waterfalls sounding far below; and as I drifted toward sleep I began to experience an uncomfortable feeling of nearness to the furred Monos. Then the full moon looked down over the edge of the cañon wall, her countenance seemingly filled with intense concern, and apparently so near as to produce a startling effect as if she had entered my bedroom, forgetting all the world, to gaze on me alone....

PART 2

Tourist Sanctuary

Tourism remade Yosemite. The landscape's sights, sounds, and smells, its flora and fauna, had been home to the Indigenous peoples who for millennia lived in and managed the valley. But with their forced removal, white settler-colonists like James Mason Hutchings and John Muir, as well as geologists and artists turned Yosemite into a visitor's haven—a place to encounter, tour, and leave, a site of temporary respite. This alteration in how these well-heeled tourists experienced Yosemite shaped in part the records they left behind of their time in the High Sierra. Private diaries and correspondence, like published travelogues, emphasize a three-part chronology: they chronicle how visitors arrived in Yosemite, what they did while there, and what they took with them when they departed. Making their trips possible were an evolving set of transportation options—stagecoaches and trains, horses and mules—as well as an increased availability of food and lodging. Just as essential was a set of illustrated guidebooks, which, when combined with oft-exhibited paintings and photographs of the valley, structured how they moved from one waterfall and granite monolith to another. At each scenic oversight, they saw what they had been prepared to see; they felt what they had been encouraged to feel. These literate visitors then put pen to paper to articulate what they observed and how they responded emotionally, material that they preserved as a keepsake (as did succeeding generations of their family). Other such reflections entered the public record when compiled into a tract or book. Either way, these documents reinforced the larger cultural conversation about Yosemite's value and virtue as a beguiling refuge in an urbanizing world. A place from which to escape civilization, even though it was the wealth generated by the booming industrial economy that enabled these tourists to travel to this remote valley in the Sierra.

i. Tourists on Horseback

James Mason Hutchings, *Scenes of Wonder and Curiosity in California* (San Francisco: J.M. Hutchings & Company, 1862)

ii. Descending into Yosemite Valley
James Mason Hutchings, *Scenes of Wonder and Curiosity in California* (San Francisco: J.M. Hutchings & Company, 1862)

iii. Yosemite Valley Panorama

James Mason Hutchings, *Scenes of Wonder and Curiosity in California* (San Francisco: J.M. Hutchings & Company, 1862)

iv. El Capitan
James Mason Hutchings, *Scenes of Wonder and Curiosity in California* (San Francisco: J.M. Hutchings & Company, 1862)

v. Pohono or Bridalveil Falls
James Mason Hutchings, *Scenes of Wonder and Curiosity in California* (San Francisco: J.M. Hutchings & Company, 1862)

vi. Yosemite Falls
James Mason Hutchings, *Scenes of Wonder and Curiosity in California* (San Francisco: J.M. Hutchings & Company, 1862)

vii. Carleton Watkins, Mirror Lake, 1865
Library of Congress, https://www.loc.gov/resource/ppmsca.09982/

DOCUMENT 12

Extracts from James Mason Hutchings, "The Yo-Ham-i-te Valley," *Hutchings' California Magazine* (1856)

> Hutchings, as part of his promotional engagement with Yosemite, lays out the tourist map of the future national park, identifying the various sites that generations of visitors have continued to seek out. He also uses romantic terms to captivate the readers of his magazine, all with an eye to luring more visitors to the valley.

ぐ

There are but few lands that possess more of the beautiful and picturesque than California. Its towering and pine-covered mountains; its widespread vallies, carpeted with flowers; its leaping waterfalls; its foaming cataracts; its rushing rivers; its placid lakes; its evergreen forests; its gently rolling hills, with shrubs and trees and flowers, make this a garden of loveliness, and a pride to her enterprising sons.

Whether one sits with religious veneration at the foot of Mt Shasta; or cools himself in the refreshing shade of the natural caves and bridges; or walks beneath the shadows of the mammoth trees of Calaveras; or stands in awe, looking upon the frowning and pine-covered heights of the Valley of the Yo-Ham-i-te—he feels that

"A thing of beauty is a joy forever."

and that the Californian's home may compare in picturesque magnificence with that of any other land.

Among the most remarkable may be classed the Yo-Ham-i-te Valley—surrounded as it is by the lofty granite mountains, exceeding three thousand feet in height, of the most fantastic shapes; now in appearance like a vast projecting tower; now standing boldly out like an immense chimney or column; then like two giant domes; yonder, a waterfall of two thousand five hundred feet; and, as it rolls over the precipice, its quivering spray is gilded with the colors of the rain-bow, the sunlight falls upon it.

From the perpendicular sides of that mountain a stunted pine tree is struggling to live, alone—a mere speck upon the landscape. Every craggy height is surrounded by shrubs or trees—every spot has its contrast of color and appearance. Upon the mountain's summit is a dense forest of lofty pines—that by distance look only as weeds or shrubs. In the valley placidly glides the transparent stream; now impinging the mountain's base; now

The Giant's Tower: Now called El Capitan, the rock face measures 3,590 feet (1,094 m) from base to peak.

The Cascade of the Rainbow: Almost as romantic is its current name, Bridalveil Fall, with a single drop of 617 feet (188 m) to the valley floor below. Its principle source is Ostrander Lake nearly 10 miles to the south.

two thousand five hundred feet: The official calculation is 2,425 feet (739 m).

biggest waterfall in the world: It is no longer granted that title, though it remains the tallest waterfall in California.

Col. G.W. Whitman: Hutchins thus credits Whitman with being the first white man to see the valley, a claim that has other contenders, including James Rutherford Walker's 1833 sighting. William P. Abrams may well have been the first white to enter the valley. His 18 October 1849 diary entry perfectly captures Yosemite Valley, Bridalveil Fall, and Half Dome: "... While at Savage's Reamer and I saw a grizzly bear tracks and went out to hunt him down getting lost in the mountains and not returning until the following evening, found our way to camp over an Indian trail that led past a valley enclosed by stupendous cliffs rising perhaps 3000 feet from their base and which gave us cause for wonder. Not far off a waterfall dropped from a cliff below three jagged peaks into the valley while farther beyond a rounded mountain stood, the valley wide of which looked as though it had been sliced with a knife as one would slice a loaf

winding its serpentine course up the fertile valley; its margin fringed with willows and flowers, that are ever blossoming, and grass that is ever green.

Upon descending the mountains towards the valley, the first object that attracts your notice, and invites your wondering admiration, is "**The Giant's Tower**," standing on the left, an immense mountain of perpendicular granite, three thousand one hundred feet in height, from the surface of the river to its outer edge—and nearly three thousand five hundred feet to the highest place upon it. On the right side of this view, is a waterfall, nine hundred and twenty-eight feet, and named "**The Cascade of the Rainbow**."

Before you is spread the beautiful green valley, nearly covered in trees, the bright river glistening and glittering out among them.

About two miles above the "Giant's Tower," on the same side, is the great Yo-Ham-i-te Falls—**two thousand five hundred feet** in height. The upper or main portion of this fall is one thousand five hundred feet—the second, or middle, is four hundred feet—and the third, or lowest fall, is six hundred feet, and all of them perpendicular. This is the **biggest waterfall in the world**.

Col. G.W. Whitman, in the spring of 1850, when in search of stock stolen by Indians from around Sonora, stood on top of these falls, and upon looking down into the deep abyss, the idea suggested to his mind was—"Is this the bottomless pit?"—and as the deep stream rolled its volumes over the edge of the precipice, he gazed with awe and admiration at the terrific chasm before him.

Advancing up the valley, and threading your way amongst the trees; now standing beneath the shadowy mountain; or crossing the river; every few steps present a change of scene, or some variety of shade and beauty.

At the upper end of the valley stand the "Twin Domes"—two immense mountains, dome-shaped, and distinct from any of the surrounding ones.[1] … Part of this dome has fallen away, and blocking the north branch of this stream, has formed a beautiful lake, and is called **Indian Lake**, being a favorite resort of the Indians, for ensnaring the speckled trout, of which there are vast numbers in its clear deep waters.

About five miles above the lake, and on the same stream, there is **another water-fall** of three hundred feet, and which, owing to the masses of rock, and bushes, is part of the way rather difficult to access.

About three miles from the head of the valley, on the main and middle branch of this river, there are **two other water-falls**, the first of which is about four hundred feet. The other is reached with difficulty, but its hoarse roaring invites the attempt; and climbing a tree, you secure safe footing, and reach the top,—and witness **another magnificent fall**, of six hundred feet.

About twenty miles above this fall is the lake spoken of below.

---

1   This is a reference to Half Dome (4,737 feet; 1,444 m) and North Dome (7,546 feet; 2,300 m).

On the east fork, there is another waterfall of several hundred feet, the elevation of which has not yet been ascertained.

The principal altitudes of the objects of wonder and interest in this valley, were taken by Mr. G.K. Peterson, engineer of the Yo-semite and Mariposa Water Company, and are doubtless very correct; and although the stupendous height of the water-falls could scarcely be realized, they have, by actual measurement, exceeded the estimates given. They now stand forth as realities, which invite the spontaneous admiration of every lover of the sublime and beautiful, who may visit the deep solitude of this interesting and remarkable valley....

of bread and which Reamer and I called the Rock of Ages." See Weldon F. Heald, ed., "The Abrams Diary," *Sierra Club Bulletin* 32, 5 (May 1947): 126–27.

Indian Lake: Mirror Lake originally covered most of the Yosemite Valley, is seasonally fed by Tenaya Creek, and due to sediment accumulation is continuing to shrink.

another water-fall: Vernal Fall (317 feet; 96 m).

two other water-falls: A reference perhaps to Illilouette Fall (370 feet; 113 m).

another magnificent fall: Nevada Fall (594 feet; 181 m).

DOCUMENT 13:

Extracts from the Diary of Sarah Haight, 20–25 May 1858[2]

Sarah Haight was a bridesmaid in the wedding of Lizzie Fry and William Ralston from two prominent San Franciscan families. She joined a large entourage of the newlyweds' friends and family on the couple's honeymoon to Yosemite. This extract from Haight's diary reveals the lure of Yosemite for those with the time and resources to visit it. It is striking that by the late 1850s it had become a well-known destination, just seven years after the Mariposa Battalion had driven Indigenous people from the valley.

May 20

Marched into church with slow and measured footsteps to the sound of solemn music. At first the impulse was strong upon me to hurry and get through as soon as possible. But fortunately, I recollected myself in time and walked with serenity and composure up to the altar where the words were pronounced which united Lizzie Fry and William Ralston in the bonds of holy matrimony. The bride looked beautiful, with just sufficient of a rose tint upon her cheek to relieve the complete whiteness of her dress.

We each went to our respective houses and laid aside our white silks, tulle, and orange flowers for something more appropriate for travelling. Four o'clock found us on board of the Stockton boat and after innumerable farewells and congratulations from friends and acquaintances we left the wharf. Received salutes from the steamships *Orizaba* and *Sierra Nevada* which fairly made my head ache. We had a very nice dinner until our arrival at Benicia, when our party separated; part to return to San Francisco and the rest to go on to the Big Trees....

May 21

... The country through which we [later] passed was undulating and picturesque and we saw miners at work in the sun digging for gold. Where there are diggings the beauty of the immediate country is destroyed—rough, unsightly mounds of earth, suggestive of freshly made graves, and piles of refuse quartz that but add to the general barren aspect of the country. I could not help moralizing a little on the somewhat stale subject of filthy

---

2 *The Diary of Miss Sarah Haight*, ed. Francis P. Farquhar (The Friends of the Bancroft Library, U of California–Berkeley, 1961).

lucre: how unsightly it makes the country appear; how few flowers or how little vegetation there is where there is gold; how it sometimes tells the same story on nations surfeited with it; and how often its blighting effects are on the human heart. The miners' cottages have none of that air of comfort and even beauty which marks that of the poorest peasant in other countries. The tavern is generally the best-looking house in the place—for a good reason, because it is the best supported.

Towards noon we passed through **Angel's Camp**, a place that seemed to me composed of quartz mills, the hammers of which gave the only sounds of life that were heard throughout the town....

Towards evening the air became more pleasant and the dust less troublesome, and before arriving at "**Murphy's**," which had been our projected stopping place, we ladies were all desirous of proceeding on to the Big Trees that night. The matter was talked over and all agreed to it. For the last few miles of our way we were gradually going up hill and the breeze which sprang up came fresh from the mountains with a freshness that was delightful after the heat of the day. We reached Murphy's about sunset and Lizzie and I stood at the door of the hotel and looked off in the distance, far over the cabins and canvas houses of the little town, and watched the sun slowly gathering the clouds around him [the sun] and then leaving them tinged with his own brightness to console the world a little while for his departure. And we watched them until their brightness, too, departed and they grew black and then grey. So have man seen and cherished fair hopes that were only bright with a departing lustre....

May 22

This morning's sun dispersed the clouds and the sweet singing of the birds dispelled any dream of wandering through dark forests without a guide, and awoke me to the beautiful realities of life. In the midnight gloom I had not realized the rise of the great monsters towering up above us. But when I stood at the base of one of the trees and looked up to the top, and when I saw how like pigmies the gentlemen looked walking around the base, the longer I looked the more their grandeur grew upon me, and then I could realize this vast handiwork of nature. "What a freak of nature," says **Mr. H.** "Wonderful are thy works, O Lord!" thought I, looking up to where the treetops seemed to extend to the blue space. One cannot help a feeling of awe in wandering among those majestic trees. Why are they there in that particular place? Did not some of the sons of Noah emigrate to California and plant them there? Or perhaps that locality was not reached by the flood. I felt an almost irresistible desire to question the great giants—but it was a consoling reflection to me that pigmy as I am, I could remember

Angel's Camp: This gold rush town, founded by Rhode Island migrant Henry Angell, is the reputed source of Mark Twain's story, "The Celebrated Jumping Frog of Calaveras County."

Murphy's: Located in Murphy, CA, in Calaveras County, the hotel had opened two years before the wedding party arrived (and remains open to this day). Then, as now, it offered access to the Big Trees that Haight refers to, many of which are now protected in Big Trees State Park.

Mr. H.: John Y. Hallock (1825–1910), yet another migrant to California in the Gold Rush years, established a successful building supply company in San Francisco, contributing to and benefitting from the city's rapid growth.

what has passed before me during my little life, while these giants of nature can do nothing but grow and sometimes hum a mournful song amid their branches....

We walked around the place as long as our time would permit and then tore ourselves away. We had not proceeded far on our way when the clouds that had been for some time threatening again poured down upon us, this time accompanied with hail. I could now see in the morning light that the trees gradually increased in height from Murphy's up to the "Big Trees" and could also have the pleasure of seeing the effect of the rain in the forest. How the old veterans seemed to enjoy it, and how they seemed to drink in the refreshing showers; and all the time we were regaled with that spicy herby fragrance that is so peculiar to California. It is not strange that mountaineers are generally such a noble race of men. I think that the clear bracing air that they breathe has much to do with it.

... After a most excellent dinner, which everyone was ready to do justice to, we again started on our winding way.... We drove by moonlight into **Columbia.** All our noisy mirth was gone, but the gentle chastened feeling that a beautiful landscape never fails to leave on most minds was upon all of us, and silently but happily we rode the next few miles on to Columbia. Along the road-side the miners were busy "panning" up, as they call it; i.e., washing out the sluices and counting the gold dust. Now Columbia to **Sonora** is but three miles, and there we drove quickly, for in addition to the other feelings, we knew that the next day we should separate and some of us go on to the Yosemite Falls and the rest return to San Francisco. We drove up to the hotel at Sonora at about eight o'clock, and about nine were all seated to a splendid supper and making farewell speeches for we knew that we should have very little time for that at our hurried breakfast the next morning. Soon after, the ladies, all but me, retired to rest. But I could not sleep, for the day has been one of excitements and impressions of beautiful things which keep me awake until this late hour, writing. While sitting in the parlor of the hotel, the Judge [McRae] came and had a low talk with me. At length I began to be sleepy and, bidding good night to the judge, I crept into my bed and was soon asleep, visions of beauty mingling with my dreams.

May 23

Messrs. Hallock, Young, Tobin, and Haven, and Mrs. Darling bid us good-bye this morning, and I fancy that was the reason why we all felt rather sad and quiet. I leaned back in my seat and pulled my bonnet over my face and pretended to go to sleep, but the exclamations of the party in regard to the scenery soon compelled me to look around me. The road wound

Columbia: Located in the Sierra Nevada foothills and founded in 1850, Columbia was yet another Gold Rush mining town with multiple hotels, stores, and banks. Today, its central district is preserved as part of Columbia State Historic Park and it is on the National Register of Historic Places.

Sonora: Sonora is yet another former mining town in the so-called California Mother Lode. Unlike other such communities, Sonora was founded by Mexican miners who joined the international throng of (mostly) men to chase their golden dreams in the Sierra. It is the closest town to Yosemite.

along the side of a mountain, curving like a horse-shoe, and many hundred feet below us they were washing out gold. It was a wild, desolate-looking country through which we passed, and during the whole day we did not meet but one team.

We arrived at **Coulterville** this evening about five o'clock and after dinner we all arrayed ourselves in our **bloomer costumes** and walked out to see the beauties of the place.... The village or town of Coulterville is named after the man who keeps the hotel of the place and is very prettily situated between high hills on every side and is a place of some mining importance.

Hazel Green, May 24

We left Coulterville at seven this morning and travelled for a little while on a dusty wagon-road until we exchanged it for a mountain trail. I have heard much of mountain scenery but had always connected with it some idea of sterility and gloom, but the Sierras certainly do not realize that in the month of May, for on all sides we passed beautiful flowers and bright green grass.

At about twelve miles from Coulterville we dismounted from our horses and were invited to take a short walk to see **the Cave**. I went rather unwillingly, for I had but little idea of what I was going to see. Here Captain Tyler joined us. The Captain was a steamboat man on the Mississippi River and a regular character in his way. He was about six feet high, stalwart as a giant, with a peculiar honest expression in his handsome face. He will be a very great addition to our party, I can see. The next in order and importance is **Captain Ackley**, our guide. The Captain has evidently been a good looking man once but is much disfigured with a sabre cut across his cheek. He has been in the Mexican War and has seen some service, but I think not quite all that he pretends to. He occasionally forgets himself and has been in too many battles at the same time and, if one can trust his own account, has performed deeds to which **Gonzalvo de Cordova** or **the Cid** were entirely unequal. Nevertheless, he is quite an addition to our party, though I observe he is never in a hurry to work....

Capt. T. led Mrs. Ralston [to the cave], and I followed. After a short ascent we came suddenly upon a flight of steps which we ascended and the beauties of the cave burst upon us. For a few moments we could do nothing but gaze, and then, the first impressions having in some degree subsided, we had leisure to look. We descended about seventy-five feet on steps constructed for that purpose before reaching the floor of the cave. Its floor on the right is covered with large rocks cushioned with green moss whose color and texture no upholsterer could rival. The cave at the top is partially open, and the trees, called boxwood elders, grow among the rocks and thrust their tops out of the opening. The rays of light that come into the cave through

Coulterville: Named after its first settler, George W. Coulter, it was one of many small mining towns that sprang up along the Sierras's many creeks, streams, and rivers—in fact, Coultersville was originally called Maxwell's Creek.

bloomer costumes: Knee-length dresses over full trousers. Women's rights activists Alice Bloomer, for whom it is named, Elizabeth Cady Stanton and Elizabeth Smith Miller, advocated that all women wear the outfit, known as the "freedom dress," as a healthy alternative to tight corsets and frilly petticoats.

the Cave: Bowers Cave, now managed as part of the Stanislaus National Forest, was a sacred site for the Miwok Nation, who believed that it was the home of the first people. By the early 1850s, when white miners and settlers arrived in the area, its then-owner, Nicholas Arni, seized on the opportunities that the road to Yosemite offered, and turned the cave into a tourist attraction. The depth of the subterranean lake that Haight describes in vivid detail remains unascertained.

Captain Ackley: Elias C. Ackley (1826–73), a veteran and adventurer, sailed around Cape Horn to arrive in California in the early 1850s, and began to flume his claim dubbed Poor Man's Creek. Family memory has him leaving California in 1854, but a description of Ackley that Haight provided in 1858 corresponds to the cheek-scar that the family also identifies.

Gonzalvo de Cordova:
Gonzalo de Córdoba (1453–1515) was a Spanish general who led the conquest of Granada and the Reconquista, and later fought in the Italian Wars (1495–1503).

the Cid: El Cid, Rodrigo Díaz de Vivar (c. 1043–99) was a Castilian nobleman and military leader in medieval Spain, a warrior and strategist of great fame.

Nicholas Arni: Arni is reputed to have been the first white person to have explored the cave and built the stairs and other amenities that enabled tourists like Haight to visit the cave as part of their Yosemite experience.

these green leaves are chastened and softened to a proper degree. The place does not want the broad glare of the sun in it. From the right-hand side, where the trees are, the ground slopes gradually to the shore of a beautiful lake, clear as crystal—though forty feet deep, every stone on its bottom is distinctly visible. There is no knowing how deep it may be underneath the rocks, for it has apparently no bottom.

There was a little boat there into which I got and Captain T. rowed me about the tiny lake. It gave me a strange feeling, like awe, to go in under the rocks where it was so cold, dark, and solitary. Sitting in the boat and looking up on the rocks, it resembled a theatre with the side scenes. There were grotesque faces and bats and owls carved in rock, but when you changed your position the resemblance would vanish. There was one figure that seemed to me to be very distinct. It was a female figure with her head bent down and clinging to the rock as if in agony. It was very satisfactory to us to see in one corner a rock cascade. There was a depression in this corner of the rock above and it looked as if there had been a fall of water there that had suddenly turned to stone. Between the cascade and the theatre there was an organ, the pipes of which were very distinct.

Going up a flight of steps to the left, we entered a spacious shanty, which bears the name of the ballroom, though I should imagine the floor somewhat rough for a dance. But my favorite place was in the little boat on the lake—to watch the rays of light as they stole in through the opening of the cave with softened rays, giving it that softened light that a painter would love. Innumerable swallows flew twittering around, and they, with some pretty little green lizard were the sole occupants of the cave. The water of the lake is beautifully clear and cold. The proprietor, **Nicholas Arni**, told us that fish put in the lake entirely disappeared, probably by some subterranean outlet. The trees, rocks, and sides of the cave are everywhere covered with beautiful green moss. The honor of naming it was conferred on Judge McRae, who called it the "Bower Cave." At last we were compelled to go away and we left with regret, but promising ourselves a visit on our return.

Again in the saddle, we rode rapidly on and passed the last Chinaman digging for gold and heard their last "How do John," and passed the last houses or shanties that we were likely to see for some time, and then we were alone with our party in the mountains. The trail was marked by the trees being "blazed," as it is called. We could not travel more than a hundred yards without crossing little mountain brooks running merrily along over their pebbly bottoms and filled with cold water.

The forests are unlike those of the Eastern states. There is no underbrush and the branches of the trees are very far from the ground. The smell of the pines, too, is very pleasant. Our trail is frequently crossed by a fallen tree that some tempest had brought down. A tempest in the mountains and among those pines must be a grand thing. How the wind would howl and roar, and how the ground would shake when one of them fell! In one place a pine tree had fallen and crushed two or three others in its fall and together they had rolled down the mountain sides....

May 25

This morning all were in the saddle at an early hour. We saw some of the most magnificent fir prospects I have ever beheld—at the foot of the mountain upon whose summits we were was a beautiful green level prairie with a little stream flowing through its midst and the trees were all like orchard trees. So cultivated did it look that we could scarcely believe that it was not cultivated. Above it on the opposite side towered a mountain covered with trees, and still beyond that rose another and another, range on range, and the last were covered with snow. How grateful the cold wind coming from the snow felt in the noon, and the snow was so pure and white that you could scarce distinguish it from the clouds resting midway on its sides. Looking back of us we could see the coast range of mountains at a distance of two hundred miles and conspicuous among them was **Mt. Diablo**. How that glimpse of the old veteran carried me home to my own room, where it is the first thing I can see on looking out of my window in the morning.

The road has been getting gradually wilder and the hills sterner. Immense granite rocks rest on the mountain above the trail with a threatening aspect. In some places they appear to have fallen and carried large pine trees along with them. In one place I saw where a large pine tree had torn up a rock in its fall, exactly as a dentist extracts a tooth with his pincers. This afternoon, when about two miles from the entrance of the valley, we saw the Bridal Veil, the first fall in the valley. It looked like a silver thread in the distance and relieved the solemn grandeur of the surrounding hills.

As we approach the valley it grows ever wilder, and when we commence the descent we compare it involuntarily to the entrance to the infernal regions. The mountains that are in view are covered with great white rocks. The trail is over rocks, and a little stream below us tumbles and rushes over its rocky bottom as if it were mad. It is without exception the wildest scene I have ever seen. The only flowers that grow here are the beautiful scarlet ice plant, as it is called, and some fungi. The steep toilsome descent is at last accomplished. We came in view of all the party stretched on the ground beneath the shade of a tree. I am sorry to say my fortitude gave way. My foot pained me. I was very tired and threw myself exhausted on the ground.

After half an hour's rest we again proceeded on our way, and what a change! The desolation of the way we had passed was not visible to us. We rode through beautiful green meadows, under the shady branches of trees,

Mt. Diablo: Located in Contra Costa County in the eastern portion of the San Francisco Bay Area, Mount Diablo rises to 3,848 feet (1,173 m); its distinct promontory remains visible from the Sierras (and vice versa).

Cathedral: Cathedral Rocks or Spires rises 6,644 feet (2,025 m) above the valley.

Sentinel: Another striking granite formation in Yosemite, Sentinel Rock reaches to 7,038 feet (2,145 m).

and the fragrance of the wild honeysuckle was a pleasant exchange for the reflection of the sun's rays from the great white rocks. To the right of us was what is called a "**Cathedral**" ... and where could there be a church more magnificent? We rode on, at our left "El Capitan," a man wrapped in a Spanish cloak with a slouched hat. We drew rein on the banks of the Merced, where it was very still and deep, and lay down on our blankets under the protection of the "**Sentinel**." Never did the beauty of the Twenty-third Psalm present itself so before me. I had been frightened and disturbed and was very weary, and the words, "He maketh me to lie down in green pastures; he leadeth me beside the still *waters*.—Yea, though I walk through the valley of the shadow of death, I will fear no evil; for thou art with me; thy rod and thy staff they comfort me," filled me with quiet and peace. We had been walking through the valley of the shadow of death, as it seemed. By my request the camp was called "Stillwater Camp."

From the camp we were not in sight of either of the falls, though we could hear them very plainly. A large fire was burning. All the party were tired and stretched themselves out in various postures, but I was so happy and so occupied with the beautiful scene that I could not sleep. Behind me was the Sentinel—it was only by lying on my back that I could see its summit 4,000 feet above me. The valley was in shade when the moonlight crepting softly downwards until it was about half-way down its sides, and then I saw the moon itself advance hesitatingly above the brow of opposite rocks. The hesitated advance withdrew and then came boldly forward. She was closely followed by a star that advanced trembling to the edge of the rocks, rose and fell several times, then followed her mistress. Gradually the moonlight advanced and covered the whole camp and shone on the beautiful river.

DOCUMENT 14:

The Yosemite Grant Act (1864)[3]

This act was signed by President Abraham Lincoln on 30 June 1864. In putting his signature to this transfer and charging the state of California with its management for "public use, resort, and recreation," the president was establishing an important precedent. This was the first time the US government had set aside land for recreation, and this set the preconditions for the 1916 establishment of the National Park Service. But this act also codified the erasure of Miwok, Numu/Paiute, and Newe/Shoshone rights to their ancestral territories. Because the state was later deemed to have failed in its responsibilities for maintain and protecting the valley, in 1890 California receded Yosemite to the US government.

ℰ

Be it enacted by the Senate and House of Representatives of the United States of America in Congress assembled, That there shall be, and is hereby, granted to the State of California the "cleft" or "gorge" in the granite peak of the Sierra Nevada Mountains, situated in the county of Mariposa, in the State aforesaid, and the headwaters of the Merced River, and known as the Yo-Semite Valley, with its branches or spurs, in estimated length fifteen miles, and in average width one mile back from the main edge of the precipice, on each side of the valley, with the stipulation, nevertheless, that the said State shall accept this grant upon the express conditions that the premises shall be held for public use, resort, and recreation; shall be inalienable for all time; but leases not exceeding ten years may be granted for portions of said premises.

All incomes derived from leases of privileges to be expended in the preservation and improvement of the property, or the roads leading thereto; the boundaries to be established at the cost of said State by the United States surveyor-general of California, whose official **plat**, when affirmed by the Commissioner of the General Land Office, shall constitute the evidence of the locus, extent, and limits of the said cleft or gorge; the premises to be managed by the governor of the State with eight other commissioners, to be appointed by the executive of California, and who shall receive no compensation for their services. And be it further enacted, That there shall likewise be, and there is hereby, granted to the said State of California the tracts embracing what is known as the "Mariposa Big Tree Grove," not to exceed the area of **four sections**, and to be taken in legal subdivisions

plat: In the United States, a plat is a map drawn to scale that identifies divisions of a piece of land.

four sections: Under the US Public Land Survey System, a section equals 640 acres (260 hectares), roughly one square mile.

---

3   United States Code, title 16, sec. 48, 1864.

of one quarter section each, with the like stipulation as expressed in the first section of this act as to the State's acceptance, with like conditions as in the first section of this act as to inalienability, yet with same lease privilege; the income to be expended in preservation, improvement, and protection of the property; the premises to be managed by commissioners as stipulated in the first section of this act, and to be taken in legal subdivisions as aforesaid; and the official plat of the United States surveyor general, when affirmed by the Commissioner of the General Land Office, to be the evidence of the locus of the said Mariposa Big Tree Grove.

DOCUMENT 15:

Extract from Frederick Law Olmsted, Preliminary Report upon the Yosemite Valley and the Mariposa Big Tree Grove (1865)[4]

Olmsted (1822–1903), the nation's leading landscape architect, briefly served as one of the commissioners appointed to manage the grant of the Yosemite Valley and the Mariposa Big Tree Grove from the US Congress to the State of California. Olmsted's report, excerpted here, argues forcefully for the power of nature to enhance human health, a claim that John Muir would make in subsequent years. Olmsted's report also underscores that beautiful scenery uplifts people's perceptions of themselves and, by extension, it became the political duty of the nation-state to protect access to a place like Yosemite so that it did not become an exclusive preserve for the rich and powerful. Parks, in short, must be open and democratic. Olmsted read the report to his fellow Commissioners at a meeting in the Yosemite Valley on 9 August 1865; ultimately intended for presentation to the state legislature, it met with indifference or hostility from other members of the Commission, and was quietly suppressed. Olmsted himself left California for good at the end of 1865; he had arrived there just a little more than two years before to assume responsibilities as Superintendent for the Mariposa Mining Estate. Only in the twentieth century has Olmsted's Preliminary Report come to be widely recognized as one of the most profound and original philosophical statements to emerge from the American conservation movement.

It is a fact of much significance with reference to the temper and spirit which ruled the loyal people of the United States during the war of the **great rebellion**, that a livelier susceptibility to the influence of art was apparent, and greater progress in the manifestations of artistic talent was made, than in any similar period before in the history of the country. The great dome of the Capitol was wholly constructed during the war, and the forces of the insurgents watched it rounding upward to completion for nearly a year before they were forced from their entrenchments on the opposite bank of the Potomac; **Crawford's great statue of Liberty** was poised upon its summit in the year that President Lincoln proclaimed the emancipation of the slaves. **Leutze's fresco** of the peopling of the Pacific States, the finest work of the painter's art in the Capitol; the noble front of the Treasury building with its long colonnades of massive monoliths; the exquisite hall of the Academy of Arts; the great park of New York, and many other works

great rebellion: The US Civil War, 1861–65.

Crawford's great statue of Liberty: This 1863 statue caps the dome of the US Capitol building; the bronze sculpture stands 19' 6" tall and weighs 15,000 pounds.

Leutze's fresco: The fresco by Emmanuel Leutze, entitled *Westward the Course of Empire Takes Its Way* (1862), is an artistic ode to westward expansion, frontier settlement, and the displacement of Indigenous peoples.

---

4   Reprinted in *Landscape Architecture* 43 (1952): 12–25.

of which the nation may be proud, were brought to completion during the same period. Others were carried steadily on, among them our own Capitol; many more were begun; and it will be hereafter remembered that the first organization formed solely for the cultivation of the fine arts on the Pacific side of the Globe, was established in California while the people of the State were not only meeting the demands of the Government for sustaining its armies in the field but were voluntarily making liberal contributions for binding up the wounds and cheering the spirits of those who were stricken in the battles of liberty.

It was during one of the darkest hours, before **Sherman** had begun the march upon Atlanta or **Grant** his terrible movement through the Wilderness, when the paintings of **Bierstadt** and the photographs of **Watkins**, both productions of the War time had given to the people on the Atlantic some idea of the sublimity of the YoSemite, and of the stateliness of the neighboring Sequoia grove, that consideration was first given to the danger that such scenes might become private property and through the false taste, the caprice or the requirements of some industrial speculation of their holders; their value to posterity be injured. To secure them against this danger Congress passed an act providing that the premises should be segregated from the general domain of the public lands, and devoted for ever to popular resort and recreation, under the administration of a Board of Commissioners, to serve without pecuniary compensation, to be appointed by the Executive of the State of California.

His Excellency the Governor in behalf of the State accepted the trust proposed and appointed the required Commissioners; the territory has been surveyed and the Commissioners have in several visits to it, and with much deliberation, endeavored to qualify themselves to present to the Legislature a sufficient description of the property, and well considered advice as to its future management.

The Commissioners have deemed it best to confine their attention during the year which has elapsed since their appointment to this simple duty of preparing themselves to suggest the legislative action proper to be taken, and having completed it purpose to present their resignation, in order to render as easy as possible the pursuance of any policy of management the adoption of which may be determined by the wisdom of the Legislature. The present report, therefore, is intended to embody as much as is practicable, the results of the labors of the Commission, which it also terminates.

... It is the will of the Nation as embodied in the act of Congress that this scenery shall never be private property but that like certain defensive points upon our coast it shall be held solely for public purposes.

Two classes of considerations may be considered to have influenced the action of Congress. The first and less important is the direct and obvious pecuniary advantage which comes to a commonwealth from the fact that it possesses objects which cannot be taken out of its domain, that are attractive to travelers and the enjoyment of which is open to all. To illustrate this it is simply necessary to refer to certain cantons of the Republic of Switzerland, a commonwealth of the most industrious and frugal people in Europe. The results of all the ingenuity and labor of this people applied to the resources of wealth which they hold in common with the people of other lands has become of insignificant value compared with that which they derive from the price which travelers gladly pay for being allowed to share with them the enjoyment of the natural scenery of their mountains. These travelers alone have caused hundreds of the best inns in the world to be established and maintained among them, have given the farmers their best and almost the only market they have for their surplus products, have spread a network of rail roads and superb carriage roads, steamboat routes and telegraphic lines over the country, have contributed direct and indirectly for many years the larger part of the state revenue, and all this without the exportation or abstraction from the country of any thing of the slightest value to the people....

That when it shall have become more accessible the Yosemite will prove an attraction of a similar character and a similar source of wealth to the whole community, not only to California but of the United States, there can be no doubt....

A more important class of considerations however, remain to be stated. These are considerations of a political duty of grave importance to which seldom if ever before has proper respect been paid by any Government in the world but the grounds of which rest on the same eternal base, of equity and benevolence with all other duties of a republican government. It is the main duty of government, if it is not the sole duty of government, to provide means of protection for all its citizens in the pursuit of happiness against the obstacles, otherwise insurmountable, which the selfishness of individuals or combinations of individuals is liable to interpose to that pursuit.

It is a scientific fact that the occasional contemplation of natural scenes of an impressive character, particularly if this contemplation occurs in connection with relief from ordinary cares, change of air and change of habits, is favorable to the health and vigor of men and especially to the health and vigor of their intellect beyond any other conditions which can be offered them, that it not only gives pleasure for the time being but increases the subsequent capacity for happiness and the means of securing happiness. The want of such occasional recreation where men and women are habitually pressed by their business or household cares often results in a class of disorders the characteristic quality of which is mental disability, sometimes taking the severe forms of softening of the brain, paralysis, palsy, monomania, or insanity, but more frequently of mental and nervous excitability, moroseness, melancholy or irascibility, incapacitating the subject for the proper exercise of the intellectual and moral forces. It is well established that where circumstances favor the use of such means of recreation as have been indicated, the reverse of this is true....

But in this country at least it is not those who have the most important responsibilities in state affairs or in commerce, who suffer most from lack of recreation; women suffer more than men, and the agricultural class is more largely represented in our insane asylums than the professional, and for this, and other reasons it is these classes to which the opportunity for such recreation is the greatest blessing.

If we analyze the operation of scenes of beauty upon the mind, and consider the intimate relation of the mind upon the nervous system and the whole physical economy, the action and reaction which constantly occurs between bodily and mental conditions, the reinvigorating which results from such scenes is readily comprehended.... The power of scenery to affect men is, in a large way, proportionate to the degree in which their taste has been cultivated. Among a thousand savages there will be a much smaller number who will show the least sign of being so affected than among a thousand persons taken from a civilized community. This is only one of the many channels in which a similar distinction between civilized and savage men is to be generally observed. The whole body of the susceptibilities of civilized men and with their susceptibilities their powers, are on the whole enlarged. But as with the bodily powers, if one group of muscles is developed by exercise exclusively, and all others neglected the result is general feebleness, so it is with the metal faculties. And men who exercise those faculties or susceptibilities of the mind which are called in play by beautiful scenery so little that they seem to be inert with them, are either in a diseased condition from excessive devotion of the mind to a limited range of interests, or their whole minds are in a savage state; that is, a state of low development. The latter class need to be drawn out generally; the former need relief from their habitual matters of interest and to be drawn out in those parts of their mental nature which have been habitually left idle and inert. But there is a special reason why the reinvigoration of those parts which are stirred into conscious activity by natural scenery is more effective upon the general development and health than that of any other, which is this: The severe and excessive exercise of the mind which leads to the greatest fatigue and is the most wearing upon the whole constitution is almost entirely caused by application to the removal of something to be apprehended in the future, or to interests beyond those of the moment, or of the individual; to the laying up of wealth, to the preparation of something, to accomplishing something in the mind of another, and especially to small and petty details which are uninteresting in themselves and which engage the attention at all only because of the bearing they have on some general end of more importance which is seen ahead. In the interest which natural scenery inspires there is the strongest contrast to this. It is for itself and at the moment it is enjoyed. The attention is aroused and the mind occupied without purpose, without a continuation of the common process of relating the present action, thought or perception to some future end. There is little else that has this quality so purely.... It therefore results that the enjoyment of the scenery employs the mind without fatigue and yet exercises it; and thus, through the influence of the mind over the body, gives the effect of refreshing rest and reinvigoration to the whole system.

Men who are rich enough and who are sufficiently free from anxiety with regard to their wealth can and do provide places of this needed recreation for themselves. They have done so from the earliest periods known in the history of the world, for the great men of the Babylonians, the Persians and the Hebrews, had their rural retreats, as large and as luxurious as those of the aristocracy of Europe at present....

The enjoyment of the choicest natural scenes in the country and the means of recreation connected with them is thus a monopoly, of a very few, very rich people. The great mass of society, including those to whom it would be of the greatest benefit, is excluded from it. In the nature of the case private parks can never be used by the mass of the people in any country nor by any considerable number even of the rich, except by the favor of a few, and in dependence on them.

Thus without [steps] ... taken by government to withhold them from the grasp of individuals, all places favorable in scenery to the recreation of the mind and body will be closed against the great body of the people. For the same reason that the water of rivers should be guarded against private appropriation and the use of it for the purpose of navigation and otherwise protected against obstruction, portions of natural scenery may therefore properly be guarded and cared for by Government. To simply reserve them from monopoly by individuals, however, it will be obvious, is not all that is necessary. It is necessary that they should be laid open to the use of the body of the people.

The establishment by Government of great public grounds for the free enjoyment of the people under certain circumstances, is thus justified and enforced as a political duty....

DOCUMENT 16:

Extracts from Alice Ives Van Schaack, "A Familiar Letter from a Daughter to Her Mother" (1871)[5]

Van Schaack (1844–1912) was the daughter of Henry C. and Adeline Van Schaack of Manlius, New York, and she visited Yosemite in the company of her brother Peter, among others. By the time Van Schaack arrived in Yosemite, steamboats and railroads made the approach to the remote site much easier than Sarah Haight had experienced in 1858. But like Haight, Van Schaack followed a prescribed tour of Yosemite, visiting all its legendary sites that James M. Hutchings identified in his guidebooks, commenting on the valley's transcendent beauty and its religious evocations, and freely discussing her traveling companions.

e

San Francisco, *August*, 1871.

My Dear Mother:

Tuesday, July 25, at four P.M., Peter, Kate, and your correspondent, took the boat for Stockton, distance 127 miles, arriving there early the next morning....

We had a lovely sail; and the next morning, at Stockton, took the seven o'clock train for Milton, distance twenty-six miles. At Milton we commenced our stage ride. For about twelve miles the trees were very stunted, but gradually increased in size, until we saw some respectable specimens before we reached Gibson's, where we dined.

Doubtless you remember our road lay through a mountainous region, and after reaching quite a high altitude, by an abrupt descent, we would soon lose all we had apparently gained.

It seemed rather discouraging; and then the *miles* (sectional miles) are exceeding long, number at least twelve furlongs to a mile, the *bends* and *curves not being counted*. We found more to interest us in the afternoon, passing through a mining country. What a desolate scene it presents!

We saw a few men engaged in **placer mining**, but quartz mining is the most popular now. Did you visit the quartz mills at Angels?

One of our party has sad associations with that place, as his father invested in those mines, lost a large property, and died shortly after, broken-hearted.

placer mining: Placer mining is a form of streambed mining in which miner's various tools, including rocker boxes, are used to separate gold from alluvial sand and gravel. This method gave way to hydraulic mining in which pressurized water was blasted to remove rock or sediment, a relatively efficient way to unearth gold embedded in rock and gravel that was also environmentally destructive. It scoured hillsides and sent tons of debris into rivers that increased their turbidity and thus compromised riparian habitats and aquatic life, from the Sierras to the San Francisco Bay.

---

5   Alice Van Schaack, "A Familiar Letter, from a Daughter to Her Mother, Describing a Few Days Spent at the Big Trees and the Yosemite" (Chicago: Horton & Leonard, 1871).

A friend of Mr. G's., a merchant at Angels, recently discovered $4000 worth of gold on the site of his store.

The water used for milling purposes is brought such a great distance, and the use of the sluices being about $2.50 per day, many of those engaged in placer mining must have made a mere pittance. The desolation they leave behind them seems a fitting monument to blighted hopes.

An intelligent elderly man in our party, who appeared familiar with mining, told us that the "Amador," which is the richest gold mine in California, changed owners a few years ago, and paid for itself in three years. Another mentioned that gold was first discovered in this State, at Sutter's mills—a fact I was ashamed I had not learned before.

There were no mountain streams to cheer us until we left Murphy's, when a cheerful little brook kept us company nearly all the way to the Big Trees, and enlivened our dusty ride of seventeen miles.

We saw some "**Digger Indians**" at Murphy's, and passed one on the road who was as motionless as a bronze statue, when he first came to view, but Peter thought he should not like to meet him "by moonlight, alone." [...] They live principally on manzanitas (little apples), acorns, and pine nuts, which are collected by the women, dried, and then ground by them in their stone mortars.

The ascent from Murphy's to the Big Trees is 2,500 feet. We arrived at the Big Trees at eight P.M., and a lady described Peter (our "Boss") as the dustiest man she had ever seen....

Wednesday evening we merely visited the house over the Big Tree stump, and the Sentinels. As I stood in the shadow of the latter and thought of the many generations that had passed away during their existence, for a moment I felt insignificant in comparison, **until I remembered** that I am *immortal*, and they are not.

Thursday, A.M., we made the tour of the Big Trees, riding on horseback through the **Father of the Forest**. I was glad to see a noble, thrifty tree named for the Empire State.... Many of the trees were marked by marble slabs. Among others, a fine representative, "**Wm. Cullen Bryant.**" Below the name is a line from his Thanatopsis:

"The groves were God's first temples."

We all rejoiced the "poet of the woods" was not forgotten. Peter was particularly interested in the "**Mother of the Forest**," the bark of which was taken to England in sections, put together in the Crystal Palace near London, where he saw it ten years ago. There is a thrifty sugar-pine growing at the top of this barkless tree. We saw some very large sugar-pines during our travels. The gum, which is quite sweet, is used for medicinal purposes....

Digger Indians: "Diggers" is a pejorative term that white settler-colonists used as a catch-all for the many different Indigenous peoples of the Sierras and the Great Basin. It functioned as a stereotype and a curse, anthropologist Allan Lönnberg has observed, and this "taxonomic stigma" was devised to describe all Indigenous people as "being treacherous, bloodthirsty, dirty, squalid, lazy, comic, and/ or pathetic." Lönnberg cites an early visitor to the region, George C. Yount, who linked the term to the Indigenous people's food sources and behavior: "From their mode of living on roots and reptiles, insects and vermin, they have been called Diggers. In fact, they almost burrow into the ground like the mole and are almost as blind to everything comely." Allan Lönnberg, "The Digger Indian Stereotype in California," *Journal of California and Great Basin Anthropology* 3, 2 (Winter 1981): 215–23.

until I remembered: Van Schaack, like Haight before her, draws on Christian conceptions of life after death to steady her nerves when confronted with the immensity and age of the Big Trees.

Father of the Forest: Many of the trees in Yosemite were, as Van Schaack notes subsequently, "named" and thus became part of a tourist's itinerary.

Wm. Cullen Bryant: William Bryant (1794–1878), was the editor of the *New York Evening Post* and a beloved poet. "Thanatopsis" (a consideration of death) was perhaps his most famous work.

We dined at Sonora. There are lead and gold mines in that vicinity, and the country on either side of the road, for miles, has been devastated in searching for those metals. Sonora is twenty miles from Murphy's, and 1,250 feet higher. We afterwards descended several hundred feet, and then ascended 1,200 feet in two miles, so you see we were forcibly reminded of the "ups and downs of life."

... It was about nine o'clock when we arrived, weary and worn, at Garrote, and, in spite of the uncomfortable thoughts suggested by the name, we slept well until half-past two, A.M., when we were roused for breakfast. Like our dear John, I felt marvelously in the mood of saying: "Thanks, but I do not care to eat in the night." By four o'clock we were again on our winding way, and the spirits of the party seemed equal for any emergency. Witness the cheerfulness and sociability during our hot, dusty, uncomfortable ride on Wednesday, and on Saturday, when we rose long before the sun.

Saturday we drove, until noon, through forests of mighty trees, passing the grove known as Tuolumne, representatives of the Sequoias, one stump being *thirty-three feet* in diameter. The Sequoias, as you are aware, can be distinguished from their neighbors by the peculiar reddish brown shade of the bark, as well as by their immense size and straightness. The Tuolumne Big Trees have more branches covered by the bright yellow lichen, than those in the Big Tree Grove. We noticed several trees which were enlivened to their very tops by this gay parasite. The contrast with the bark is very fine. We carried away some beautiful trophies. There were several of us who thought we should advise tourists, whose time is limited, to content themselves with seeing the Tuolumne Grove.

At midday we reached a small hotel in the midst of the forest, and dined on half a bear. Bruin, who was only twenty months old, was killed near by.... Shortly before reaching Tamarack Flat, we arrived at the summit, 7,000 feet above the sea. On either side are massive rocks, many assuming fantastic forms.... We rode on horseback two miles over a good carriage road...

Before we began the descent we stopped on a cliff overlooking the valley, to drink our fill of a wondrously lovely scene. I felt Heaven itself could not be much lovelier.

We then began the descent, our well trained Mustangs carefully picking their way, each following literally in the footsteps of the other. It took us two hours to descend the Sierras, three miles. The honored "Counsellor" left the reins loose on his horse's neck, calmly folded his arms, and trusted implicitly to his faithful steed. Several of the gentlemen walked part of the way. We will be generous, and say it was to carry out Mr. Hutchings' suggestion, to be merciful to his horses! Kate and I concluded ours were more familiar with the trail than ourselves, and neither dismounted, nor indulged in feminine shrieks. For fear the "Boss" should forget to mention in his addenda that he was proud of us, I will merely allude to it in passing, and add, his heart was in his mouth until we reached the foot in safety, when that *elastic member* bounded back to its place again. The chief of the Yo-Semites—that nearly extinct tribe—and a young Spanish boy were our guides. The latter, Emmanuel, regarded me as his peculiar charge, I being the greatest novice in riding, and was so kind and attentive while we were in the valley, I was really sorry to part with him. He used to speak quite encouragingly of my improvement, even when you could have seen "daylight between me and the saddle." However, after riding a few miles I gained sufficient confidence so as to be able to enjoy each opening view.

... As you will see by referring to the map, page III, Hutchings' Yo-Semite Guide Book,[6] we took the Coulterville trail, following the left bank of the crystal waters of the Merced. It is well named, for mercy is ever pure.

Opposite us was the Bridal Veil, now a mere ribbon, while the Ribbon Fall itself is only observable by the dark outline its waters have left on the rock. It was quite a disappointment to us all. I cannot describe, or even give you a faint idea of the grandeur of the huge masses of granite on either side of the Merced. After passing **Tu-tock-ah-nu-lah**, we came to Pom-pom-pa-sus—"three mountains playing leap frog"—otherwise known as the Three Brothers. Then we crossed the dry bed of a branch of the Merced, riding slowly along, studying the Cathedral Rocks which hemmed us in on the other side, the noble El Capitan on the left, the Sentinel on the right, a bold peak almost under the shadow of which nestles Hutchings' hotel and cottages. Only one lady has ventured to climb this mountain, and she was a bride. It seems strange she should venture her life so soon after giving it into the keeping of another....

Mrs. H.B. Stanton came into the dining-room while we were at breakfast, and described her journey down the mountain in such a sprightly way we were all greatly entertained. She and **Miss Anthony** reached there the Thursday previous, and both experienced much difficulty in making the descent. In fact, as Mrs. S. expressed herself, "It was a hard day's work." Mrs. Stanton's figure is too portly for horseback, but she was surprised she could not ride with as much ease as twenty years ago. Susan is too long-limbed to be the personification of grace and elegance; besides, she was mounted astride. Well, I was very anxious to converse with Mrs. Stanton, whom I remembered seeing in Bloomer costume when a child, but I did not introduce myself until shortly before lunch. We occupied the same cottage, and when Kate and I passed in on our return from our Sunday morning ramble, she invited Kate to sit with her. (I came up another stoop.) K. declined,

Tu-tock-ah-nu-lah: See Document 3, p. 000.

Mrs. H.B. Stanton: Elizabeth Cady Stanton (1815–1902) was an early American feminist, author, and lecturer who wrote the *Declaration of Sentiments* (1848), considered the opening salvo in defining women's rights. She was married to Henry Beecher Stanton (1805–77), an abolitionist, reformer, journalist, and politician.

Miss Anthony: Susan B. Anthony (1820–1906), like Stanton, was a critical force in the development of the early women's movement in the United States. Like Stanton, she was an ardent abolitionist, organizer, and writer. Their friendship spanned more than 50 years.

---

6   James M. Hutchings, *Scenes of Wonder and Curiosity in California* (San Francisco: J.M. Hutchings, 1862).

and I did not have the courage to speak then; but ventured to do so after brushing off the dust....

It seems the "Counsellor" has a great horror of "strong-minded women," even of Mrs. Stanton, one of their brightest ornaments....

But to return to our Sunday morning ramble. About ten o'clock the "Boss," Kate, the "Buckeyes," and your correspondent, started on foot, under the escort of our host, to visit the Yo-Semite Falls.... After crossing the crystal Merced, we visited the log cabin in which Mr. Hutchings and his family spent the winter. It is a rude structure containing two rooms. The first you enter is a good sized apartment, with a loft above the rear, which is reached by a ladder, and probably used as a bed-room. An immense fireplace attracted our attention. On one side are shelves containing books, among others a copy of *Hutchings' Magazine*, which he edited five years before making his home in the valley, and, strange to say, the opening article in the first number is about the Yo-Semite. The inner room is used as a kitchen. In these limited quarters Mr. H. and his family have spent many winters. Mr. Hutchings has lived in the valley sixteen years. Last winter his wife, mother and two children, were alone in this cabin five months, while he was attending to business in Washington, concerning his **land claim** in the valley. They say Mrs. H. is an attractive, accomplished woman. She was only eighteen when she married Mr. H., a bachelor of thirty-six. The "Boss" says Mr. Hutchings is an "enthusiast," and he declares his wife is quite as enthusiastic about the valley as himself. He is certainly an interesting man, and his wife must be a lovely woman, to bear so severe a test as this secluded life, and retain his love through all.... Father will be interested in hearing that even the inhabitants of this quiet valley are not free from litigation, and that Mr. Hutchings, though a pioneer, has his title disputed.

After passing through the vegetable garden, we climbed rocks for some distance, until we finally had a view of the Falls. There are three, but the lower one is considered too insignificant to be counted. Last winter was unusually **open**, and Mr. H. told us that when the snow bank at the head of the upper fall is melted, which he thinks will be before long, there will be no more water to supply the Falls. Even now the volume is very slight. May and June are the months to see these Falls in their beauty. Large trout were sporting in the clear waters of the basin below—a tempting sport for fishermen....

We then retraced our steps to the hotel, lunched, and as there was to be no service until evening, Peter, Kate, and I decided to go to Mirror Lake, a ride in all of six miles. We passed a very small mirror lake on our way to Lake Mono, the mirror lake proper; but we did not dismount until we reached the second, which we crossed in a leaky boat, and then waited patiently until its surface was undisturbed by a ripple, when we were rewarded by

land claim: Hutchings' legal struggle culminated in 1873, when the US Supreme Court rejected his claim to ownership of land in the valley. Jen A. Huntley, *The Making of Yosemite: James Mason Hutchings and the Origins of America's Most Popular National Park* (Lawrence: UP of Kansas, 2011), 129.

open: By this, he means that less snow fell.

two perfect dissolving views of the North and South Domes. The trees on their summits formed a fringe of living green. It was the most exquisite sight, I think, we saw in our wanderings. That reminds me of the Claude Lorraine glass, **Mr. King**, the artist, showed us. It is solid plate glass, black throughout, and the reflections of the landscape on it are lovely.

Lake Mono should be visited at sunrise. It is a small sheet of water, only covering two acres. Peter's only regret, in connection with our trip, is, he failed to secure a piece of the "petrified foam," which is sold on its banks! We passed the **Royal Arches** both in going and returning. I confess I was disappointed in them, having expected the arches to stand in bold relief, instead of being as they are, devices in that form....

Sunday evening we had a delightful service in the parlor of our cottage, the Rev. Dr. Hunt, a Presbyterian missionary pioneer in California, conducting it. He offered a prayer, read the 104th Psalm from my Church Service, made some very good remarks, and led in the singing. He mentioned that when a lady who had climbed Inspiration Point, was asked what she saw, answered: "I see God." This remark, he said, we should take home to ourselves, and be nobler and wiser after seeing some of the grandest, most awe-inspiring of our Creator's works.... Afterwards I had a good Sunday talk with the "Deacon," during which a cannon was fired to show the power and wonderful reverberations of thunder in the valley. Surely it sounded like "Heaven's artillery." Then we joined our party who had gone to see the moon rise. The trees on the summit of the mountains often partially obscured the disc, and it was fascinating to watch how as one tree disappeared, as the moon slowly and majestically rose above the peaks, another would take its place. Kate compared it to moss agate.... I shall never forget it, or indeed anything of interest connected with our trip; it was pure, unalloyed pleasure, such as we rarely taste in this life, but, I trust, may ever be ours in the world to come.

Monday morning, bright and early, we took horses for Mirror Lake, Vernal, and Nevada Falls. [...] Of course, we saw all the falls at an unfavorable season, there was, however, a sufficient volume of water to give us pleasure, and I enjoyed watching the spray as it was blown down the stream. We then went on foot down a shorter trail (our horses being sent around), and had a fine view of the Vernal Fall from below. If you notice a lack of adjectives, please remember it was said I exhausted my stack in the valley....

We had an easy ride up the Sierras [the next day], and I was sufficiently accustomed to riding to enjoy each disappearing view. I still prefer the first glimpse of the Yo-Semite from Prospect Point.

Mr. King: George W. King (1836–1922) was a US artist who, like Van Schaack, hailed from New York State. A good friend of John Muir and William Keith, he painted a number of important "views" of Yosemite. A Claude Lorrain glass is a painting tool: it is a convex mirror, often made of black glass, and is used to view a reflected landscape; it is named for its eponymous inventor, the French painter (1600–82).

Royal Arches: A cliff containing naturally occurring granite exfoliation arches, located below North Dome. Today it is one of the premiere rock-climbing sites.

"'Tis like a little heaven below."[7]

At the Flat we took stages for Chinese Camp, where we arrived at 9 p.m. [...] A young lady in the stage mentioned that, last summer, the guests in the Yo-Semite hotels were alarmed when they heard Piutes (I do not know how to spell it) were on the war path. The supplies they had counted on for coming winter had failed them, the whites having allowed their cattle to browse on their favorite wild vegetable, and there being a decrease of a kind of insect they were accustomed to collect on the lake, they became desperate. The "pale faces" fled, but no one was attacked, I believe. The Piutes roasted deer and had their war dances near Hutchings'; was it not frightful?

Wednesday, A.M., we left Chinese Camp, taking a crossroad through Copperopolis to Milton, thence by cars to Stockton, where we took the boat for San Francisco, arriving here in safety early on Thursday.

Good-bye to thee, Yo-Semite!

---

7   From the hymn "Lord, how delightful 'tis to see." Written in 1715 by Isaac Watts (1674–1748) and included in various editions of the *Primitive Methodist Sabbath-School Hymn Book*.

DOCUMENT 17:

Extracts from Helen Hunt, *Bits of Travel at Home* (Boston, MA: Roberts Brothers, 1878), Chapters 8–10

Hunt later became more famous as Helen Hunt Jackson (1830–85) due to her advocacy of the rights of Indigenous nations in California. *A Century of Dishonor* (1881) offered a blistering critique of the mistreatment of Indigenous people in Southern California, and Jackson's novel *Ramona* (1884), wildly successful, fictionalized many of the same issues. She is less sensitive in this earlier account to the plight of the Ahwahnechee, though disparages Bunnell's renaming of the valley.

$\wp$

Ah-wah-ne! Does not the name vindicate itself at first sight and sound? Shall we ever forgive the Dr. Bunnell, who, not content with volunteer duty in killing off Indians in the great Merced River Valley, must needs name it the Yo-sem-i-te, and who adds to his account of his fighting campaigns the following naïve paragraph?

> "It is acknowledged that Ah-wah-ne is the old Indian name for the valley, and that Ah-wah-ne-chee is the name of the original occupants; but, as this was discovered by the writer long after he had named the valley, and as it was the wish of every volunteer with whom he conversed that the name Yo-semite be retained, he said very little about it. He will only say, in conclusion, that the principal facts are before the public, and that it is for them to decide whether they will retain the name Yo-semite or have some other."

It is easy to do and impossible to undo this species of mischief. No concerted action of "the public," no legislation of repentant authorities, will ever give back to the valley its own melodious name; but I think its true lovers will forever call it Ah-wah-ne. The name seems to have in its very sound the same subtle blending of solemnity, tenderness, and ineffable joy with which the valley's atmosphere is, filled. Ahwahne! Blessed Ahwahne! [...]

... Falstaff's men could find their proper mount at Gentry's when the saddle train comes up from Ah-wah-ne. Ten, twenty, thirty, horses, mustangs, mules, rusty black, dingy white, streaked red; ungroomed, unfed, untrained; harmless only because they are feeble from hunger; sure to keep on, if their strength holds out, to the end of the journey, simply because their one instinct is to escape somewhere.... You stand on the piazza, at Gentry's, and watch the procession come slowly up. Nose after nose comes into sight, followed by reluctant, stumbling fore-feet; so slow they climb it seems to take a good while before you see the whole of any one horse.

They stop long before they reach the piazza, thinking that their riders may as well get off a minute or two sooner. The guides whack their haunches and push them up to the steps, and the Ah-wah-ne pilgrims slip or spring from their saddles with sighs of relief.

You, who were longing for these to come out, that you might go in, look on with dismay. On all sides you hear ejaculations from the people waiting. "I'll never go on that horse;" "nor on that;" "that poor creature will never live to go down again." Everybody gazes intently toward the crest of the hill, over which the pathetic file is still coming. Everybody hopes to see a horse better than these. But there is not a pin's choice between them, when they are all there. Wherever their riders leave them, there they stand, stock-still, till they are pushed or dragged away. Heads down, tails limp, legs out, abject, pitiable things,—you feel as if cruelty personified could not have the heart to lay a feather's weight on their backs.

With the timid reverence natural in the mind of one going toward Ah-wah-ne for one coming from it, you approach the newly arrived and ask concerning these horses. Your pity and horror deepen when you are told that the poor creatures are never fed, never sheltered. They are worked all day without food, often being out from six in the morning until six at night, carrying people over steep, stony trails; then they are turned loose to shift for themselves in the meadows all night. By four or five o'clock in the morning the guides are out scouring the meadows to drive them in again. And so their days go on. There was but one alleviation to this narrative. It was the statement that every morning a good many horses cannot be found. They trot all night to find fields out of reach of their tormentors, or they swim off to little islands in the Merced and hide. Mr. Hutchings has lost seventy horses in this way since last year....

...We set out at three o'clock. Our first sensations were not agreeable. We had seen how steep it looked when horse and rider disappeared over that hill-crest. It felt steeper. To an unaccustomed rider it is not pleasant to sit on a horse whose heels are much higher than his head. One's first impulse is to clutch, to brace, to cling, and to guide the horse. But there is neither comfort nor safety till you leave off doing so. With a perfectly loose rein and every muscle relaxed, sitting as you would sit in a rocking-chair, leaning back when the horse rocks down, leaning forward when he rocks up, and forgetting him altogether, riding down precipices is as comfortable and safe as riding on a turnpike. I do not say that it is altogether easy in the outset to follow these simple directions. But, if you are wise, it soon becomes so, and you look with impatient pity on the obstinacy of women who persist in grasping pommels, and sitting so stark stiff that it seems as if a sudden lurch of the horse must inevitably send them off, before or behind.

The first two miles and a half of the path down the wall of Ah-wah-ne are steep,—so steep that it is best not to try to say how steep. It is a narrow path, zig-zagging down on ledges, among boulders, through thickets. It is dusty and stony; it comes out suddenly on **opens**, from which you look over and down thousands, yes, thousands of feet; it plunges into tangles of trees, where a rider must lay his head on the horse's neck to get through, for oaks and pines and firs grow on this precipice; high ceanothus bushes, fragrant with blossom, make wall-like sides to the path, and bend in as if trying to arch it. In some places the rocks are bright with flowers and ferns, which look as if they were holding on for dear life and climbing up: they project so nearly at right angles from the steep surfaces. With almost every step we get a new view,—more depth, more valley, more wall, more towering rock. The small cleared spaces in the valley are vivid light green; they seem sunken like emerald-paved wells among the masses of dark firs and pines, whose tops lie solid and black below us. The opposite wall of the valley looks steeper than the wall we are descending. It seems within stone's throw, or as if we might call across; it is less than a half-mile distant. Its top seems far higher than the point from which we set out; for it lies in full sunshine, and we are in shadow. One waterfall after another comes into view, streaming over its edge like smooth silver bands. The guide calls out their names: "Inspiration Fall," "Bridal Veil Fall." The words seem singularly meaningless, face to face with the falls. How do men dare to name things so confidently?

... It takes an hour to reach the bottom of the wall. As we near it, the opposite wall appears to lift and grow and stretch, till the sky seems pushed higher. Our trail lies along the bank of the river, on sandy stretches of low meadow, shaded by oaks and willows and bordered by alders. Occasionally we come to fields of boulders and stones, which have broken and rolled down from the walls above; then we pass through green bits of grass-grown land, threaded by little streams, which we ford; then we ride through great groves of pines and firs, two and three hundred feet high. These feel dark and damp, though the ground is sandy, for it is long past sunset here; but the gray spires and domes and pinnacles of the eastern wall of the valley are still bright in sunlight.... Mile by mile the grand rocks, whose shapes and names we already knew, rose up on either hand: The Cathedral Rocks, The Spires, El Capitan, The Three Brothers, The Sentinel. Already the twilight wrapped the western wall. The front of El Capitan looked black; but its upper edge was lined with light, as sometimes a dark cloud will be when the sun is shining behind. The eastern wall was carved and wrought into gigantic forms, which in the lessening light grew more and more fantastic and weird every moment. Bars and beams of sunlight fell, quivered, and

opens: Views.

vanished on summit after summit, as we passed. At last we heard the sound of waters ahead to the left. Soon we saw the white line, indistinct, waving, ghostly, coming down apparently from the clouds, for it was too dark to see distinctly the lip of a fall two thousand and seven hundred feet up in the air. This was the great Yosemite Fall. Its sound is unlike that of any other fall I have seen. It is not so loud as one would expect, and it is not continuous or even in tone. Listening to it intently, one hears strange rhythmic emphases of undertone on a much lower key. They are grand. They are like the notes of a gigantic violoncello,—booming, surging, filling full and rounding out the harmony of supernatural music. Sometimes they have an impatient and crashing twist, as if the bow escaped the player's hand; sometimes, for an hour, they are regular and alike, as the beats of a metronome. Men have said that these sounds are made by rocks thundering down under the water. They may be. I would rather not know.

For the last mile before reaching Hutchings's Hotel, the trail is little more than a sandy path, winding in and among huge granite boulders, under and around oak and pine trees, and over and through little runs and pools, when the Merced River is high. It ends abruptly, in a rough and dusty place, partly cleared of boulders, partly cleared of trees. Here are four buildings, which stand apparently where they happened to, between the rocks and trees. Three of these make up Hutchings's Hotel. Two of them are cottages, used only for lodgings. One of these is called "The Cottage by the River," and stands closer than is safe to the banks of the Merced; the other is called "The Cottage in the Rocks," and seems half barricaded by granite boulders. "Oh, Mr. Hutchings!" we exclaimed. Put us in the 'Cottage by the River.' We cannot be happy anywhere else."

... They do not dawn like days elsewhere. How should they, seeing that the sun has been long up before he looks over into Ah-wah-ne? They burst, they flash, they begin like a trumpet peal. One moment it is morning twilight. The swaying torrent of the Great [Yosemite] Fall looks dim at the edges, and the pines and firs, high in the air by its side, look black. The next moment it is broad day. The Fall shines like molten silver under the streaming sunlight, and the firs and pines are changed in a twinkling from black to green. This miracle of dayspring was the first sight I saw in Ah-wah-ne. I was but half awake. From my pillow I looked out on the upper half of the Great Fall. An oval of gray sky; white foam pouring from it, and falling into a bed of black fir-tops; waving branches of near trees just beyond my window,—these were all I saw. Boom! boom! boom! sounded the mysterious violoncello accompaniment, measuring and making rhythmical the roar of the Fall. Suddenly, as suddenly as a light-house flashes its first beam seaward, came a great blaze of yellow light from the east, making the water dazzling bright, and throwing out into relief every green spire fir or pine on the precipice.

With the sudden flood of light seemed to come a sudden flood of louder sound. I sprang to the window in wonder, which was not without a vague terror; but in that very second the transformation was past, the quiet look of full day had settled on all things. Almost I doubted the vision I had seen. It was simply broad daylight; that was all. The air was full of fleecy-winged seeds from Balm of Gilead trees. They went slowly, sinking and rising, but steadily to the north, like a snowy flock following an invisible shepherd. As they passed, they seemed to spin fine silken lines athwart the Fall; and they came so fast and thick they hindered my seeing. There was a strange sweetness of peace and promise in their presence. The Great Fall so loud, so vast: they so small, so still. Three thousand feet from my window-sill up to the top of the wall over which the torrent of waters fell; within my hand's reach, the current, silent, irresistible, unmeasured, on which centuries of forest were gliding into place.

This was the first beginning of my first day in Ah-wah-ne. Two hours later was the second beginning of the same day. It is odd how much bustle there can be in Ah-wah-ne. Sit on the hotelward piazza of Hutchings's River Cottage from seven till nine, and no moment goes by empty. The little clearing is dusty; the sun beats down; people crossing from house to house, zigzag, to get into shade of the oaks or into dust an inch or so less deep. On every piazza sit groups ready to set out on excursions, and waiting for their guides to bring up the horses and mules. Under the trees, beyond the hotel, is a long line of the unfortunate beasts, saddled hap-hazard and tied to the fence, waiting the evil that may betide them. They have been saddled since four or five o'clock; perhaps they will stand there till three. Now and then a man comes riding over the bridge, driving in a few more, which he has just caught. Poor things! They miscalculated distances, and did not run away quite far enough in the night. Sometimes a wiry, weather-beaten old guide dashes round and round the clearing (I think I will call it plaza, since I do not know what name the Ah-wah-ne-chee had for little clearings)—dashes round the plaza, trying to break in a vicious mule or mustang. Sometimes the mustang gets the better; sometimes the guide. Then comes the laundry wagon, tilting up and down on its two big wheels, stopping at everybody's door for clothes for the laundry. It is painted bright blue, and, being the only thing seen going about on wheels in Ah-wah-ne, looks marvelously queer.

Then comes along an Indian woman, with a papoose on her back. Half naked, dirty beyond words, her stiff, vicious-looking hair falling around her forehead like fringed eaves, her soulless eyes darting quick glances to right and left, in search of a possible charity, she strides through the plaza, and disappears among the thickets and boulders. She belongs to a colony which has camped half a mile below. They will dance a hideous dance for a few pennies. They are descendants of Tenaya, no doubt; but

Tenaya would scorn them: Although Hunt would later excoriate the mistreatment of Indigenous people in California, here she fails to contextualize the impact of 20 years of settler-colonists' dispossession and mistreatment of the Indigenous peoples of the Yosemite region. See also Document 10, p. 000.

Tenaya would scorn them to-day.... Mealtime at Hutchings's is a species of secular pass-over: breakfast is a freebooting foray, lunch a quieter foraging excursion, dinner a picnic. As soon as one learns the order or disorder of the thing, one can get on; but it is droll to watch the newly arrived or the obstinately fastidious traveler, sitting in blank astonishment at the absence of most which he expects to find in a dining-room. Mr. Hutchings is an enthusiast, a dreamer, a visionary. He loved Ah-wah-ne well enough years ago to make his home in its uninhabited solitude, and find in its grand silences all the companionship he needed. He loves it well enough to-day to feel all the instinct of loving hospitality in his welcome to every traveler who has journeyed to find it by reason of the fame of its beauty. All this is plainly to be seen in his mobile, artistic face, and in the affectionate ring of every word that he speaks of the Valley....

PART 3

Battle for Wilderness

The violent dispossession of Indigenous populations in Yosemite, when combined with the subsequent development of the valley as a tourist destination, set the condition for the early-twentieth-century debate that would erupt over San Francisco's desire to build a dam-and-reservoir complex in the Hetch Hetchy Valley. The section opens with two discussions of the valley—scientific and discursive—that in different ways helped place Hetch Hetchy on the map, a charting of its geology and hydrology, beauty and solitude that would figure later in the contested analyses of this granite-walled landscape as a dam site. The initial political context of these analyses and the arguments they spawned are reflected in the 1907 correspondence between John Muir and President Theodore Roosevelt, as well as in the formal petition of the City of San Francisco to the Secretary of the Interior for permission to construct the dam and that cabinet officer's response. They are embedded, too, in the flurry of petitions, pro and con, that a number of leading conservation groups and social organizations entered into the public record. This thrust and counter thrust escalated in 1912 as Congress began the final consideration of legislation that would permit the inundation of the Hetch Hetchy Valley. The public hearings generated considerable attention, and as the extracts of the statements to congressional public lands committee indicates there was a remarkable range of opinion and conviction that went well beyond a simple narrative that the dam was good or bad, that it was necessary or nefarious. The level of engagement across the country is also striking: conservationists disagreed with one another, and labor unions, women's clubs, and university professors from different parts of the country weighed in. Collectively these testimonials underscored how important environmental issues had become by the early twentieth century, and offer a foreshadowing of their continued centrality over the next century.

DOCUMENT 18:

Charles Frederick Hoffmann, "Notes on Hetch-Hetchy Valley," *Proceedings of the California Academy of Sciences* (San Francisco: CAS, 1868), series 1, 3:5, pp. 368–70

Hoffmann (1838–1913), a German-born and -trained engineer, migrated to the US before the Civil War. As a member of the California Geological Survey, he produced the first series of topographical maps of the Sierra Nevada. Mount Hoffmann (10,855 feet), a prominent peak in Yosemite National Park, is named for him. This may be the first discussion of Hetch Hetchy to appear in print and may have provided the impetus for John Muir to hike to the valley four years later.

⨍

Hetch-Hetchy: *Iyaydz* is the Paiute name for the valley. Joseph Screech, a rancher who may have been the first white person to enter the valley, misinterpreted the name as Hetch Hetchy: see Joseph Lent, "Bridgeport Yosemite Paiutes: Who We Are," in *Voices of the People* by The Traditionally Associated Tribes of Yosemite National Park (Yosemite Conservancy, 2019), 101–02.

chain: A chain is a unit of measure in surveying equal to 66 feet or 22 yards.

Tuolumne Valley, or **Hetch-Hetchy**, as it is called by the Indians (the meaning of this word I was unable to ascertain) is situated on Tuolumne River about fifteen miles in a straight line below Tuolumne Meadows and Soda Springs, and about twelve miles north of Yosemite Valley. Its elevation above the sea is from 3,800 to 3,900 feet, a little less than that of Yosemite. The valley is three miles long running nearly east and west, with but little fall in this distance. Near its center it is cut in two by a low spur of shelving granite coming from the south. The lower part forms a large open meadow with excellent grass; one mile in length, and gradually increasing from ten **chains** to a little over half a mile in width, and only timbered along the edges. The lower part of this meadow terminates in a very narrow cañon, the hills sloping down to the river at an angle of from 40° to 60°, only leaving a channel from six to ten feet wide; the river in the valley having an average width of about fifty feet. This is the principal cause of the overflow in spring time of the lower part of the valley, and probably also has given rise to the report of there being a large lake in the valley. Below this cañon is another small meadow, with a pond. The upper part of Hetch-Hetchy, east of the granite spur, forms a meadow one and three-fourths miles in length, varying from ten to thirty chains in width, well timbered and affording good grazing. The scenery resembles very much that of the Yosemite, although the bluffs are not as high, nor do they extend as far. On the north side of the valley, opposite the granite spur we first have a perpendicular bluff, the top of which is 1,800 feet above the valley.... In the spring when the snows are melting a large creek precipitates itself over the western part of this bluff. I was told that this fall is one of the grandest features of the valley, sending its spray all over its lower portion. It was dry, however, at the time of my visit, the fall is 1,000 feet perpendicular after which it strikes the debris and loses itself among the rocks. About thirty chains further east we come to the Hetch-Hetchy fall; its height above the valley is 1,700 feet. This fall is not perpendicular, although it appears so from the front, as may be seen from the photograph by Mr. Harris. It falls in a series of cascades at an angle of about 70°. At the time of my visit the volume of water was much greater than that of Yosemite fall, and I was told that in the spring its roarings can be heard for miles.

Still further east we have two peaks, shaped very much like "The Three Brothers," in the Yosemite. Their base forms a large, naked and sloping granite wall on the north side of the valley, broken by two timbered shelves, which run horizontally the whole length of the wall. Up to the lower shelf or bend, about eight hundred feet high, the wall, which slopes at an angle of from 45° to 70°, is polished by glaciers, and probably these markings extend still higher up, as on entering the valley the trail followed back of and along a **moraine** for several miles, the height of which was about 1,200 feet above the valley. The same polish shows itself in places all along the bluffs on both sides, and particularly fine on the granite spur crossing the valley. There is no doubt that the largest branch of the great glacier which originated near Mt. Dana and Mount Lyell, made its way by Soda Springs to this valley. A singular feature of this valley is the total absence of talus or debris at the base of the bluffs, excepting at one place in front of the falls. Another remarkable rock, corresponding with Cathedral Rock in the Yosemite, stands on the south side of the valley, directly opposite Hetch-Hetchy fall; its height is 2,270 feet above the valley....

At the upper end of the valley the river forks, one branch, nearly as large as the main river, coming from near Castle Peak, the main river itself from Soda Springs. About half a mile up the main cañon, the river forms some cascades, the highest being about thirty feet.

The valley was first visited, in 1850, by **Mr. Joseph Screech**, a mountaineer of this region, who found it occupied by Indians. This gentleman informed me that, up to a very recent date, this valley was disputed ground between the **Pah Utah** Indians from the eastern slope and the Big Creek Indians from the western slope of the Sierras; they had several fights, in which the Pah Utahs proved victorious. The latter still visit the valley every fall to gather acorns, which abound in this locality. Here I may also mention that the Indians speak of a **lake of very salt water**, on their trail from here to Castle Peak. Mr. Screech also informed me of the existence of a fall, about a hundred feet high, on the Tuolumne River, about four miles below this valley, and which prevents fish from coming at any higher. The climate is said to be milder in winter than that of the Yosemite Valley, as is also indicated by a larger number of oaks and a great number of *Pinus Sabiniana*. The principal tree

moraine: A moraine is a glacially formed accumulation of debris. What is significant about Hoffmann's report is that it pre-dates John Muir's glacier studies. Muir is often credited with promoting the idea that glaciers played a significant role in construction of the Sierra, but clearly did so in the wake of Hoffmann's earlier report.

Mr. Joseph Screech: Joseph Screech and his brothers Nate and William grazed cattle and sheep in the valley in the 1850s.

Pah Utah: Numu/Paiute.

lake of very salt water: Mono Lake.

of the valley is *Pinus ponderosa*; besides this we have *P. Sabiniana*, Cedar, *Q. Sonomensis, Q. crassipocula*; also poplar and cottonwood.

The valley can he reached easily from Big Oak Flat by taking the regular Yosemite trail, by Sprague's Ranch and Big Flume, as far as Mr. Hardin's fence, between south and middle fork of Tuolumne River, about eighteen miles from Big Oat Flat. Here the trail turns off to the left, going to Wade's Meadows or Big Meadows, sometimes called Reservoir Meadows, the distance being about seven miles. From Wade's Ranch the trail crosses the middle fork of Tuolumne and goes to the Hogg Ranch, five miles; thence up the divide between the middle fork and main river, about two miles, to another little ranch called "The Cañon." From here the trail winds down through rocks for six miles to Tuolumne Cañon. This trail is **well blazed**, and was made by Mr. Screech and others, for the purpose of driving sheep and cattle to the valley. The whole distance from Big Oak Flat is thirty-eight miles.

Another trail equally good, but a little longer, leaves the Yosemite trail about half a mile beyond the crossing of the south fork, thence crosses the middle fork within about one and a half miles of the south fork crossing, and follows up the divide between the middle fork and the main river, joining the first-named trail at the Hogg Ranch.

well blazed: Note the assumption that Screech blazed the trail; as Lent makes clear this and others had been used by the Paiute and other Indigenous peoples for centuries. Lent, "Bridgeport Yosemite Paiutes: Who We Are," in *Voices of the People*, 99–101.

DOCUMENT 19:

John Muir, "The Hetch Hetchy Valley," *Boston Weekly Transcript*, 25 March 1873

> This is John Muir's first essay about Hetch Hetchy, an account of his fall 1872 10-day trek through the Sierra backcountry ending up in Hetch Hetchy. As was characteristic of many of Muir's essay, this one meanders along at a pace that reflected his gait. It stops, as he did, to observe and record, a delightful narrative format. Muir references Hoffmann's 1868 California Geological Survey report on the valley, and adds to his own cataloging of the landscape's botanical riches and urges tourists coming to Yosemite to follow his lead into Hetch Hetchy.

e

Hetch Hetchy is one of a magnificent brotherhood of Yosemite Valleys, distant from Yosemite Valley, so-called, eighteen or twenty miles in a north-westerly direction, but by the only trail the distance is not less than forty miles.

In the first week of last November, I set out from here on an excursion of this wonderful valley. My "proper route" was by the Big Oak Flat road as far as Hardin's Mills, thence by a trail which mazes among rocks and chaparral, past "Wade's and the Hogg Ranch," but as I never follow trails when I may walk the living granite, and as I was moreover anxious to see as much as possible of the cañons of Cascade Creek on my way, I set out straight across the mountains leaving Yosemite by Indian Cañon. There was some little danger of being caught in snow thus late in the season, but as I was afoot and had no companion to fear for, I felt confident that I could force my way out of any common storm. I carried one pair of woolen blankets and three loaves of bread—I reckoned that two loaves would be sufficient for the trip, provided all went sunnily, the third was a big round extra that I called my storm loaf. In case of being snowed in, it would last me three days, or, if necessary, six days. Besides those "breads," I carried their complementary coffee and a two-ounce mug of the **Fray Bentos Extractum Carnis of Baron Liebig**. Thus grandly allowanced, I was ready to enjoy my ten days' journey of any kind of calm or storm.

On reaching the top of Indian Cañon I bore off to the left, crossed Yosemite Creek about a mile back of the falls, and slanted up the side of El Capitan Mountain towards the gap, through which the mono trail passes. By the time I reached the summit it was sundown, and as I found an old friend of a brooklet still living, and plenty of dry logs, I concluded to camp, that is, to set fire to a log and cut an armful of pine or fir branches for a bed.

Fray Bentos Extractum Carnis of Baron Liebig: A reference to tinned corn beef; named for Justus von Liebig, an organic chemist, who invented a method for the industrial production of beef extract.

Most of the next day was spent in crossing parallel rows of ice-polished cañons belonging to the basin of Cascade Creek. Night overtook me in a magnificent grove of silver fir, in which I camped.

Next morning, after climbing a long timbered slope and crossing a few groove-shaped valleys I came upon the precipitous rim of the great Tuolumne Cañon, a mile or two above Hetch Hetchy. I had explored a few miles of the central portion of this stupendous cañon in one of my former excursions. It is a Yosemite Valley in depth and in width, and is over twenty miles in length, abounding in falls and cascades, and glacial rock forms. Hetch Hetchy is only an expanded lower portion of this vast Yosemite. The view from my first standpoint is one of the very grandest I ever beheld. From the great cañon as a sort of base line, extends a most sublime map of mountains rising gradually higher, dome over dome, crest over crest, to the summit of the range, and the whole glorious engraving is reposed at such an angle that you look full upon its surface near and far. To one unacquainted with the hidden life and tenderness of the high sierra, the first impression is one of intense soul-crushing desolation. Robert Burns described the Scottish Highlands as "a country where savage streams tumble over savage mountains," and nothing but the same (outside) savageness and confusion is apparent here. Castaway heaps of dead, broken mountains outspread, cold and gray, like a storm sky of winter. But, venture to the midst of these bleached mountain bones—dwell with them, and every death taint will disappear, you will find them living joyously, with lakes, and forests, and a thousand flowers, their hardest domes pulsing with life, breathing in atmospheres of beauty and love.

After I had carefully scanned a mile or two of the cañon wall I discovered a curve that seemed climbable all the way to the bottom, which I concluded to test. After I had descended two or three hundred yards, I struck a well-worn trail that mazed down to the cañon just where I wished to go. At first I took it to be an Indian trail, but after following it a short distance, I discovered certain hieroglyphics which suggested the possibility of its belonging to the bears. It was plain that a broadfooted mother and a family of cubs had been the last to pass over it.

It is dangerous to come suddenly upon an affectionate family of bears, but this seldom happens, if one walks noisily, for bears have excellent ears, and they are acquainted with caves and thickets, to which they gladly retire for the sake of peace.

A little below this discovery of paws, I was startled by a noise close in front. Of course in so grizzly a place, the noise was speedily clothed upon by a bear skin, but it was only the bounding of a frightened deer which I had cornered, and compelled to make a desperate leap in order to pass me. In its hurried flight up the mountain, it started several heavy boulders that came crashing and thumping uncomfortably near.

A little further on, I came to a most interesting group of glacial records, which led me away from the trail to the edge of a sheer precipice, which, by comparison with my recollections of those of Yosemite, must be betwixt two and three thousand feet in depth. Peering cautiously over the wall, I noticed a narrow ledge fringed with dwarf live oaks, which I made out to reach; my hope was, that by following this ledge along the face of the wall I would strike my neighbor's highway, in which I had full confidence, believing that I could climb any rock that a bear could. But it soon proved that this was not unconditionally true, for in scrambling through the brush fringe of my narrow way, I observed a solitary bear track; the rugged author of those broad prints had gone in the same direction as I was going, and there was no return track. This made me more hopeful than before of being able to creep along the wall to the main traveled road, but the track appeared fresh, and the possibility of meeting long claws upon so conquer-or-die a place made me uneasy. I moved forward with great caution until I came to a recess where a few trees were anchored. Here I found that my pioneer had climbed to a sloping place on the wall above, by a dead pine that leaned against it like a ladder. Had I been empty handed like him I would have followed by the same way, but my blankets encumbered my limbs and kept them out of balance. A little farther on I was positively halted by a sheer wall, and my hour's scramble in this direction, so far as getting to the bottom was concerned, was worse than useless. Escaping from this rigid bench by the same way as I found it, I made out to zigzag down a fissured portion of the wall to another bushy seam, still hoping to reach the bear road by creeping along the face of the rock, but this second shelf terminated like the first. I was now tired of cut-offs, and decided to seek my way back up the mountain to where I first wandered from the trail. In groping through brush and fissures I found a rock cup which contained a few quarts of water, and as it was now past noon, and there was a flat place close by where I could unroll my blankets, I made a fire with chaparral twigs, and boiled a tin cupful of coffee. After dining and resting upon this lofty rock table, I continued my return climb up the rocks at a slow pace, careful to avoid thirst, in case I might be compelled to pass the night on the mountain without water. However, I encountered no extraordinary difficulties, and by two or three o'clock was safe in Bear Cañon, with fair prospects of reaching the bottom before dark. I was not on a good road and I made fast time, careful always to make abundance of admonitory noise for the benefit of Mother Bruin and her muffy cubs.

They followed the windings of the trail, in Indian file, with great fidelity, scraping it clear of sticks and pine needles, at steep places, where they had been compelled to adopt a shuffling gait to keep from rolling head over heels. Thin crumbs of dirt, around the edges of their tracks, were still moist.

I could not help thinking, at times, that so remarkably well worn and well directed a trail must formerly have belonged to the Indians; but on reaching a long slope of debris, near the bottom of the cañon, it suddenly branched and melted out in all directions into densest thickets of chaparral, as Indian trails never do, and when at length I touched bottom on the level cañon floor, so good a highway was easily accounted for. Here are fine groves of black oak, and the ground was brown with acorns. At the upper end of the road are extensive fields of manzanita bushes, which yield the berries of which they are so fond; a manzanita orchard at one terminus, an acorn orchard at the other. It was plain that I had near neighbors, but they caused no alarm, as they never choose to eat men where acorns are plentiful.

I selected a camping ground near the river, in the middle of a close group of cedars, whose lower boughs drooped to the ground. I cut off some of their flat, spicy plumes for a bed, gathered a store of wood, and made a cordial fire, and was at home in this vast **unhandselled** Yosemite. Night gathered, in most impressive repose; my blazing fire illumined the grand brown columns of my compassing cedars and a few withered briers and goldenrods that leaned forward between them, as if eager to drink the light. Stars glinted here and there through the rich plumes of my ceiling, and in front I could see a portion of the mighty cañon walls, dark against the sky, making me feel as if at the bottom of a sea. Few sounds reached me, excepting a few broken scraps of song from distant cascades. My weariness and the near soothing hush of the river made me drowsy. The breath of my cedar pillow was delicious, and I quickly drifted deep into the land of sleep.

Next morning I was up betimes, ate my usual crust, and stared down the river bank to Hetch Hetchy, which I reached in about an hour. Hetch Hetchy bears are early risers, for they had been out in the open valley printing the hoar frost before I arrived.

This valley is situated on the main Tuolumne River, just as Yosemite is on the Merced. It is about three miles in length, with a width varying from an eighth to half a mile; most of its surface is level as a lake, and lies at an elevation of 3800 feet above the sea. Its course is mostly from east to west, but it is bent northward in the middle like Yosemite. At the end of the valley the river enters a narrow cañon which cannot devour spring floods sufficiently fast to prevent the lower half of the valley from becoming a lake. Beginning at the west end of the valley where the Hardin trail comes in, the first conspicuous rocks on the right are a group like the Cathedral Rocks of Yosemite, and occupying the same relative position to the valley. The lowest member of the group which stands out well isolated above, exactly like the corresponding rock of the Yosemite group, is, according to the State geological survey, about 2270 feet in height. The two higher members are not so separate as those of Yosemite. They are best seen from the top of the

unhandselled: This refers to a gift or token of good luck, and in this context appears to mean Muir's joy at experiencing Yosemite's beauty and sanctity.

wall a mile or two farther east. On the north side of the valley there is a vast perpendicular rock front 1800 feet high, which resembles El Capitan of Yosemite. In spring a large stream pours over its brow with a clear fall of at least one thousand feet. East of this, on the same side, is the Hetch Hetchy Fall, occupying a position relative to the valley like that of Yosemite Fall. It is about seventeen hundred feet in height, but not in one unbroken fall. It is said to have a much larger body of water than the Yosemite Fall, but at the time of my visit (November), it was nearly dry. The wall of the valley above this fall has two benches fringed with liveoak, which correspond with astonishing minuteness to the **benches** of the same relative portion of the Yosemite wall.

benches: A bench is a long, relatively narrow strip of relatively level or gently inclined land that is bounded by distinctly steeper slopes above and below.

At the upper end of the valley a stream comes in from the northwest which is large enough to be considered a fork of the river. Its cañon is exceedingly rich in rock forms, of which a good view may be had from the south side of the valley. The surface of Hetch Hetchy is diversified with groves and meadows in the same manner as Yosemite, and the trees are identical in species. The dryer and warmer portions have fine groves of the black oak (Quercus sonomensis) with a few sugar pines (P. lambertiania). The Sabine pine (P. sabiniana) which grows on the north side of the valley in sun-beaten rocks, is not found in Yosemite. Upon the debris slopes, and in the small side cañons of the south wall, dwell the two silver firs (Picea amabilis and grandis). The white cedar (Libocedrus decurrens) and Douglas spruce (Abies douglasii) are noble trees and pretty generally distributed throughout the valley. Thickets of azalea and the brier rose are common and extensive tracts along the edges of the meadows are covered with the common bracken (Pteris aquilina). I measured several specimens of this fern that exceeded eight feet in height, and the fissured walls of the valley, from top to bottom, abound in tufted rock ferns of rare beauty, which we have not space to enumerate. The crystal river glides between sheltering groves of alder and poplar and flowering dogwood. Where there is a few inches of fall it ripples and sparkles songfully, but it flows gently in most places, often with a lingering expression, as if half inclined to become a lake. Many of these river nooks are gloriously bordered with ferns and sedges and drooping willows; some were enlivened with ducks that blended charmingly into the picture, only it seemed wonderful that mountain water, so pure and so light like, could be sufficiently substantial to float a duck.

It is estimated that about **7000 persons** have seen Yosemite. If this multitude were to be gathered again, and set down in Hetch Hetchy perhaps less than one percent of the whole number would doubt their being in Yosemite. They would see rocks and waterfalls, meadows and groves, of Yosemite size and kind, and grouped in Yosemite style. Amid so vast an assemblage of

7000 persons: Muir, here, means white visitors. Given that the Hetch Hetchy Valley was a key Numu/Paiute landscape, managed and stewarded for millennia, the numbers of those who had "seen" Hetch Hetchy would have been countless.

sublime mountain forms, only the more calm and careful observers would be able to fix upon special differences.

The trail from Hardin's enters the valley on the south side, upon a slope which corresponds to that upon which the Mariposa trail enters Yosemite. It was made by the well-known hunter "Joe Screech" for the purpose of driving stock into the meadow. The whole valley is at present claimed by the "Smith brothers" as a summer sheep range. Sheep are driven into Hetch Hetchy every spring, about the same time that a nearly equal number of tourists are driven into Yosemite; another coincident which is remarkably suggestive.

We have no room here to discuss the formation of this valley; we will only state as our opinion that it is an inseparable portion of the great Glacier Cañon of the Tuolumne, and that its level bottom is one of a chain of lake basins extending throughout the cañon, which have been no great time ago filled up with glacial drift. The Yosemite Valley is a cañon of exactly the same origin.

Mr. Screech first visited this valley in the year 1850, one year before Yosemite was entered by Captain Boling and his party. At present there are a couple of shepherds' cabins and a group of Indian huts in the valley, which I believe is all that will come under the head of improvements.

In returning to Yosemite, I left the valley by the trail, which I followed a few miles, then turned southward, intending to cross the head cañons of the south and middle forks of the Tuolumne to Tamarac, thence to drift along the north side of Yosemite and dive to the lower world of home by some one of the side cañons.

Shortly after I had gained the summit of the divide between the main river and the middle fork, the sky, which had been growing dark and opaque all the forenoon, began to yield snowflakes. I at once hastened to a sheltered hollow which was groved with firs and watered by a tiny brook. I searched until I found a place where a number of large trees had fallen, which in case the storm should be severe would afford abundance of fire. At the stump of one of these trees, which had splintered in falling, I found plenty of laths from two to ten feet long, with which I could make a hut, but I had not sufficient time, as the snow began to fall fast. Beneath one of my fire logs I hastily burrowed a sort of bear's nest, and lined it with branchlets of fir—that was home. Then I gathered up a large pile of dry limbs in my front yard, and made a fire before the door, and boiled a cup of coffee, and went into the house. The storm was earnest, and I most intensely enjoyed its growing magnificence.

Towards night the wind, which had been making grand songs in the fir tops and upon the edges of the hollow, began to slacken, the flakes came softly, in a sauntering mood. It seemed as if snow dust were falling from the forest ceiling, and that I had crept beneath a straw on the floor.

It was delightful to lie and look out from my ample windows to the forest. Scores of firs in my front yard were over 200 feet in height. How nobly and unreservedly they gave themselves to the storm. Heart and voice, soul and body, sang to the flowering sky, each frond tip seemed to bestow a separate welcome to every **ward** of the wind, and to every snowflake as they arrived. How perfectly would the pure soul of Thoreau have mingled with those glorious trees, and he would have been content with my log house. I did not expect company in such unfavorable weather; nevertheless I was visited towards evening by a brown nugget of a wren. He came in, without knocking, by the back door, which, happily, he found high enough for his upslanted tail. He nodded, mannerly enough, when he reached the middle of the floor, and I invited him to stay over night. He made no direct reply; but judging from his fussy gestures around my boots, I thought he intended lodging beneath them, or in one of the legs. I crumbled bread for him, but he had already dined in his own home, and required none of my clumsy cares.

ward: In this case means every direction from which the wind comes.

The night became cold, and I had frequently to rise to mend my fire. Towards midnight the stars shone out, and I no longer planned concerning a snowbound. Only a few inches of snow had fallen, just sufficient to droop the whorled branches of the firs, and felt a smooth cloth for the ground.

Morning came to the snow-blossomed mountains in most surpassing splendor. The forest was one dazzling field of snow-flowers, and the ground was silvered and printed like a photographer's plate, with trees and groves and all their life. Before I had gone a hundred and fifty yards from my fire I came upon the tracks of a herd of deer that had been feeding on the branches of the ceanothus. Deer were exceedingly abundant all the way to Tamarac. In many places the ground was broidered with the footprints of foxes, squirrels, coyotes, etc.

I found that the cañons of the middle and south forks of the Tuolumne were very deep and numerous, and by the time I reached Tamarac I was glad to camp. On the sixth day of this excursion I rambled along the edge of Yosemite, and at night swooped to the bottom and home. Thus easily and safely may we mingle ourselves with the so-called frightful rocks and bears of the two Yosemites of Tuolumne and Merced.

Tourists who can afford the time ought to visit Hetch Hetchy on their way to or from Yosemite. The trail from Hardin's will be found as good as mountain trails usually are, and it certainly is worth while riding a few miles out of a direct course to assure one's self that the world is so rich as to possess at least two Yosemites instead of one.

An Act to Set Apart Certain Tracts of Land in the State of California as Forest Reservations (1890)[1]

Because California had not fully abided by the requirements of the 1864 grant of Yosemite to carefully manage the site for recreation and as a park, activists in the state, including John Muir, argued that the state should return the land to the people of the United States. After negotiations between the two governments, in 1890 Congress withdrew rights of settlement from all the land surrounding—but not including—the Yosemite Valley and the Mariposa Big-Tree Grove as a vital first step. Its stewardship was placed under the authority of the Secretary of the Interior. It would take another 16 years before the state and the federal government would complete the transfer of the valley and the grove to the national park.

Be it enacted by the Senate and the House of Representatives of the United States of America in Congress assembled, That the tracts of land in the State of California known as described as follows ... are hereby reserved and withdrawn from settlement, occupancy, or sale under the laws of the United States, and set apart as reserved forest lands; and all persons who shall locate or settle upon, or occupy the same or any part thereof, except as hereinafter provided, shall be considered trespassers and removed therefrom: Provided, however, That nothing in this act shall be construed as anywise affecting the grant of lands to the State of California by virtue of the act entitled "An act authorizing a grant to the State of California of the Yosemite Valley, and of the land embracing the Mariposa Big-Tree Grove, approved June thirtieth, eighteen hundred and sixty-four; or as affecting any bona-fide entry of land made within the limits above described under any law of the United States prior to this approval of this act.

Sec. 2. That said reservation will be under the exclusive control of the Secretary of the Interior, whose duty it shall be, as soon as practicable, to make and publish such rules and regulations he may deem necessary or proper for the care and management of the same. Such regulations will provide for the preservation from injury of all timber, mineral deposits, natural curiosities, or wonders within such reservation, and their retention in their natural condition. The Secretary may, at his discretion, grant leases for building purposes for terms not exceeding ten years of small parcels of

---

1   Fifty-First Congress, Session I, Chapter 1263.

ground not exceeding five acres; at such places in said reservation, as shall require the erection of buildings for the accommodation of visitors; all of the proceeds of said leases and other revenues that may be derived from any source connected with said reservation to be expended under his direction in the management of the same and the construction of roads and paths therein. He shall provide against the wanton destruction of the fish, and game, found within said reservation, and against their capture or destruction, for the purpose of merchandise or profit. He shall also cause all persons trespassing upon the same after the passage of this act to be removed therefrom, and, generally, shall be authorized to take all such measures as shall be necessary and proper to fully carry out the objects and purposes of this act.

Sec. 3. There shall also be and is hereby reserved and withdrawn from settlement, occupancy or sale under the laws of the United States, and shall be set apart as reserved forest lands as hereinbefore provided, and subject to all the limitations and provisions herein contained, the following addition lands.... Nothing in this act shall authorize rules or contracts touching the protection and improvement of said reservations, beyond the sums that may be received by the Secretary of the Interior under the forgoing provisions or authorize any charge against the Treasury of the United States.

Approved, October 1, 1890.

DOCUMENT 21:

Letter from John Muir to Theodore Roosevelt, 9 September 1907[2]

John Muir and Theodore Roosevelt first met in May 1903, when they arranged to take a three-day camping trip in Yosemite National Park.[3] Their time in the majestic landscape helped forge a close friendship and it was on the basis of their relationship—which Muir alludes to in a postscript—that Muir felt comfortable urging the president to protect Hetch Hetchy from the ravages of commercialism. Note Muir's use of religious imagery and rhetoric in his arguments countering those of pro-dam boosters.

Dear Mr. President:

I am anxious that the Yosemite National Park may be saved from all sorts of commercialism and marks of man's work other than roads, hotels etc. required to make its wonders and blessings available. For as far as I have seen there is not in all of the wonderful Sierra, or indeed the world another so grand and wonderful and useful a block of Nature's mountain handiwork.

There is now under consideration, as doubtless you well know, an application of San Francisco supervisors for the use of the Hetch Hetchy Valley and Lake Eleanor as storage reservoirs for a City water supply. This application should I think be denied, especially the Hetch Hetchy part, for this valley … is a counterpart of Yosemite, and one of the most sublime and beautiful and important features of the Park, and to dam and submerge it would be hardly less destructive and deplorable in its effects on the Park in general than would be the damming of Yosemite itself. For its falls and groves and delightful camp-grounds are surpassed or equaled only in Yosemite: and furthermore, it is the hall of entrance to the grand Tuolumne Canyon which opens a wonderful way to the magnificent Tuolumne Meadows, the focus of pleasure travel in the High Sierra of the Park and grand-central camp-ground. If Hetch Hetchy should be submerged as proposed to the depth of 175 feet, not only would it be made utterly inaccessible, but this glorious canyon way to the High Sierra would be blocked.

I am heartily in favor of a Sierra or even Tuolumne water supply for San Francisco but all the water required can be obtained from sources outside the Park, leaving the twin Valleys Hetch Hetchy and Yosemite to the use

---

2   John Muir Correspondence, Muir-Hanna Trust, University of the Pacific.

3   Theodore Roosevelt, "John Muir: An Appreciation," *Outlook* 109 (16 January 1915): 27–28, discusses their camping experience in Yosemite.

they were intended for when the Park was established. For every argument advanced for making one into a reservoir would apply with equal force for the other excepting the cost of the required dam. The few promoters of the present scheme are not unknown around the boundaries of the Park, for they have been trying to break through for years. However able they be as capitalists, engineers, lawyers, or even philanthropists ... they all show forth the proud sort of confidence that comes of a good sound substantial irrefragable ignorance. For example, the capitalist, Mr. **James D. Phelan**, says "there are a thousand places equally beautiful as Hetch Hetchy, it is inaccessible nine months of the year, and it is an unlivable place the other three months because of mosquitoes." On the contrary there is not another of its kind in all the Park excepting Yosemite.... And so the fight goes on. Ever since the Park was established it has called for defense, and however much it may be invaded or its boundaries shorn, while a single mountain or tree or waterfall is left the poor stub of the park will still need protection. The first forest reserve was in Eden and although its boundaries were drawn by the Lord, and angels set to guard it, even that most moderate reservation was attacked.

I pray therefore that the people of California be granted time to be heard before the reservoir question is decided: for I believe that as soon as the light is cast upon it, nine-tenths or more of even the citizens of San Francisco would be opposed to it. And what the public opinion of the world may be guessed by the case of **Niagara Falls**.

O for a tranquil camp hour with you like those beneath the Sequoias in memorable 1903.

James D. Phelan: Phelan (1861–1930) was the mayor of San Francisco and a key advocate for the Hetch Hetchy Dam.

Niagara Falls: Muir is referring to the hydroelectric works that were constructed to take advantage of the immense generating power of these great cataracts. Late-nineteenth-century activists protested against the implementation of the Canadian and US operations, to no avail.

DOCUMENT 22:

Letter of Theodore Roosevelt to John Muir, 16 September 1907[4]

In his reply to Muir, President Roosevelt conveys two important points. That he is quite willing to protect Hetch Hetchy, as he had been doing to other sites around the country. But any such protection required public opinion in support of such preservation designations—and at the moment, Roosevelt had seen little evidence that there was a groundswell in favor of Hetch Hetchy. He was counseling Muir, then, to do a better job of convincing the public of his position; and in the next years Muir indeed would help build a national campaign to protect his beloved valley.

My Dear Mr. Muir:

I gather that **Garfield** and **Pinchot** are rather favorable to the Hetch Hetchy plan, but not definitely so. I have sent them your letter with a request for a report on it. I will do everything in my power to protect not only the Yosemite, which we already have protected, but other similar great natural beauties of this country; but you must remember that it is out of the question permanently to protect them unless we have a certain degree of friendliness toward them on the part of the people of the State in which they are situated; and if they are used so as to interfere with the permanent material development of the State instead of helping the permanent development, the result will be bad. I would not have any difficulty at all if, as you say, nine-tenths of the citizens took ground against the Hetch Hetchy project; but so far everyone that has appeared has been for it and I have been in the disagreeable position of seeming to interfere with the development of the State for the sake of keeping a valley, which apparently hardly anyone wanted to have kept, under **national control**.

I wish I could see you in person; and how I do wish I were again with you camping out under those great sequoia or in the snow under the silver firs.[5]

Garfield: James Garfield served as Roosevelt's secretary of the interior between 1907 and 1909.

Pinchot: Gifford Pinchot was the first chief of the US Forest Service, an agency established in 1905 with management oversight of what would become the national forest system.

national control: Roosevelt is advising Muir that developing a groundswell of *national* opinion in opposition to the Hetch Hetchy dam project is essential because the state clearly wanted the dam built; Char Miller, *Gifford Pinchot and the Making of Modern Environmentalism* (Washington, DC: Island Press, 2001), 139–41, 170–73.

---

4 John Muir Correspondence, UC Berkeley, Bancroft Library.

5 Roosevelt's reference to their 1903 camping experience.

DOCUMENT 23:

Petition of Marsden Manson, City Engineer of San Francisco, on Behalf of the City and County of San Francisco, to the Secretary of the Interior Department, Washington, DC, to Reopen the Matter of the Application of James D. Phelan for Reservoir Rights of Way in the Hetch Hetchy Valley and Lake Eleanor Sites in the Yosemite Park, 7 May 1908[6]

Manson (1850–1931) received his PhD in engineering from the University of California–Berkeley in 1893, and was the civic engineer for the city of San Francisco at the time of the Hetch Hetchy hearings. He provides a year-by-year accounting of the steps that San Francisco had taken to secure rights to the land and waters of the Hetch Hetchy Valley. His appeal, framed around what he describes as "years of careful and scientific study of the sites themselves and information concerning the capacity of the sites applied for and the tributary drainage areas," also contains the nine stipulations that the city was willing to accept as part of an agreement with the federal government to build the dam-and-reservoir complex. The hearing was held before the Committee on the Public Lands of the House of Representatives on 16 December 1908 on House Joint Resolution 184, Part II.

Washington, D.C., *May 7, 1908*

The honorable Secretary of the Interior.

Sir: On behalf of the city and county of San Francisco, I respectfully petition you to exercise your supervisory authority and reopen the matter of the application of James D. Phelan for reservoir rights of way in the Hetch Hetchy Valley and Lake Eleanor sites in the Yosemite National Park. This application was made October 15, 1901, by James D. Phelan, then mayor, in conjunction with an effort that was being made to secure an adequate and pure supply of water for the city and county of San Francisco, and was assigned to said city and county February 20, 1903, in order to carry out the original intent in making the application and that the city might be of record as the successor to any rights that may have been gained by the application. Subsequently, on December 22, 1903, the application was rejected on the ground that the Secretary of the Interior did not have power to allow such right of way within the Yosemite National Park. Thereafter I, as the

---

6 Virtual Museum of the City of San Francisco, accessed 19 September 2019.

representative of the said city and county, came to Washington and asked for a reconsideration of the matter. This reconsideration was granted in the form of a request for an opinion from the Attorney-General concerning the Secretary's contention that he did not have the power. The Attorney-General held that the Secretary of the Interior had full power, and that it was merely a matter of administrative judgment as to whether the application for rights of way should or should not be granted.

I was of the opinion that the steps taken by the city and county of San Francisco, through me, to have this matter reconsidered was a formal action which kept the application alive, but it seems that, according to the technical and strict interpretation of the rules of practice of the Department of the Interior, my supposition was incorrect and that the maps of location were formally rejected and returned to the city and county, where they remained and were destroyed by fire following the earthquake in April, 1906. I learned recently that the case was technically closed, but I find that the practice of your department will permit, through the exercise of supervisory authority, the curing of a technical action made final through mistake of an applicant, especially when great public interests and equities are involved.

I caused exact retracements of certified copies of the original maps of location to be made and Mr. Phelan filed them in your department in 1907. As the city engineer, directly in charge of these matters, I have certified that they are exact reproductions made under my personal direction of the original maps of location. I therefore ask that you treat them as though they were originals, and in view of all the circumstances mentioned above, the great needs of the city of San Francisco for an adequate and pure water supply, and the fact that I have been authorized to act for the city in this matter by a resolution of the board of supervisors (a certified copy of which resolution I will obtain from San Francisco at the earliest practicable moment and file with this petition), urge that you treat the application of James D. Phelan, afterwards assigned to the city of San Francisco, as though it had never technically lapsed.

As the engineer of the city, I have gathered from years of careful and scientific study of the sites themselves information concerning the capacity of the sites applied for and the tributary drainage areas, and I am confident that the city could not afford to develop the Lake Eleanor site alone without every assurance possible to be given by the Government that the Hetch Hetchy site will be available as soon as the needs of the city exceed the Lake Eleanor storage capacity. For that reason I urge that the right to use both sites be now granted in order that the city may proceed in its work with a degree of security.

If the application for both reservoir sites is granted, I offer and agree on behalf of the city that its application for the two reservoir sites may be approved upon the basis of the following conditions which will be furnished if you desire, in the form of a stipulation, approved by resolution of the board of supervisors, and duly executed under the seal of the city of San Francisco.

The city and county of San Francisco will agree to the following stipulations:

1. The city of San Francisco practically owns all the patented land in the floor of the Hetch Hetchy reservoir site and sufficient adjacent areas in the Yosemite National Park and the Sierra National Forest to equal the remainder of that reservoir area. The city will surrender to the United States equivalent areas outside of the reservoir sites and within the national park and adjacent reserves in exchange for the remaining land in the reservoir sites, for which authority from Congress will be obtained if necessary.

2. The city and county of San Francisco distinctly understands and agrees that all the rules and regulations for the government of the park, now or hereafter in force, shall be applicable to its holdings within the park and that, except to the extent that the necessary use of its holdings for the exclusive purpose of storing and protecting water for the uses herein specified will be interfered with, the public may have the full enjoyment thereof, under regulations fixed by the Secretary of the Interior.

3. The city and county of San Francisco will develop the Lake Eleanor site to its full capacity before beginning the development of the Hetch Hetchy site, and the development of the latter will be begun only when the needs of the city and county of San Francisco and adjacent cities, which may join with it in obtaining a common water supply, may require such further development. As the drainage area tributary to Lake Eleanor will not yield, under the conditions herein imposed, sufficient run-off in dry years to replenish the reservoir, a diverting dam and canal from Cherry Creek to Lake Eleanor reservoir for the conduct of waste, flood, or extra-seasonal waters to said reservoir is essential for the development of the site to its full capacity, and will be constructed if permission is given by the Secretary of the Interior.

4. The city and county of San Francisco, and any other city or cities which may, with the approval of the municipal authorities, join with said city and county of San Francisco in obtaining a common water supply, will not interfere in the slightest particular with the right of the Modesto irrigation district and the Turlock irrigation district to use the natural flow of the Tuolumne River and its branches to the full extent of their claims, as follows: Turlock irrigation district, 1,500 **second-feet**; Modesto irrigation

second-feet: The volume of water represented by a flow of 1 cubic foot per second for 24 hours; equal to 86,400 cubic feet.

district, 850 second-feet; these districts having, respectively, appropriated the foregoing amounts of water under the laws of the State of California.

To the end that these rights may be fully protected, San Francisco will stipulate not to store nor cause to be stored, divert nor cause to be diverted from the Tuolumne River or any of its branches any of the natural flow of said river when desired for use by said districts, for any beneficial purpose, unless this natural flow of the river and tributaries above La Grange dam be in excess of the actual capacities of the canals of said districts, even when they shall have been brought up to the full volumes named—1,500 second-feet for the Turlock irrigation district and 850 second-feet for the Modesto irrigation district.

5. The city and county of San Francisco will in no way interfere with the storage of flood waters in sites other than Hetch Hetchy and Lake Eleanor by the Modesto and Turlock irrigation districts or either of said districts for use in said districts, and will return to the Tuolumne River above the La Grange dam, for the use of said irrigation districts, all surplus or waste flow of the river which may be used for power.

6. The city of San Francisco will, upon request, sell to said Modesto and Turlock irrigation districts for the use of any land owner or owners therein for pumping subsurface water for drainage or irrigation any excess of electric power which may be generated such as may not be used for the water supply herein provided and for the actual municipal purposes of the city and county of San Francisco (which purposes shall not include sale to private persons nor to corporations), at such price as will actually reimburse the said city and county for developing and transmitting the surplus electrical energy thus sold, the price in case of dispute to be fixed by the Secretary of the Interior; and no power plant shall be interposed on the line of flow except by the said city and county except for the purposes and under the limitations above set forth.

7. The city and county of San Francisco will agree that the Secretary of the Interior shall, at his discretion, or when called upon by either the city or the districts to do so, direct the apportionment and measurement of the water in accordance with the terms of the preceding clauses of this stipulation.

8. The city and county of San Francisco, when it begins the development of the Hetch Hetchy site, will undertake and vigorously prosecute to completion a dam at least 150 feet high, with a foundation capable of supporting the dam when built to its greatest economic and safe height, and whenever, in the opinion of the engineer in charge of the reservoirs on behalf of

said city and county and of the municipalities sharing in this supply, the volume of water on storage in the reservoirs herein applied for is in excess of the seasonal requirements of said municipalities, and that it is safe to do so, that such excess will be liberated at such times and in such amounts as said districts may designate, at a price to said districts not to exceed the proportionate cost of storage and sinking fund chargeable to the volumes thus liberated, the price in case of dispute to be fixed by the Secretary of the Interior; provided, that no prescriptive or other right shall ever inure or attach to said districts by user or otherwise to the water thus liberated.

9. The city and county of San Francisco will, within two years after the grant by the Secretary of the Interior of the rights hereby applied for, submit the question of said water supply to the vote of its citizens as required by its charter, and within three years thereafter, if such vote be affirmative, will commence the actual construction of the Lake Eleanor dam and will carry the same to completion with all diligence, so that said reservoir may be completed within five years after the commencement thereof, unless such times herein before specified shall be extended by the Secretary of the Interior for cause shown by the city, or the construction delayed by litigation; and unless the construction of said reservoir is authorized by a vote of the said city and county and said work is commenced, carried on, and completed within the times herein specified, all rights granted hereunder shall revert to the Government.

Marsden Manson

DOCUMENT 24:

Decision of the Secretary of the Interior Department, Washington, DC, Granting the City and County of San Francisco, Subject to Certain Conditions, Reservoir Sites and Rights of Way at Lake Eleanor and Hetch Hetchy Valley in the Yosemite Park, 11 May 1908[7]

> Secretary of the Interior James Garfield offers a favorable response to San Francisco's request for rights of way within Yosemite National Park to build and maintain the Hetch Hetchy reservoir and related sites. Garfield, after assessing prior congressional sanction of the rights of way for the purpose of building water-storage facilities, indicates that the only decision he needed to consider was "the effect of granting the application upon 'the public interest.'" He concluded that the city's need for water must take priority over the protection of the valley.

e

Department of the Interior,
Washington, May 11, 1908.

Water supply, city of San Francisco–Application for Lake Eleanor and Hetch Hetchy Valley reservoir sites, act of February 15, 1901.

The Commissioner of the General Land Office.

Sir: October 15, 1901, James D. Phelan, then mayor of the city of San Francisco, filed application for reservoir rights of way within the Yosemite National Park upon what are known as the **Lake Eleanor** and Hetch Hetchy Valley reservoir sites. This application was made under the act of February 15, 1901, and was in fact the application of the city made in the name of James D. Phelan to avoid the difficulties which beset a city if it must announce its business intentions to the public before securing options and rights necessary for its project. This is not disputed, and the fact is corroborated by his assigning to the city and county of San Francisco, on February 20, 1903, all his rights under the above application.

This application was considered by the Secretary of the Interior and, on December 22, 1903, rejected on the ground that he did not have the legal power to allow such a right of way within the Yosemite National Park. From that time to this the city has, with practical continuity, pressed its request for a permit to use these reservoir sites. The city failed, however, to take steps

Lake Eleanor: Lake Eleanor, so named in the 1860s for the daughter of geologist Josiah Whitney director of the California Geological Survey, was dammed in 1918 to supply water and power to San Francisco.

---

7   Virtual Museum of the City of San Francisco, accessed 19 September 2019.

to reopen this case in the form prescribed by the rules of practice of this department, and for that reason technically had no application on file after December 22, 1903. On the other hand, the city's evident good faith and the strong evidence that it supposed its application was alive in the department is shown by the fact that at its request and solicitation the question of the power of the Secretary of the Interior to grant the rights of way applied for was referred to the Attorney-General, who, on October 28, 1905, held definitely that the Secretary of the Interior had full discretionary power to grant rights of way for reservoir, irrigation, or hydro-electric purposes within the park.

When the Secretary's decision of December 22, 1903, was made final, the maps of location for the two reservoir sites were returned to the city, and unfortunately were destroyed by the fire which followed the earthquake of 1906. Fortunately, however, exact tracings of these maps had been made by the city engineer for use in court proceedings, and for that reason it has been possible to file exact reproductions of the original maps, certified by the city engineer. When the attention of the city's representative was called to the fact that technically the city had no application before the department, he, on May 7, 1908, formally filed a petition requesting the Secretary of the Interior to exercise his supervisory authority and reopen the matter of the application of James D. Phelan for the reservoir rights in question, thus treating it as though it had never lapsed. I have given the most careful consideration to this petition, and have decided that the facts mentioned above are ample grounds for exercising my supervisory power, and therefore reinstate the application of James D. Phelan, assigned to the city, as though the case had been technically kept alive since December 22, 1903, by specific compliance with the rules of practice of the department. To this end the tracings of the original maps of location as recertified by Marsden Manson, city engineer, on April 22, 1908, will be accepted in lieu of the original and treated accordingly.

Congress, on February 15, 1901, provided specifically:

> "The Secretary of the Interior ... is authorized ... to permit the use of rights of way through ... the Yosemite, Sequoia, and General Grant national parks, California, for ... water conduits and for water plants, dams, and reservoirs used to promote ... the supply of water for domestic, public, or other beneficial uses ... provided that such permits shall be allowed within or through any of said parks ... only upon the approval of the chief officer of the department, under whose supervision such park or reservation falls, and upon a finding by him that the same is not incompatible with the public interest."

By these words Congress has given power to the Secretary of the Interior to grant the rights applied for by the city of San Francisco, if he finds that the permit is "not incompatible with the public interest." Therefore I need only consider the effect of granting the application upon "the public interest."

In construing the words of a statute the evident and ordinary meaning should be taken, when such meaning is reasonable and not repugnant to the evident purpose of the law itself. On this broad principle the words "the public interest" should not be confined merely to the public interest in the Yosemite National Park for use as a park only, but rather the broader public interest which requires these reservoir sites to be utilized for the highest good to the greatest number of people. If Congress had intended to restrict the meaning to the mere interest on the public in the park as such, it surely would have used specific words to show that intent. At the time the act was passed there was no authority of law for the granting of privileges of this character in the Yosemite National Park. Congress recognized the interest of the public in the utilization of the great water resources of the park and specifically gave power to the Secretary of the Interior to permit such use. The proviso was evidently added merely as a reminder that he should weigh well the public interest both in and out of the park before making his decision.

The present water supply of the city of San Francisco is both inadequate and unsatisfactory. This fact has been known for a number of years and has led to a very extensive consideration of the various possible sources of supply. The search for water for the city has been prosecuted from two diametrically opposite points of view. On the one side, the water companies, interested in supplying the city with water for their own profit, have taken advantage of the long delay since it was first proposed to bring water from the Yosemite to San Francisco to look up and get control, so far as they could, of the available sources in order to sell them to the city. On the other hand, both the National Government and the city of San Francisco have made careful study of the possible sources of supply for the city. Four or five years ago the hydrographic branch of the Geological Survey, after a careful examination by engineers of character and ability, reached the conclusion that the Tuolumne River offered a desirable and available supply for the city. The same conclusion was reached by the engineers of the city of San Francisco after years of exhaustive investigation.

I appreciate keenly the interest of the public in preserving the natural wonders of the park and am unwilling that the Hetch Hetchy Valley site should be developed until the needs of the city are greater than can be supplied from the Lake Eleanor site when developed to its full capacity. Domestic use, however, especially for a municipal supply, is the highest use to which water and available storage basins therefor can be put. Recognizing this the city has expressed a willingness to regard the public interest in the Hetch Hetchy Valley and defer its use as long as possible.

The next great use of water and water resources is irrigation. There are in the San Joaquin Valley two large irrigation districts, the Turlock and Modesto, which have already appropriated under state law 2,350 second-feet of the normal flow of water through Lake Eleanor and Hetch Hetchy. The representatives of these districts protested strongly against the granting of the permit to San Francisco, being fearful that the future complete development of these irrigation communities would be materially hampered by the city's use of water. After repeated conferences, however, with the representatives of these irrigation districts I believe their rights can be fully safeguarded, provided certain definite stipulations to protect the irrigators are entered into by the city. Fortunately, the city can agree to this, and the interest of the two users will not conflict. On the contrary, the city in developing its water supply will to a considerable extent help the irrigation districts in their further development.

The only other source of objection, except that from persons and corporations who have no rights to protect but merely the hope of financial gain if the application of the city is denied, comes from those who have a special interest in our national parks from the standpoint of scenic effects, natural wonders, and health and pleasure resorts. I appreciate fully the feeling of these protestants and have considered their protests and arguments with great interest and sympathy. The use of these sites for reservoir purposes would interfere with the present condition of the park, and that consideration should be weighed carefully against the great use which the city can make of the permit. I am convinced, however, that "the public interest" will be much better conserved by granting the permit. Hetch Hetchy Valley is great and beautiful in its natural and scenic effects. If it were also unique, sentiment for its preservation in an absolutely natural state would be far greater. In the mere vicinity, however, much more accessible to the public and more wonderful and beautiful, is the Yosemite Valley itself. Furthermore, the reservoir will not destroy Hetch Hetchy. It will scarcely affect the canyon walls. It will not reach the foot of the various falls which descend from the sides of the canyon. The prime change will be that, instead of a beautiful but somewhat unusable "meadow" floor, the valley will be a lake of rare beauty.

As against this partial loss to the scenic effect of the park, the advantages to the public from the change are many and great. The city of San Francisco and probably the other cities on San Francisco Bay would have one of the finest and purest water supplies in the world. The irrigable land in the Tuolumne and San Joaquin valleys would be helped out by the use of the excess stored water, and by using the electrical power not needed by the city for municipal purposes to pump subterranean water for the irrigation of additional areas the city would have a cheap and bountiful supply of electric energy for pumping its water supply and lighting the city and its municipal buildings. The public would have a highway at its disposal to reach this beautiful region of the park herefore practically inaccessible. This road would be built and maintained by the city without expense to the Government or the general public. The city has options on land held in private ownership within the Yosemite National Park, and would purchase this land and make it available to the public for camping purposes. The settlers and entrymen who acquired this land naturally chose the finest localities and at present have power to exclude the public from the best camping places, and, further, the city in protecting its water supply would furnish to the public a patrol to save this part of the park from destructive and disfiguring forest fires.

The floor of the Hetch Hetchy Valley, part of which is owned privately and used as a cattle ranch, would become a lake bordered by vertical granite walls or steep banks of broken granite. Therefore, when the water is drawn very low it will leave few muddy edges exposed. This lake, however, would be practically full during the greater part of the tourist season in each year, and there would be practically no difficulty in making trails and roads for the use of the tourists around the edges of the valley above high-water mark. The city of San Francisco, through its regularly authorized representative, has, in order to protect the interests most directly involved, agreed to file with the Secretary of the Interior a stipulation approved by specific resolution of the board of supervisors and duly executed under the seal of the city of San Francisco as follows:

"1. The city of San Francisco practically owns all the patented land in the floor of the Hetch Hetchy Reservoir site and sufficient adjacent areas in the Yosemite National Park and the Sierra National Forest to equal the remainder of that reservoir area. The city will surrender to the United States equivalent areas outside of the reservoir sites and within the national park and adjacent reserves in exchange for the remaining land in the reservoir sites, for which authority from Congress will be obtained if necessary.

"2. The city and county of San Francisco distinctly understands and agrees that all the rules and regulations for the government of the park, now or hereafter in force, shall be applicable to its holdings within the park, and that, except to the extent that the necessary use of its holdings for the exclusive purpose of storing and protecting water for the uses herein specified will be interfered with, the public may have the full enjoyment thereof, under regulations fixed by the Secretary of the Interior.

"3. The city and county of San Francisco will develop the Lake Eleanor site to its full capacity before beginning the development of the Hetch Hetchy site, and the development of the latter will be begun only when the needs of the city and county of San Francisco and adjacent cities, which may join with it in obtaining a common water supply, may require such further development. As the drainage area tributary to Lake Eleanor will not yield, under the conditions herein imposed, sufficient run-off in dry years to replenish the reservoir, a diverting dam and canal from Cherry Creek to Lake Eleanor Reservoir for the conduct of waste flood or extra-seasonal waters to said reservoir is essential for the development of the site to its full capacity, and will be constructed if permission is given by the Secretary of the Interior.

"4. The city and county of San Francisco, and any other city or cities which may, with the approval of the municipal authorities, join with said city and county of San Francisco in obtaining a common water supply, will not interfere in the slightest particular with the right of the Modesto irrigation district and the Turlock irrigation district to use the natural flow of the Tuolumne River and its branches to the full extent of their claims, as follows: Turlock irrigation district, 1,500 second-feet; Modesto irrigation district, 850 second-feet, these districts having, respectively, appropriated the foregoing amounts of water under the laws of the State of California.

"To the end that these rights may be fully protected, San Francisco will stipulate not to store nor cause to be diverted from the Tuolumne River or any of its branches, any of the natural flow of said river when desired for use by said districts for any beneficial purpose, unless this natural flow of the river and tributaries above La Grange dam be in excess of the actual capacities of the canals of said districts, even when they shall have been brought up to the full volumes named, 1,500 second-feet for the Turlock irrigation district and 850 second-feet for the Modesto irrigation district.

"5. The city and county of San Francisco will in no way interfere with the storage of flood waters, in sites other than Hetch Hetchy and Lake Eleanor by the Modesto and Turlock irrigation districts or either of said districts for use in said districts, and will return to the Tuolumne River above the La Grange dam, for the use of said irrigation districts, all surplus or waste flow of the river which may be used for power.

"6. The city of San Francisco will upon request sell to said Modesto and Turlock irrigation districts for the use of any land owner or owners therein for pumping subsurface water for drainage or irrigation and any excess of electric power which may be generated such as may not be used for the water supply herein provided and for the actual municipal purposes of the city and county of San Francisco (which purposes shall not include sale to private persons nor to corporations), at such price as will actually reimburse the said city and county for developing and transmitting the surplus electric energy thus sold the price in case of dispute to be fixed by the Secretary of the Interior; and no power plant shall be interposed on the line of flow except by the said city and county except for the purposes and under the limitations above set forth.

"7. The city and county of San Francisco will agree that the Secretary of the Interior shall, at his discretion, or when called upon by either the city or the districts to do so, direct the apportionment and measurement of the water in accordance with the terms of the preceding clauses of this stipulation.

"8. The city and county of San Francisco, when it begins the development of the Hetch Hetchy site, will undertake and vigorously prosecute to completion a dam at least 150 feet high, with a foundation capable of supporting the dam when built to its greatest economic and safe height, and whenever, in the opinion of the engineer in charge of the reservoirs on behalf of said city and county and of the municipalities sharing in this supply, the volume of water on storage in the reservoirs herein applied for is in excess of the seasonal requirements of said municipalities, and that it is safe to do so, that such excess will be liberated at such times and in such amounts as said districts may designate, at a price to said districts not to exceed the proportionate cost of storage and sinking fund chargeable to the volumes thus liberated, the price in case of dispute to be fixed by the Secretary of the Interior; provided, that no prescriptive or other right shall ever inure or attach to said districts by user or otherwise to the water thus liberated.

"9. The city and county of San Francisco will, within two years after the grant by the Secretary of the Interior of the right hereby applied for, submit the question of said water supply to the vote of its citizens as required by its charter, and within three years thereafter, if such vote be affirmative, will commence the actual construction of the Lake Eleanor dam and will carry the same to completion with all reasonable diligence, so that said reservoir may be completed within five years after the commencement thereof, unless such times herein before specified shall be extended by the Secretary of the Interior for cause shown by the city, or the construction delayed by litigation; and unless the construction of said reservoir is authorized by a vote of the said city and county and said work is commenced, carried on, and completed within the times herein specified, all rights granted hereunder shall revert to the Government."

In considering the reinstated application of the city of San Francisco, I do not need to pass upon the claim that this is the only practicable and reasonable source of water supply for the city. It is sufficient that after careful and competent study the officials of the city insist that such is the case. By granting the application opportunity will be given for the city, by obtaining the necessary two-thirds majority vote, to demonstrate the practical question as to whether or not this is the water supply desired and needed by the residents of San Francisco.

I therefore approve the maps of location for the Lake Eleanor and Hetch Hetchy reservoir sites as filed by James D. Phelan and assigned to the city of San Francisco, subject to the filing by the city of the former stipulation set forth above, and the fulfillment of the conditions therein contained.

Very respectfully,
James R. Garfield,
Secretary.

DOCUMENT 25:

Letter of the American Civic Association to the Committee on Public Lands, 15 December 1908[8]

The American Civic Association was a national municipal reform organization, whose mission was "the cultivation of higher ideals of civic life and beauty in America, the promotion of city, town and neighborhood improvement, the preservation and development of landscape and the advancement of outdoor art." Its president, J. Horace McFarland (1859–1948), a journalist and activist, fought to protect Niagara Falls as well as Yosemite. Here he joined with other conservationists fighting to protect the Hetch Hetchy Valley and urged the Congress, and by extension the Roosevelt administration, to launch a full "most careful consideration of the matter."

&

American Civic Association
Harrisburg, Pa., December 15, 1908.

Hon. Frank W. Mondell:
Frank Wheeler Mondell
(1860–1939) represented
Wyoming in the US
Congress from 1899–1923.

Hon. Frank W. Mondell
Chairman Committee on the Public Lands,
House of Representatives, Washington, D.C.

Dear Sir: On behalf of the American Civic Association I wish to urge the most careful and intimate consideration of the problem before you in connection with a hearing on Wednesday of this week, to be given to officials of the city of San Francisco, in advocacy of the bill to confirm a grant made by the Secretary of the Interior to that city for the use of Lake Eleanor and the Hetch Hetchy Valley of the Yosemite National Park

While much evidence in favor of this grant has been brought before the Secretary of the Interior, I do not know that there has ever been any call for evidence as to the effect of the grant on the general interests of the American public as the owners of the Yosemite National Park.

I respectfully urge upon your committee the consideration of the fact that the United States has now all too few reservations of a public nature, supposedly to be held as public parks; that of these the Yosemite National Park is esteemed to be among the greatest; and that once passed from its possession it is practically impossible to regain these areas for public use. I would urge that our increased population makes more necessary advance provision, in the wisdom of the Federal Government, of broad areas for

---

8   Virtual Museum of the City of San Francisco, accessed 19 September 2019.

recreation and the regaining of health through access to the wonders of nature. I would also urge that the Yosemite National Park is unique and that no portion of it can be spared to any use unless that use benefits the whole public.

The statement has been made that the creation of a lake in the Hetch Hetchy Valley to promote the interests of the city of San Francisco by impounding therein a great volume of water would add to the scenic beauty of the valley; but it is also known that the flooding of this valley would make such beauty, if so created, inaccessible. Moreover, I would respectfully insist that any claims made by any parties whatever to the effect that a public reservoir, to impound waters for domestic uses, should be allowed to be open to indiscriminate travel, is based on complete ignorance of modern methods of proper safeguarding of the water supply. If this valley is given up to San Francisco it must be utterly given up, and any suggestions as to its accessibility to tourists should be taken into consideration with the fact that such accessibility would introduce the danger of contamination, and make a remedy for San Francisco's supposed loss in the matter of a water supply worse than the difficulty which has caused those ills.

Moreover, if this valley is given up for this purpose, whether or not it is so stated, inevitably in the future all the tributary watershed supplying the water impounded must be given up to the purpose of the water supply of the city of San Francisco, and therefore must be removed completely from public use. Any other treatment would be suicidal and wrong, and I beg of you not to be deceived by any statements which may be made by those either unfamiliar with the circumstances or who do not realize the necessities of a modern city water supply, to the purport that the creation of the proposed reservoir will do other than withdraw this great portion of the public domain from the public use to which it was once dedicated by Congress.

If it should be found that San Francisco cannot have a water supply anywhere else than in the Hetch Hetchy Valley which will properly serve her purposes, and if, in the belief of your committee and Congress, it is more important for San Francisco to have the Hetch Hetchy Valley than for the whole country to have the Hetch Hetchy Valley, then the grant should be confirmed, but under no specious suggestion of a possible increase in picturesqueness or of any possible dual use of the location for both reservoir and the purpose to which it was once set aside by Congress.

For the above reasons I now again urge the fullest and most careful consideration of the matter, with an invitation to others than the citizens of San Francisco to participate in the hearing, so that the truth may be fully brought out. I would suggest that various associations concerned with the protection of American scenery be invited to attend a hearing arranged for the purpose, and among these I would name the Appalachian Mountain

Club, of Boston; the American Civic Association, of Philadelphia; the Sierra Club, of San Francisco. I would suggest further that citizens who have knowledge of the conditions be likewise invited, and among these I would name Richard Underwood Johnson, the associate editor of the Century Magazine; John Muir, the eminent naturalist; and others whose great achievements and high reputation place their motives above criticism.

With the hope that the Committee on Public Lands will not deem it wise to favorably report the approval of the grant until after full public opportunity has been offered to present all the facts, apparently not now completely made known, I am,

Very respectfully yours,
J. Horace McFarland
President.

DOCUMENT 26:

Letter of the Appalachian Mountain Club to the Committee on Public Lands, 15 December 1908[9]

> The Appalachian Club, founded in 1876, is the oldest conservation and outdoor recreation organization in the United States. Its efforts to promote the expansion of recreational activities in the mountains close to the burgeoning eastern cities is of a piece with the arguments this letter makes about preserving the Sierra and "notable scenery as these parks contain as national assets of value."

ℰ

Appalachian Mountain Club
Boston, Mass., December 15, 1908.

Committee on the Public Lands,
House of Representatives, Washington, D.C.

Gentlemen: Being advised that a hearing is to be granted to-morrow by your committee upon the petition of the city of San Francisco for a confirmation of a grant of flowage rights in certain valleys within the Yosemite National Park, said petition being represented by House Joint Resolution 184 dated May 12, 1908, I beg leave to herewith file with you a protest, on behalf of the Appalachian Mountain Club, against this grant and its confirmation.

Permit me to state that I have authority to thus speak on behalf of the club by virtue of a vote passed by our governing board on October 22, 1907. The matter was at that time before the Secretary of the Interior, and a formal protest was filed with him.

Allow me also to state that we are not speaking upon this subject without definite knowledge of the conditions both political and physical. Many of us have visited the Hetch Hetchy Valley, and in fact have traversed the entire length of the Tuolumne Canyon from Soda Springs meadows to Hetch Hetchy. Moreover, we have examined in detail all the printed evidence gathered upon the subject by the Hon. **E.A. Hitchcock,** who, as Secretary of the Interior, considered this petition in 1902; we have corresponded with the present **Secretary of the Interior,** with the **Chief of the Forest Service,** and with prominent citizens of San Francisco and other bay cities upon the matter. The writer has also had personal interviews on two or three occasions with two noted hydraulic engineers who had served as consulting authorities

E.A. Hitchcock: Ethan Allen Hitchcock (1835–1909) served presidents William B. McKinley and Theodore Roosevelt as secretary of the interior from 1898 to 1907.

Secretary of the Interior: James R. Garfield (1865–1950), son of the assassinated president, served as Theodore Roosevelt's secretary of the interior from 1907 to 1909.

Chief of the Forest Service: Gifford Pinchot.

9   Sierra Club Archives online, accessed 19 September 2019.

upon this subject of added water supply for San Francisco. We have, in short, taken the utmost pains to inform ourselves as to the merits of both sides of the case, and have kept posted constantly through all the proceedings.

It is our belief that Mr. Hitchcock took the only proper stand upon this petition. It was his endeavor to ascertain whether or no there was any public necessity which would justify him in surrendering to any community special rights which would tend to injure the natural beauties of the park. The act of October, 1890, requires the Secretary of the Interior to "provide for the preservation from injury of all timber, mineral deposits, natural curiosities, or wonders ... and their retention in their natural condition."

It is true that the act gives him power to make grants such as that now under consideration, but only when it "is not incompatible with the public interest."

Mr. Hitchcock, after taking much testimony, decided that this was not the only reasonable source of water supply for the city, and that he was not justified, therefore, in granting flowage rights which would of necessity involve the mutilation of the natural wonders of the park.

Mr. Garfield, however, declined to rule upon the claim of the city that this was the only reasonable source of water supply, stating that in his judgment "it is sufficient that after careful and competent study the city officials insist that such is the case."

In this we feel that Mr. Garfield erred. What constitutes "careful and competent study"?

Two of the very best authorities on municipal water supply in the country were consulted by the opposing sides in this matter. For the city, Mr. Desmond Fitz Gerald, of Boston, made an examination and report. For the opposition, Mr. Frederick P. Stearns, also of this city, likewise made examination and report. Both engineers considered not only the present water supply but several proposed new supplies among others the Hetch Hetchy and Lake Eleanor watersheds. Mr. Fitz Gerald favored the Tuolumne source, while Mr. Stearns reported that the present supply with the extensions which can readily be made, is in all respects adequate for many years to come.

Was not the study of the opposition therefore equally "careful and competent"?

We would not array ourselves knowingly in opposition to granting any community a proper water supply, but we feel that here is a point of fundamental importance which should be proved beyond peradventure before the Hetch Hetchy grant is confirmed. Is the Tuolumne supply the only reasonable one for San Francisco?

The mere assertion of either side that it is or that it is not, however positively made, should not be accepted as conclusive evidence. It is our hope that your committee will avail itself of the personal testimony of the two engineers named above.

We believe that you will agree with us that the resources of our national parks should not be carelessly opened to exploitation and that you will also appreciate the importance of conserving such notable scenery as these parks contain as national assets of value. Switzerland long ago appreciated the commercial and sanitary value of scenery and legislated for its conservation to her great and lasting profit. Our people are more and more coming to appreciate the value of their national scenic treasures. The Yosemite Park is year by year visited by increasing numbers. An examination of the recent reports of the superintendent of the park will show that the tide of travel has greatly increased there since the completion of the railroad to El Portal. The hotels in the main valley are already inadequate, and camping parties find it increasingly difficult to secure.

Hetch Hetchy Valley is admitted to be a natural wonder, but little inferior to the Yosemite proper, while the Tuolumne Canyon, through which flows and plunges the main river from the great mountain meadows at Soda Springs, is one of the big natural features of the Sierra and of the park.

The old Yosemite is soon to prove inadequate in every way to keep the throngs that will journey to those mountain regions. With better roads to Soda Springs and to Hetch Hetchy the present pressure upon Yosemite will be relieved. Civil engineers who are members of this club and who have recently traveled over the trails of the park, state that it would be a comparatively simple matter to thus open up those sections to the public. The public merely awaits the facilities. With a reservoir at Hetch Hetchy one of these great camping grounds will be extinguished, and the scenery which would attract the people thence will, in our opinion, be seriously marred. We are unable to agree with those who profess to think that a vast artificial lake, subject to heavy drafts by the water users and by evaporation in dry summers, with the attendant bare and slimy shores, will prove equally attractive to those who seek relaxation amid pleasant scenes.

It is even doubtful if the users of the water would long allow the camping upon those shores of hundreds of tourists and their animals, owing to the danger of the contamination of the supply. And will not the same hold true of the camping privilege in the Tuolumne Canyon and on the mountain meadows above? The tendency of water boards everywhere is to relieve the watersheds under their care of even a suspicion of a contaminating influence.

We regret that we are unable to be personally represented at the hearing, but we trust that this letter may be allowed to go in as a part of your record, and that your committee will take no hasty action upon the petition of the city.

Respectfully,
Allen Chamberlain,
Councillor of Exploration and Forestry.

Allen Chamberlain:
Chamberlain was a key eastern voice in defense of the Hetch Hetchy Valley.

Telegram from the Sierra Club to the Committee on Public Lands, 16 December 1908[10]

In an effort to forestall the secretary of the interior's 1908 decision to grant San Francisco the right to build Hetch Hetchy, the Sierra Club joined with its conservationist allies across the country to challenge Secretary Garfield's action. This telegram rebuts the pro-dam argument that the reservoir would be a recreational bonanza and the claim that building in Hetch Hetchy would save San Francisco considerable expense—and demanded an impartial investigation. This larger effort helped stall the outgoing Roosevelt administration's willingness to push the project in the final months of its tenure.

Chairman of Public Lands Committee,
House of Representatives, Washington, D.C.:

The Yosemite National Park was created in order that the unrivaled aggregation of scenic features of this great natural wonderland should be preserved in pure wildness for all time for the benefit of the entire nation, and Hetch Hetchy Valley is a counterpart of Yosemite; and a great and wonderful feature of the park, next to Yosemite in beauty, grandeur, and importance, is the floor of Hetch Hetchy, which, like that of Yosemite, is a beautiful landscape park, diversified by magnificent groves, gardens, and flowery meadows in charming combinations specially adapted for pleasure camping, and this wonderful valley is the focus of pleasure travel in the large surrounding area of the park, and all the trails from both the south and the north lead into and through this magnificent camp ground, and though now accessible only by trails it is visited by large numbers of campers and travelers every summer, and after a wagon road has been made into it and its wonders become better known it will be visited by countless thousands of admiring travelers from all parts of the world.

If dammed and submerged as proposed, Hetch Hetchy would be rendered utterly inaccessible for travel, since no road could be built around the borders of the reservoir without tunneling through solid granite cliffs, and these camp grounds would be destroyed and access to other important places to the north and south of the valley interfered with, and the high Sierra gateway of the sublime Tuolumne Canyon leading up to the central

---

10   Virtual Museum of the City of San Francisco, accessed 19 September 2019.

camp ground of the upper Tuolumne Valley would be completely blocked and closed. Such use would defeat the purpose and nullify the effect of the law creating the park. The proponents of the San Francisco water scheme desire the use of Hetch Hetchy not because water as pure and abundant can not be obtained elsewhere, but because, as they themselves admit, the cost would be less, for there are fourteen sources of supply available. We do not believe that the vital interests of the nation at large should be sacrificed and so important a part of its national park destroyed to save a few dollars for local interests. Therefore we are opposed to the use of Hetch Hetchy Valley as a reservoir site as unnecessary, as impartial investigation will demonstrate.

John Muir, *President*
E.T. Parsons
J.N. Leconte
Wm. F. Bade
Directors of the Sierra Club.

E.T. Parsons: Edward Taylor Parsons (1861–1914) was on the board of directors of the Sierra Club and an innovator of its outings program.

J.N. Leconte: Joseph Nisbet LeConte (1870–1950) was an engineer and mountaineer and served as the Sierra Club's second president. LeConte Point in Yosemite National Park is named for him.

Wm. F. Bade: William F. Bade (1871–1936), a theologian, mountaineer, and literary executor for John Muir, was a lifelong member of the Sierra Club.

IMAGE GALLERY: 1910 RESOLUTIONS
ON HETCH HETCHY

Portsmouth, N.H., February 4, 1910.

Hon. Jacob H. Gallinger,
    Senate Chamber,
        Washington, D.C.

Sir:-

        The following resolution has been adopted by the
Graffort Club of Portsmouth, N. H.:-

        "WHEREAS: The Hetch-Hetchy Valley is one of the grandest
and most important features of the great Yosemite National Park
belonging to the ninety millions of people composing the American
public;

        WHEREAS: This valley is threatened with destruction
by those seeking a water supply for San Francisco and the use of
the park by the public would thereby be seriously restricted;

        WHEREAS: The precedent thus established would destroy
the integrity of our whole national park system;

        WHEREAS: The need for great public playgrounds is
becoming vastly greater instead of diminishing;

        WHEREAS: Eminent engineers report that this proposed
invasion of a national wonderland is wholly unnecessary and that
San Francisco can get an abundance of pure water elsewhere;

        NOW THEREFORE BE IT RESOLVED: That we are earnestly
opposed to such a needless local use of a priceless national
possession in which the entire citizenship is interested, and we
petition the President and the Secretary of the Interior to revoke
the revocable permit now existing and urge all Senators and Representatives, especially those composing the Public Lands Committees,
to defeat any bill which proposes to confirm any such invasion;
and that a copy of this resolution be sent to the Secretary of
the Interior and our Representatives in Congress."

        Very respectfully,

          Anne F. Howard

               Secretary.

i. Resolution of the Graffort Club of Portsmouth, NH

Women's clubs provided some of the strongest opposition. Perceived as being tied to women's larger effort to extend their traditional "housekeeping" role into the public sector, resolutions like this one from the Graffort Women's Club of Portsmouth argued that the Hetch Hetchy Valley belonged to all people as a public playground. The General Federation of Women's Clubs drafted the language for this petition, and dozens of affiliated clubs submitted their own versions.

Committee on the Conservation of Natural Resources; Petitions and Memorials (SEN 61A-J13); Records of the US Senate, Record Group 46; NAID 7268048

San Francisco, February 2, 1910.

Hon. Frank P. Flint.
    U. S. Senator.

Dear Sir:-

    The Hypatia Women's Club of San Francisco has voted to request that the permission granted by the Government to San Francisco to take water from Lake Eleanor and the Hetch-Hetchy Valley be *not* revoked, for the following reasons:-

    1st. San Francisco has no other available supply of pure water that is sufficient.

    2nd. Under the permit Lake Eleanor is to be first developed.

    3rd. The Yosemite Park is an immense tract, while the Hetch-Hetchy Valley, where a reservoir is proposed, is a very small space not over a mile wide and not more than three or four miles long and is often flooded for long periods during storms and high water and the making the same as a permanent reservoir rather beautifies than injures this small piece of land.

    4th. Yosemite Park of which this valley is so minute a portion, is a vast domain of almost inaccessible mountains, lakes and streams at a very high altitude and largely a region of perpetual snow. It is not, or never will be visited by large numbers of people at any one time.

    5th. This vast supply of pure water is running away to the ocean while San Francisco is suffering for a supply of pure water.

    6th. The individual who adores every bush or tree that has ever become a familiar object and who would sacrifice the rights and needs of a great city for pure water to a more aesthetic desire to permit the slightest modification of scene, is irrational and unjust.

    7th. This matter has been fully discussed in every phase at Washington, D. C., for many years before the permit was granted and Government experts have fully reported to President Roosevelt's Administration favorably.

    8th. After complete campaigns in San Francisco, the vote to issue bonds for such a water supply was substantially unanimous.

    9th. It is not at all denied that at all times since this permit was first applied for, that its chief and open opponent has been the Spring Valley Water Co., which has a monopoly of the present undesirable and inadequate water supply of San Francisco.

            Respectfully submitted by

                    Edith Webster.

                    Secretary Hypatia Women's Club,
                                San Francisco,
                                    California.

ii. Resolution from the Hypatia Women's Club of San Francisco

Committee on the Conservation of Natural Resources; Petitions and Memorials (SEN 61A-J13); Records of the US Senate, Record Group 46; NAID 7268040

Extract from John Muir, *The Yosemite* (New York: Century, 1912), 255–57, 260–62

> This text powerfully reflects Muir's pronounced ability to present the moral arguments against the Hetch Hetchy project and to utilize biblical references to persuade readers of the justness of his position.

᠕

Hetch Hetchy Valley, far from being a plain, common, rock-bound meadow, as many who have not seen it seem to suppose, is a grand landscape garden, one of Nature's rarest and most precious mountain temples. As in Yosemite, the sublime rocks of its walls seem to glow with life, whether leaning back in repose or standing erect in thoughtful attitudes, giving welcome to storms and calms alike, their brows in the sky, their feet set in the groves and gay flowery meadows, while birds, bees, and butterflies help the river and waterfalls to stir all the air into music—things frail and fleeting and types of permanence meeting here and blending, just as they do in Yosemite, to draw her lovers into close and confiding communion with her.

Sad to say, this most precious and sublime feature of the Yosemite National Park, one of the greatest of all our natural resources for the uplifting joy and peace and health of the people, is in danger of being dammed and made into a reservoir to help supply San Francisco with water and light, thus flooding it from wall to wall and burying its gardens and groves one or two hundred feet deep. This grossly destructive commercial scheme has long been planned and urged (though water as pure and abundant can be got from sources outside of the people's park, in a dozen different places), because of the comparative cheapness of the dam and of the territory which it is sought to divert from the great uses to which it was dedicated in the Act of 1890 establishing the Yosemite National Park.

The making of gardens and parks goes on with civilization all over the world, and they increase both in size and number as their value is recognized. Everybody needs beauty as well as bread, places to play in and pray in, where Nature may heal and cheer and give strength to body and soul alike. This natural beauty-hunger is made manifest in the little window-sill gardens of the poor, though perhaps only a geranium slip in a broken cup, as well as in the carefully tended rose and lily gardens of the rich, the thousands of spacious city parks and botanical gardens, and in our magnificent National parks—the Yellowstone, Yosemite, Sequoia, etc.—Nature's sublime wonderlands, the admiration and joy of the world. Nevertheless, like anything else worthwhile, from the very beginning, however well guarded, they have always been subject to attack by despoiling gain-seekers and mischief-makers of every degree from Satan to Senators, eagerly trying to make everything immediately and selfishly commercial, with schemes disguised in smug-smiling philanthropy, industriously, shampiously crying, "Conservation, conservation, **panutilization**," that man and beast may be fed and the dear Nation made great. Thus long ago a few enterprising merchants utilized the Jerusalem temple as a place of business instead of a place of prayer, changing money, buying and selling cattle and sheep and doves; and earlier still; the first forest reservation, including only one tree, was likewise despoiled. Ever since the establishment of the Yosemite National Park, strife has been going on around its borders and I suppose this will go on as part of the universal battle between right and wrong, however much its boundaries may be shorn, or its wild beauty destroyed....

That anyone would try to destroy [Hetch Hetchy Valley] seems incredible; but sad experience shows that there are people good enough and bad enough for anything. The proponents of the dam scheme bring forward a lot of bad arguments to prove that the only righteous thing to do with the people's parks is to destroy them bit by bit as they are able. Their arguments are curiously like those of the devil, devised for the destruction of the **first garden**....

These temple destroyers, devotees of ravaging commercialism, seem to have a perfect contempt for Nature, and, instead of lifting their eyes to the God of the mountains, lift them to the Almighty Dollar.

Dam Hetch Hetchy! As well dam for water-tanks the people's cathedrals and churches, for no holier temple has ever been consecrated by the heart of man.

panutilization: Muir enjoyed making up words and this is one of them—a concept that for him meant ultra-utilization.

first garden: A reference to the Garden of Eden, Genesis 2.

DOCUMENT 29:

AN ACT Granting to the city and county of San Francisco certain rights of way in, over and through certain public lands, the Yosemite National Park, and Stanislaus National Forest, and certain lands in the Yosemite National Park, the Stanislaus National Forest, and the public lands in the State of California, and for other purposes (1913)[11]

Also known as the Raker Act, and named for its lead sponsor, John E. Raker (1863–1926; he represented two different California districts in the US Congress between 1911 and 1926), this legislation represented Raker's attempt—successful as it turned out—to break the impasse between pro- and anti-dam forces. It grants San Francisco the right to purchase land in the Hetch Hetchy Valley and related sites but also sets in play a series of provisions that the city must agree to and which must be vetted by the secretaries of Agriculture (which oversees the national forests) and Interior (which manages the national parks). The Raker Act served as the basis for the negotiations and statements that brought the debate to its crescendo.

Be it enacted by the Senate and House of Representatives of the United States of America in Congress assembled, That there is hereby granted to the city and county of San Francisco, a municipal corporation in the State of California, all necessary rights of way along such locations and of such width, not to exceed two hundred and fifty feet, as in the judgment of the Secretary of the Interior may be required for the purposes of this act, in, over, and through the public lands of the United States in the counties of Tuolumne, Stanislaus, San Joaquin, and Alameda, in the State of California, and in, over, and through the Yosemite National Park and the Stanislaus National Forest, or portions thereof, lying within the said counties, for the purpose of constructing, operating, and maintaining aqueducts, canals, ditches, pipes, pipe lines, flumes, tunnels, and conduits for conveying water for domestic purposes and uses to the city and county of San Francisco and such other municipalities and water districts as, with the consent of the city and county of San Francisco, or in accordance with the laws of the State of California in force at the time application is made, may hereafter participate in the beneficial use of the rights and privileges granted by this act: for the purpose of constructing, operating, and maintaining power and electric plants, poles, and lines for generation and sale and distribution of electric energy; also for the purpose of constructing, operating, and maintaining telephone and

---

11 Sixty-Third Congress, Session II, Chap. 4, 1913.

telegraph lines, for the purpose of constructing, operating, and maintaining roads, trails, bridges, tramways, railroads, and other means of locomotion, transportation, and communication, such as may be necessary or proper in the construction, maintenance, and operation of the works constructed by the grantee herein; together with such lands in the Hetch Hetchy Valley and Lake Eleanor Basin within the Yosemite National Park, and the Cherry Valley within the Stanislaus National Forest, irrespective of the width or extent of said lands, as may be determined by the Secretary of the Interior to be actually necessary for surface or underground reservoirs, diverting and storage dams; together with such lands as the Secretary of the Interior may determine to be actually necessary for power houses, and all other structures or buildings necessary or properly incident to the construction, operation, and maintenance of said water-power and electric plants, telephone and telegraph lines, and such means of locomotion, transportation, and communication as may be established; together with the right to take, free of cost, from the public lands, the Yosemite National Park, and the Stanislaus National Forest adjacent to its right of way, within such distance as the Secretary of the Interior and the Secretary of Agriculture may determine, stone, earth, gravel, sand, **tufa**, and other materials of like character actually necessary to be used in the construction, operation, and repair of its said water-power and electric plants, its said telephone and telegraph lines, and its said means of locomotion, transportation, or communication, under such conditions and regulations as may be fixed by the Secretary of the Interior and the Secretary of Agriculture, within their respective jurisdictions for the protection of the public lands, the Yosemite National Park, and the Stanislaus National Forest:

tufa: A porous rock composed of calcium carbonate and formed by precipitation from water, for instance, around mineral springs.

Provided, That said grantee shall file, as hereinafter provided, a map or maps showing the boundaries, location, and extent of said proposed rights of way and lands for the purposes hereinabove set forth:

Provided further, That the Secretary of the Interior shall approve no location or change of location in the national forests unless said location or change of location shall have been approved in writing by the Secretary of Agriculture.

Sec. 2. That within three years after the passage of this act said grantee shall file with the registers of the United States land offices, in the districts where said rights of way or lands are located, a map or maps showing the boundaries, locations, and extent of said proposed rights of way and lands required for the purposes stated in section one of this act; but no permanent construction work shall be commenced on said land until such map or maps shall have been filed as herein provided and approved by the Secretary of the Interior:

Provided, however, That any changes of location of any of said rights of way or lands may be made by said grantee before the final completion of any of said work permitted in section one hereof, by filing such additional map or maps as may be necessary to show such changes of location, said additional map or maps to be filed in the same manner as the original map or maps; but no change of location shall become valid until approved by the Secretary of the Interior, and the approval by the Secretary of the Interior of said map or maps showing changes of location of said rights of way or lands shall operate as an abandonment by the city and county of San Francisco to the extent of such change or changes of any of the rights of way or lands indicated on the original maps:

And provided further, That any rights inuring to the grantee under this act shall, on the approval of the map and maps referred to herein by the Secretary of the Interior, relate back to the date of the filing of said map or maps with the register of the United States Land Office as provided herein, or to the date of the filing of such maps as they may be copies of as provided for herein:

And provided further, That with reference to any map or maps heretofore filed by said city and county of San Francisco or its grantor with any officer of the Department of the Interior or the Department of Agriculture, and approved by said department, the provisions hereof will be considered complied with by the filing by said grantee of copies of any of such map or maps with the register of the United States Land Office as provided for herein, which said map or maps and locations shall as in all other cases be subject to the approval of the Secretary of the Interior.

Sec. 3. That the rights of way hereby granted shall not be effective over any lands upon which homestead, mining, or other existing valid claim or claims shall have been filed or made and which now in law constitute prior rights to any claim of the grantee until said grantee shall have purchased such portion or portions of such homestead, mining, or other existing valid claims as it may require for right-of-way purposes and other purposes herein set forth, and shall have procured proper relinquishments of such portion or portions of such claims, or acquired title by due process of law and just compensation paid to said entrymen or claimants, and caused proper evidence of such fact to be filed with the Commissioner of the General Land Office, and the right of such entrymen or claimants to sell and of said grantee to purchase such portion or portions of such claims are hereby granted:

Provided, however, That this act shall not apply to any lands embraced in rights of way heretofore approved under any act of Congress for the benefit of any parties other than said grantee or its predecessors in interest.

Sec. 4. That the said grantee shall conform to all regulations adopted and prescribed by the Secretary of the Interior governing the Yosemite National Park and by the Secretary of Agriculture governing the Stanislaus National Forest, and shall not take, cut, or destroy any timber within the Yosemite National Park or the Stanislaus National Forest, except such as may be actually necessary in order to construct, repair, and operate said reservoirs, dams, power plants, water power and electric works, and other structures above mentioned, but no timber shall be cut or removed from lands outside of the right of way until designated by the Secretary of the Interior or the Secretary of Agriculture, respectively; and it shall pay to the United States the full value of all timber and wood cut, injured, or destroyed on or adjacent to any of the rights of way and lands, as required by the Secretary of the Interior or the Secretary of Agriculture:

Provided, That no timber shall be cut by the grantee in the Yosemite National Park except from land to be submerged or which constitutes an actual obstruction to the right or rights of way or to any road or trail provided in this act:

Provided further, That for and in consideration of the rights and privileges hereby granted to it the said grantee shall construct and maintain in good repair such bridges or other practicable crossings over its rights of way within the Stanislaus National Forest as may be prescribed in writing by the Secretary of Agriculture, and elsewhere on public lands along the line of said works, and within the Yosemite National Park as may be prescribed in writing by the Secretary of the Interior; and said grantee shall, as said waterworks are completed, if directed in writing by the Secretary of the Interior or the Secretary of Agriculture, construct and maintain along each side of said right of way a lawful fence of such character as may be prescribed by the proper Secretary, with such suitable lanes or crossings as the aforesaid officers shall prescribe:

And provided further, That the said grantee shall clear its rights of way within the Yosemite National Park and the Stanislaus National Forest and over any public land of any debris or inflammable material as directed by the Secretary of the Interior and the Secretary of Agriculture, respectively; and said grantee shall permit any road or trail which it may construct over the public lands, the Yosemite National Park, or the Stanislaus National Forest to be freely used by the officials of the Government and by the public, and shall permit officials of the Government, for official business only, the free use of any telephone or telegraph lines, or equipment, or railroads that it may construct and maintain within the Yosemite National Park and the Stanislaus National Forest, or on the public lands, together with the right to connect with any such telephone or telegraph lines private telephone wires for the exclusive use of said Government officials:

And provided further, That all reservoirs, dams, conduits, power plants, water power and electric works, bridges, fences, and other structures not of a temporary character shall be sightly and of suitable exterior design and finish so as to harmonize with the surrounding landscape and its use as a park; and for this purpose all plans and designs shall be submitted for approval to the Secretary of the Interior....

DOCUMENT 30:

Extracts from the Statement of Mr. W.C. Lehane, of California, to the Committee on Public Lands (1913)[12]

W.C. Lehane represented the interests of a series of major irrigation districts in the Central Valley that abutted the Tuolumne River and had senior rights to its flow. He identified the districts as follows: "I will say, gentlemen, that the Modesto irrigation district lies north and west of the Tuolumne River. The Turlock irrigation district lies south and east, and the Turlock irrigation district is twice as large as our district. We have 81,000 acres; they have 176,000 acres. On the west side of the Tuolumne River is a strip of country, probably 8 or 10 miles wide, which runs down the San Joaquin River, down beyond Tracy. They are organized there now into what is known as the Tracy district." These districts large and small had disputed San Francisco's proposed Hetch Hetchy project, believing it would rob them of their water and their profitable use of it, and in the process give San Francisco the upper hand in determining who received how much water. This debate continues to shape relations between agricultural interests in the Central Valley and urban users.

The Chairman. Now, Mr. Lehane, the committee will hear from you.

Mr. Lehane. Mr. Chairman and gentlemen of the committee, I hope you will excuse me if I do not make as connected a statement as you might wish. I left home sick, and I have been in poor shape ever since. It is almost impossible for me to present even an outline of my view of this matter in the time allotted to me. However, I will try and skeletonize it as well as I can. There are some things in connection with this matter of which you will have to ask me afterwards, because it will be impossible for me to more than merely touch upon all the points that are involved.

... Our position is this: First, that if you give this water to San Francisco we farmers down there [in the Central Valley] will not have water enough to irrigate our lands. I say "we farmers" because I am a farmer. Every year I have gone out with a shovel to help distribute the water and to help in checking it, and I own land in a good many States. We homesteaded in northwestern Iowa when I was a boy. I have always owned land and taken an active interest in land matters. Therefore what I have to say to you to-day I say largely from personal knowledge; not only personal knowledge of

12   W.C. Lehane's testimony was before the Senate Committee on Public Lands, Sixty-Third Congress, Session I, September 1913.

farming in California and of irrigation of California, but of irrigation in Idaho, Utah, and elsewhere.

... The question is whether they will need all this water. I want to answer that in the light of experience and actual experiments and practice. I have a **booklet** with me here that shows Stanislaus County, the most beautiful county in the State. If we had water for the full season there is not a word or a statement in that booklet that would not be verified. What is the actual condition? We have water for only half the season. We begin irrigating in March—we make a cutting in April, and we make another cutting in May, and the next cutting some time in June, and a later cutting in July.

Senator Norris. You are speaking of alfalfa?

Mr. Lehane. Yes; I am speaking of alfalfa. Alfalfa is our chief crop. We are the leading dairy county because we have the best alfalfa in the State. There is one creamery there in Modesto which makes four or five thousand pounds of butter a day. We are a town which has grown from 2,000 to 7,000 people in 10 years. We have just built a six-story hotel. You do not find that in every town of 7,000 population. We are not the most prosperous part of the State of California, and we never can be if our water is taken away from us. We went in there, all of us, with the understanding that the water of the Tuolumne River belonged on the Tuolumne watershed, and we have built that country up. We went into that on the understanding that whenever we needed the water we could get it by storage.... The point that I wish to make is that half of the water we use must be used between the latter part of the season and the 1st of July.

Our water users are going on trying to perfect their system. You may say, "Didn't you know that all the time when you went in there; didn't you expect anybody else to go in there, too"? I answer, No, sir; we did not."

... Where are we going to get water? ... I will tell you how you can get water. If you are giving away Government lands and Government dam sites, give it to us.... Why can not we store the cheapest water there in the Sierras. The Turlock irrigation board is **bonded** right now for less than $15 per acre; the Modesto irrigation board is bonded for about $20 per acre; right across the river on the San Joaquin they are bonded for $56 per acre, and the right above us, between us and the La Grange Dam, is the Waterford irrigation district, organized with 20,000 acres, lying ahead. They would be tickled to death to be bonded to get water. We would use the districts right around in there, ... and the farmers are anxious and willing to get in and bond their lands to take from the Hetch Hetchy a water supply for that dry land.

I was very much pleased to hear the gentlemen express his tender solicitude for the land close up to the Tuolumne River and his statement that it

booklet: Lehane is probably referring to promotional materials about the county, located in the Central Valley of California.

bonded: Lehane is referring to the cost that each irrigation board is able to charge for water per acre.

ought to be protected. I feel that I have friends on this committee; I feel that I am at home here; I feel that I am at the right place. Whenever I would go to San Francisco, they would talk to me very much like you would talk to a hayseed and a farmer. At least I have come to the place where the farmer is the party at interest; where a bunch of farmers trying to make homes can have their claims considered. We want to show you, and we can show you, that we need all this water for our lands. It seems to me that it is not fair to us to have San Francisco take the water which the man on the little 40-acre piece needs to make a living with. It means everything to him. He went in there a tenderfoot from the East. When he went there, what did he see? He saw that big river, and he was told "Why, there is all the water you want when you need it," that is what the real estate men say. They say, "The water goes with the end." That is their battle cry. Then, just as that man begins to feel rich and prosperous some fellow comes along in August, and it is as dry as a bone, and says: "What the matter?" The farmer says: "Well, next year we are going to get our reservoir." We are trying to do what we can, but it takes five years to do what a business man would do in a year.

Yet in spite of all the obstacles, in spite of all the opposition, we have made progress, we have made development in the last 10 years which is something phenomenal, and I think as great, if not greater, than that which has gone on all over the State of California, and, if you will just give us this water, I know that we will make my section the most prosperous part of the United States. The question is, How can you do this thing? It is the easiest thing in the world. The district will issue bonds. We built the dam, the La Grange Dam, in common with the Turlock side. We are making progress there. We have come to a time when we must consolidate lots of our interest in the work of the irrigation districts. We are going to work pretty soon. We are beginning by employing an expert engineer. The cooperative plan is coming stronger and stronger up there every day. In our irrigation deals we have to have high-priced talent. Our interests are all together. We have hired a man who goes out and follows legislative matters; we have hired another man who goes out and assists in other matters; we are getting to cooperate in all those matters. Now we can do things we could not do 10 years ago, because we have learned how to do them.

... Now, I will tell you just what you people could do if you wanted to do it, and what you people could do if you would let us do it. We could store 300,000 acre-feet of water up in the Hetch Hetchy Dam. I do not know how much water power that would generate. San Francisco has the greatest habit of putting everything in a kind of conglomeration in here. For instance, they include the Eleanor and Cherry Creek, and Hetch Hetchy.... But they not only want Lake Eleanor and Cherry Creek, but they want to take the last available site away, take away our water and our power, and you tell about giving things to the people. I want to know what is the matter with the people of our country down here. We have miles and miles of country. What is the matter with giving the water to the people to put on that land? It belongs to us just as much as it does to the people of San Francisco. In fact, it is all we have. The people of San Francisco have the whole Sacramento Valley to go into and get power. The people of San Francisco have the whole Sacramento Valley to go to and get water; and I tell you it was an unfortunate day for us when they turned their covetous eyes upon our country. It was an unfortunate day for us when they determined they would make a depredation upon us.

DOCUMENT 31:

Extracts from Gifford Pinchot's Testimony before the Committee on Public Lands (1913)[13]

Although Pinchot was no longer the chief of the US Forest Service, under whose aegis he had testified in support of the Hetch Hetchy project before Congress, he was asked to speak once more. As he did in earlier sessions of Congress, here he underscores the conservationist credo: to make use of natural resources for human benefit. He concedes that "the men who assert that it is better to leave a piece of natural scenery in its natural condition have rather the better of the argument," except in a case such as this when San Francisco's need for water takes priority to preserving nature.

The CHAIRMAN: [Scott Ferris, Congressman from Oklahoma.] In deference to Mr. Pinchot's wishes, as he desires to leave the city, he will be permitted to address the committee at this time if there is no objection.

Mr. PINCHOT: Mr. Chairman and gentlemen of the committee, my testimony will be very short. I presume that you very seldom have the opportunity of passing upon any measure before the Committee on the Public Lands which has been so thoroughly thrashed out as this one. This question has been up now, I should say, more than 10 years, and the reasons for and against the proposition have not only been discussed over and over again, but a great deal of the objections which could be composed have been composed, until finally there remains simply the one question of the objection of the **Spring Valley Water Co**. I understand that the much more important objection of the Tuolumne irrigation districts have been overcome. There is, I understand, objection on the part of other irrigators, but that does not go to the question of using the water, but merely to the distribution of the water. So we come now face to face with the perfectly clean question of what is the best use to which this water that flows out of the Sierras can be put. As we all know, there is no use of water that is higher than the domestic use. Then, if there is, as the engineers tell us, no other source of supply that is anything like so reasonably available as this one; if this is the best, and, within reasonable limits of cost, the only means of supplying San Francisco with water, we come straight to the question of whether the advantage of leaving this valley

Spring Valley Water Co.:
The Spring Valley Water Co., a private company, controlled San Francisco's water supply beginning in 1860. Notorious for its corruption of local officials, its monopoly ended in 1930 when the city purchased its waterworks operations and four years later Hetch Hetchy water became the single most important source for the city; public ownership of this resource was a crucial element in the city's proposal to dam Hetch Hetchy.

---

13 House Committee on the Public Lands, *Hetch Hetchy Dam Site*, Sixty-Third Congress, Session I (25–28 June 1913; 7 July 1913) (Washington, DC: Government Printing Office, 1913).

in a state of nature is greater than the advantage of using it for the benefit of the city of San Francisco.

Now, the fundamental principle of the whole conservation policy is that of use, to take every part of the land and its resources and put it to that use in which it will best serve the most people, and I think there can be no question at all but that in this case we have an instance in which all weighty considerations demand the passage of the bill. There are, of course, a very large number of incidental changes that will arise after the passage of the bill. The construction of roads, trails, and telephone systems which will follow the passage of this bill will be a very important help in the park and forest reserves. The national forest telephone system and the roads and trails to which this bill will lead will form an important additional help in fighting fire in the forest reserves. As has already been set forth by the two Secretaries, the presence of these additional means of communication will mean that the national forest and the national park will be visited by very large numbers of people who cannot visit them now. I think that the men who assert that it is better to leave a piece of natural scenery in its natural condition have rather the better of the argument, and I believe if we had nothing else to consider than the delight of the few men and women who would yearly go into the Hetch Hetchy Valley, then it should be left in its natural condition. But the considerations on the other side of the question to my mind are simply overwhelming, and so much so that I have never been able to see that there was any reasonable argument against the use of this water supply by the city of San Francisco....

Mr. RAKER: Taking the scenic beauty of the park as it now stands, and the fact that the valley is sometimes swamped along in June and July, is it not a fact that if a beautiful dam is put there, as is contemplated, and as the picture is given by the engineers, with the roads contemplated around the reservoir and with other trails, it will be more beautiful than it is now, and give more opportunity for the use of the park?

Mr. PINCHOT: Whether it will be more beautiful, I doubt, but the use of the park will be enormously increased. I think there is no doubt about that.

Mr. RAKER: In other words, to put it a different way, there will be more beauty accessible than there is now?

Mr. PINCHOT: Much more beauty will be accessible than now.

Mr. RAKER: And by putting in roads and trails the Government, as well as the citizens of the Government, will get more pleasure out of it than at the present time?

Mr. PINCHOT: You might say from the standpoint of enjoyment of beauty and the greatest good to the greatest number, they will be conserved by the passage of this bill, and there will be a great deal more use of the beauty of the park than there is now.

Mr. RAKER: Have you seen Mr. John Muir's criticism of the bill? You know him?

Mr. PINCHOT: Yes, sir; I know him very well. He is an old and a very good friend of mine. I have never been able to agree with him in his attitude toward the Sierras for the reason that my point of view has never appealed to him at all. When I became Forester and denied the right to exclude sheep and cows from the Sierras, Mr. Muir thought I had made a great mistake, because I allowed the use by an acquired right of a large number of people to interfere with what would have been the utmost beauty of the forest. In this case I think he has unduly given away to beauty as against use.

Mr. RAKER: Would that be practically the same as to the position of the Sierras [sic] Club?

Mr. PINCHOT: I am told that there is a very considerable difference of opinion in the club on this subject.

Mr. RAKER: Among themselves?

Mr. PINCHOT: Yes, sir.

Mr. RAKER: You think then, as a matter of fact, that the provisions of this bill carried out would relieve the situation; in other words, that there is no valid objection which they could make?

Mr. PINCHOT: That is my judgment....

DOCUMENT 32:

Extracts from the Statement of Hon. Herbert Parsons, of New York City, before the Committee on Public Lands (1913)[14]

> Herbert Parsons (1869–1925) was a US representative from New York from 1905 to 1911. Here, Rep. Parsons, a self-confessed "nature lover," appeals to his congressional colleagues on esthetic grounds: that the Hetch Hetchy Valley's beauty is worth preserving for its own sake. He also challenges the dam's proponents' belief that a reservoir would improve the valley's appearance and that such an intrusion into a national park would be a public benefit.

e

Mr. Parsons. Mr. Chairman, I appear in opposition to the bill. I appear as a nature lover. I was a member of the Sixtieth Congress and of the Public Lands Committee of the House of Representatives of that Congress. The matter of Hetch Hetchy as a reservoir for San Francisco, being taken up, was exhaustively considered by the Public Lands Committee of the House of Representatives in the Sixtieth Congress. Every person interested was heard, and elaborate reports were prepared by members of the committee. I submitted a report myself in opposition to the bill. I took the position then that if San Francisco absolutely needed Hetch Hetchy Valley as a reservoir, San Francisco should have it, but the burden of proof was on San Francisco to show that she could not get another source of supply.

One argument made then before that committee was that instead of the reservoir spoiling Hetch Hetchy it would make it still more beautiful. I made up my mind that at the first opportunity I would go there to see for myself, and so in August, 1910, I visited Hetch Hetchy Valley, Lake Eleanor, and the Stanislaus National Forest. I first went to the Yosemite and up to the Merced River, then over the Vogelsang Pass into Lyell Park, down the Tuolumne Meadows and then back to some of the lakes, Benson Lake among them, then to Hetch Hetchy itself, and camped on the banks of the Tuolumne River for the night. Then the next day I went on the Lake Eleanor.

The beauty of the Hetch Hetchy is the floor of the valley. The valley gives you a parklike effect. There is a considerable variety of trees, I see that that is admitted, I think, by **Col. Biddle** in the House hearings. The beauty of the valley consists in the meadows and trees, combined with the rocks and the river meandering through; and then, there is a waterfall there, although that really was not such a great feature when I was there, because it was late in August and there had been no rainfall for three months and a half.

Col. Biddle: John Biddle (1859–1936) served in the US Army Corps of Engineers, and between 1907 and 1912 was stationed in San Francisco. He was a senior member of the board appointed under Act of Congress to report, under direction of the secretary of the interior, on San Francisco Water Supply, 1910–12—which is why he was invited to speak on the congressional committee about Hetch Hetchy.

---

14 Virtual Museum of the City of San Francisco, accessed 19 September 2019.

You do not need a lake in the Hetch Hetchy Valley in order to induce people to go there. The valley of Yosemite Park is filled with lakes. There are lakes everywhere. I spent 10 nights, I think, traveling through the park, and half of those nights, I think, we camped on the shores of lakes. They are all rock-bound lakes, with the exception of those like Lake Eleanor, which have wooded shores.

You do not need a reservoir in Hetch Hetchy in order to have a rock-bound lake. The impressive part of Hetch Hetchy is that, after you have traveled through the park, through what you might call its waste portions and its rock-bound lakes, you come down to this gem of a valley, with its meadows, ferns, and trees, and the river meandering through. So that, with all due respect to the contention of my friend, **Secretary Lane**, anyone who has been there unprejudiced—and I think I was unprejudiced; there was no reason why I should be prejudiced—will realize that [the] ... beauty of the floor of the valley ... will be absolutely destroyed by the reservoir.

You get better perspectives of the rocks and the trees and the floor of the valley and the river in the Hetch Hetchy than you do in the Yosemite itself. It has a charm which the Yosemite has not.

There is another feature which was recalled to my mind when I read over the diary I kept on that trip, and that is that in the Hetch Hetchy there are more nature sounds than there are in any other part of the park which I visited.

Senator Thomas. More what?

Mr. Parsons. Nature sounds—the fish and deer and particularly the birds. I suppose that is natural in view of the features of the valley and its being a place where birds would naturally come.

Now, one argument in opposition. It comes down to a question whether this valley, having been taken by the people of the United States because of its remarkable scenery and having been preserved in that way, is to be given to San Francisco for a reservoir when San Francisco does not absolutely need it. As I understand from Col. Biddle's testimony before the House committee, San Francisco can get a water supply elsewhere, but it is cheaper to get it here.

Senator Thomas. Now, right there—

Mr. Parsons. May I just finish the statement?

Senator Thomas. I was going to ask how much cheaper; that is all.

Secretary Lane: Franklin K. Lane (1864–1921) served as secretary of the interior in the Woodrow Wilson administration, from 1913 to 1920.

Mr. Parsons. I think $20,000,000. The expense there, I believe, would be about $60,000,000. Is not that correct?

Mr. Raker. $77,000,000.

Mr. Parsons. $77,000,000. In other words, it is $77,000,000 as against $97,000,000, if you can compel them to go somewhere else. It is a pure gift; it is a gift by the people of the United States, and it is in direct contravention of the purposes for which Hetch Hetchy was put in a park. The very fact that it was put in a park is the reason, I venture to say now, why some individual or a number of individuals have not control there. If it had not been put in a park, then, in my judgment, from my experience on the Public Lands Committee and my travel through national forests, and so on, somehow or other private individuals would have got hold of it; so that if San Francisco wanted to take the Hetch Hetchy for a reservoir it would cost San Francisco just about as much as another water supply; but now if San Francisco gets it it will not cost her so much, because the people of the United States have preserved it for the people of the United States.

It does not seem to me, with all due respect to San Francisco, that it is a fair proposition to all the people of the United States that they should give up to San Francisco what they have preserved for scenic purposes, when if it had not been preserved for scenic purposes it probably would have cost San Francisco just as much as any other source, and there is only a question of 20 or 25 per cent difference in cost at any rate.

I know the objection is made that very few people go into the valley. Well, that is true of all reservations. We have found it so in New York; but we find that after a while people commence to come in greater numbers, and there is no question but that in time the numbers who go to Hetch Hetchy Valley will enormously multiply....

DOCUMENT 33:

Extracts from James Phelan's Testimony before the Committee on Public Lands (1913)[15]

Appearing as a private citizen, Phelan was a former mayor of San Francisco and in that position had been deeply involved in developing the city's case for its acquisition of the Hetch Hetchy Valley. He appeals to the congressional committee on several bases. Among them was the fact that the city would pay for the project itself, that its population was growing rapidly despite the massive earthquake and fire that destroyed the community but six years earlier, and that its project would not mar but enhance the recreational possibilities in the Yosemite region.

The CHAIRMAN: Mr. Phelan, please state what official connection you have had with the city of San Francisco.

Mr. PHELAN: I was mayor of San Francisco for five years, my term ending in 1902.

The CHAIRMAN: Are you connected with the administration in any way now?

Mr. PHELAN: No, sir; except as a member of this commission which has been sent to Washington, appointed by the mayor of San Francisco, to represent in part the city of San Francisco in this water investigation.... The mayor asked me to appear because I am familiar with the needs of the city of San Francisco, where I was born and of which I have been ever since a resident, and because during my incumbency of the office of mayor the first filings were made on this Hetch Hetchy Valley and on the Tuolumne River. I have also participated in the several hearings which have been had on this subject. I realize that the committee has gone into all the questions at this hearing, and I do not wish to delay the committee a moment longer than is necessary, so I will only emphasize the fact that the needs of San Francisco are pressing and urgent. San Francisco is expanding with tremendous rapidity due to the development of the interior of California and to the prospect of the early opening of the canal and the building of the exposition, and already, notwithstanding the threat of a water famine,

15 House Committee on the Public Lands, *Hetch Hetchy Dam Site*, Sixty-Third Congress, Session I (25–28 June 1913; 7 July 1913) (Washington, DC: Government Printing Office, 1913).

the outlying district, which never before was developed, is being cut up into suburban tracts.

A large number of our population has been lost to Oakland, Alameda, and Berkeley, by reason of the fact that we have never had adequate facilities either of transportation or of water supply to meet what would otherwise be a demand for residences on the peninsula. There are disadvantages in crossing the bay. So San Francisco, the chief Federal city on the Pacific coast, asks the Federal Government for assistance in this matter by grant and not by money. It has obligated itself to pay $70,000,000 for a water supply. We have endeavored to satisfy the needs of the irrigationists in good faith, as well as the local water monopoly, and we come this year to Washington, I think, with the good will of those heretofore opposed, possibly with the exception of the gentlemen who are devoted to the preservation of the beauties of nature.

As Californians, we rather resent gentlemen from different parts of the country outside of California telling us that we are invading the beautiful natural resources of the State or in any way marring or detracting from them. We have a greater pride than they in the beauties of California, in the valleys, in the big trees, in the rivers, and in the high mountains. We have the highest mountain in the United States in California, Mount Whitney, 15,000 feet above the sea, as we have the lowest land, in Death Valley, 300 feet below the sea. We have the highest tree known in the world, and the oldest tree. Its history goes back 2,000 years, I believe, judged by the internal evidences; as we have the youngest in the world, Luther Burbank's plumcot.

All of this is of tremendous pride, and even for a water supply we would not injure the great resources which have made our State the playground of the world. By constructing a dam at this very narrow gorge in the Hetch Hetchy Valley, about 700 feet across, we create, not a reservoir, but a lake, because Mr. Freeman, who has studied the situation in Manchester or Birmingham, where there is a similar case, has shown that by planting trees or vines over the dam, the idea of a dam, the appearance of a dam, is entirely lost; so, coming upon it, it will look like an emerald gem in the mountains; and one of the few things in which California is deficient, especially in the Sierras, is lakes, and in this way we will contribute, in a large measure, to the scenic grandeur and beauty of California. I suppose nature lovers, suspecting a dam there not made by the Creator, will think it of no value, in their estimation, but I submit, man can imitate the Creator—a worthy exemplar.

Mr. [James] GRAHAM: [Illinois. Congressman] In that they are mistaken by a dam site?

Mr. PHELAN. They are mistaken by a dam site, and after it is constructed, as somebody said, not wishing to be outdone in profanity, "It will be the damdest finest sight you ever saw."

... To provide for the little children, men, and women of the 800,000 population who swarm the shores of San Francisco Bay is a matter of much greater importance than encouraging the few who, in solitary loneliness, will sit on the peak of the Sierras loafing around the throne of the God of nature and singing His praise. A benign father loves his children above all things. There is no comparison between the highest use of the water—the domestic supply—and the mere scenic value of the mountains. When you decide that affirmatively, as you must, and then, on top of that, that we are not detracting from the scenic value of the mountains, but enhancing it, I think there is nothing left to be said. That is all.

DOCUMENT 34:

Extracts from the Statement of Mr. Richard B. Watrous, of Washington, DC, Secretary of the American Civic Association, to the Committee on Public Lands (1913)[16]

> In his testimony on behalf of the American Civic Association, Richard Watrous does not doubt San Francisco's need for a secure water supply. But he also stresses—as does the organization's president, Horace McFarland, whose insights Waltrous quotes at length—that citizens of an industrializing and urbanizing society must have open space. This document casts doubt, finally, on the city's demands set against the nation's public interest.

ge

Mr Watrous. I am going to be very brief. I am secretary of the American Civic Association, with my office here in Washington.

I desire to say, Mr. Chairman, that the American Civic Association, from the start, has been a national organization, with thousands of individual members and many hundreds of societies, and our principal object is and has been from the first to work for a beautiful America, both in the cities and in the development of parks and the preservation of natural scenery. The American Civic Association has had more or less to do with the Yosemite National Park, which we are considering here to-day. The matter was beginning to come before the attention of the Interior Department in 1909, and at our convention in Cincinnati we passed resolutions, of which I am going to read a part, which is at follows. This was sent to **Secretary Ballinger**. [Reading:]

> Recognizing the wisdom of the Congress in setting aside for public use the great national parks and believing that any avoidable interference with the scenic integrity of these parks is in the highest degree undesirable, the American Civic Association, in the convention assembled, urges the Secretary of the Interior to revoke the permit and the Congress to refuse to confirm such permit under which the city of San Francisco is assuming to control eventually for a domestic water supply more than 500 square miles of the best of the Yosemite National Park, unless after a full and impartial inquiry it shall be shown to the satisfaction of the Congress that no other sufficient source of water supply is available to San Francisco. We further respectfully insist that the

Secretary Ballinger:
Richard Achilles Ballinger (1858–1922) served as President William Howard Taft's secretary of the interior from 1909 to 1911. Taft and Ballinger opposed the Hetch Hetchy project and refused to grant San Francisco the right to build it. Ballinger and Gifford Pinchot would square off on another conservation battle concerning the administration's leasing of coal lands in Alaska, which Pinchot opposed. The so-called Ballinger-Pinchot affair erupted as a result, consuming the Taft Administration and was partly a reason why Taft lost the 1912 election. Miller, *Gifford Pinchot and the Making of Modern Environmentalism* (Washington, DC: Island Press, 2001), 208–15.

---

16   Virtual Museum of the City of San Francisco, accessed 19 September 2019.

granting and confirmation of such a permit to invade the public domain would create a most dangerous precedent under which other scenic possessions on the United States would be unsafe from individual or corporate assault.

J. Horace McFarland, *President.*
Richard B. Watrous, *Secretary.*

Now, Mr. Chairman, one of the men who has been at all of the hearings before the Secretary of the Interior, who was at the hearings when this matter was brought up before Congress, is the gentleman who has been president of the American Civic Association for the past six or seven years, Mr. J. Horace McFarland. Mr. McFarland has been in the Hetch Hetchy Valley; he has attended all these hearings, and he has sent me a letter which I desire to read to the committee. He was unable to be at the hearings had this summer for the reason that for the first time in his life he has been a sick man. The letter which he has asked me to read to you is brief, but it brings out many of the points that have been asked about, and for the benefit of the Senator from Wyoming, I may say that I think this answers the demand for arguments [reading]:

Dear Mr. Watrous:

I deeply regret the conditions of health which will not permit me to appear for the American Civic Association at the hearing set for Wednesday, September 24, before the Senate Committee on Trouble on Public Lands, in relation to the so-called Hetch Hetchy matter.

Owing to the absence attendant upon my illness, I have not had the opportunity to see or read the bill which I understand has passed the House and is now before the Senate Committee, intended to give to San Francisco the right to proceed contrary to the permit of the Secretary of the Interior, given May 11, 1908, which permit specified that the Lake Eleanor reservoir site must be first developed to its full capacity before the Hetch Hetchy Valley could be used as a reservoir.

It seems proper to record the position of the American Civic Association upon two points: First, we cannot and do not doubt the sincerity of Congress in setting aside, under the act of October 1, 1890, the territory now generally called Yosemite National Park, with the specific provision that the Secretary of the Interior shall "provide for the preservation from injury of all timber, mineral deposits, natural curiosities or wonders within said reservation, and their retention in their natural condition."

Second, with all right-minded people, the American Civic Association agrees that the highest use of water is the domestic use, and therefore if the city of San Francisco can secure a pure, safe, and ample water supply nowhere else than in the Hetch Hetchy Valley, I should feel that despite the expressed purpose of Congress to preserve the Yosemite National Park, of which the Hetch Hetchy Valley is so important a part, the city should be permitted to do that which it desires to do.

In view, however, of the distinctly expressed intent of Congress to preserve the Yosemite National Park, and in view of the limit in the qualifying act of February 15, 1901, under which attempts have been made before the Secretary of the Interior to secure access to the Park, it is at least reasonable to insist that inquiry be made as to the necessity under which San Francisco now applies....

The propriety and necessity of a complete and impartial investigation as to alternative sources of water supply available to the city of San Francisco before a favorable report is made upon a bill which, if it should become law would undoubtedly result in practically cutting in half the reservation included in the act of October 1, 1890, constructively creating the Yosemite National Park.

It is easy enough to talk about our getting other areas in California for park purposes; but you gentlemen in Congress know that that is not so easy a matter; that it is no easy matter to set in motion machinery which creates a new park. We have an existing park; the machinery was set in motion and we have it there. We are in danger of taking a backward step and encroaching upon that park. [Reading:]

Walter L. Fisher: Walter L. Fisher (1862–1935) replaced Ballinger as Taft's interior secretary, serving from 1911 to 1913. He made the critical decision that only Congress could determine whether San Francisco's proposal for the Hetch Hetchy project was legal. This set up the final set of hearings and congressional votes that permitted the city to construct the O'Shaughnessy Dam.

I have read volumes of literature on this subject, and have been present at nearly all of the hearings had upon it in Washington before the various Secretaries of the Interior who have dealt with it. I have heard and read the statements of the engineers, and I have also had the advantage of seeing the situation on the ground, in company with the recent Secretary of the Interior, Hon. **Walter L. Fisher**, as well as with the recent city engineer of San Francisco to Mr. Marsden Manson. I have noted the complete absence of consistency between the claims then made by Mr. Manson and now made by the city of San Francisco, through its present engineers and advisers.

It has not been hard to discern in the figures submitted as to the cost of alternative water supplies very large differences as to cost factors, as that the conclusion has been forced upon me that in figuring the cost of the Hetch Hetchy water supply San Francisco has adopted a most sanguine view and made the expense very much less than it is likely to be; while in considering the cost of alternative supplies, upon which after nearly 11 years of investigation seemingly no adequate information is yet available, she has used factors very much larger than those in the first instance, with the result of greatly magnifying the possible cost of any of these supplies.

Taking all these matters into account, I cannot avoid the feeling that for herself San Francisco is making a great mistake in now insisting at this special session of Congress called for other purposes upon the passage of an enabling act to permit her to do that which is almost certain to prove inadvisable when the facts are fully known.

Further, the conclusion cannot be avoided that it would be a misfortune—indeed, a catastrophe—to have half a great national park, involving natural features not found anywhere else in the world, segregated to the purposes of a municipal water supply, without the clearest and most definite showing of absolute necessity on the part of the community to be benefited.

If, under the conditions existing, San Francisco should prevail in her present contention, it is obvious that there can be no safety whatever for any part of any national park upon which municipal engineers may cast a wishful eye. I do not believe that the American public is desirous of diverting to the use of a very small percentage of its entire population these natural wonders which are increasingly a source of pleasure, recreation, and enormous revenue to the Nation as a whole, except and only upon such a showing of absolute necessity as shall be generally and completely conclusive.

I sincerely trust wise counsels will prevail in the committee, and that the act will be reported with a negative recommendation, so that Congress can in due course inform itself upon this matter without dependence upon prejudiced statements, such as those which will doubtless be made before the committee by the representatives of San Francisco.

Yours, truly,
J. Horace McFarland,
President.

DOCUMENT 35:

Extracts from the Statement of Mr. John R. Freeman, of Boston, Mass., Engineer in Charge of the Hetch Hetchy Project (1913)[17]

John Ripley Freeman (1855–1932) was a civil and hydraulic engineer involved in major water projects across the United States; he served as president of the American Society of Civil Engineers and the American Society of Mechanical Engineers. John Freeman's testimony was a crucial element in the 1913 debate in large part because he was a renowned engineer whose on-the-ground analyses supported the pro-dam forces' contention that the current water supply controlled by the Spring Valley Water Co. was insufficient to the San Francisco's needs, and that Hetch Hetchy offered an unparalleled opportunity to all the city's future needs.

℮

Senator Thomas: Charles Spalding Thomas (1849–1934) was a US senator from Colorado.

Senator Thomas. Mr. Freeman, it was stated that there was an available source of supply from the Coast Range in connection with the Spring Valley works, close by in that section of the State and contiguous to San Francisco, which would give an available daily supply of 230,000,000 gallons of water to these communities. I would like to know something about that.

Mr. Freeman. That matter has been investigated most carefully, and I am as certain as I am of any engineering fact that no such quantity of water can be obtained. If anything approaching that quantity were to be obtained it would render sterile large areas in the Livermore Valley.

Senator Norris: George William Norris (1861–1944) was a US senator from Nebraska.

Senator Norris. That would be obtained by pumping?

Mr. Freeman. It would be obtained largely by pumping, partly by dams.

Senator Thomas. And by tunneling?

Mr. Freeman. Yes; and by tunneling.

Senator Norris. How would that take the water away? You mean they would not have enough left to irrigate with?

---

17 24 September 1913, Hearing before the Senate Committee on Public Lands (Sixty-Third Congress, Session I) on H.R. 7207, a bill "granting to the city and county of San Francisco certain rights of way in, over, and through certain public lands, the Yosemite National Park and Stanislaus National Forest, and certain lands in the Yosemite National Park, the Stanislaus National Forest, and the public lands in the state of California, and for other purposes."

Mr. Freeman. Yes. The amount of water is being lowered by the diversions of the Spring Valley Co., and if they were to take away any such quantity as has been estimated it would very seriously injure the agricultural lands in the Livermore Valley.

When an estimate is made which takes in the supply which can be obtained from the coast streams, like San Gregorio and Pescadero, and the coast creeks it is misleading. It looks like there is a lot of water there on paper. The Spring Valley Water Co. has consistently turned its back on developing those resources and has gone all the way across the bay. To develop that water it would require very long tunnels, storage facilities, and other engineering difficulties, which makes this source on the west side of the Coast Range and its cost so utterly impracticable for the supply of the city that it ought never to be considered.

Senator Thompson. Is there any other place where they can get such a supply as at the Hetch Hetchy?

Mr. Freeman. No....

The Chairman [**Henry L. Myers**]. Are there any further questions?

Mr. Freeman. ... When I was first approached by the city engineer of San Francisco [Marsden Manson] to make my investigations ... over three years ago, I declined the city's retainer, because I had read many times in magazine articles of this plan, and I believed that I did not feel in sympathy with what they proposed to do. He replied to me, "Wait until you get out there and then decide." The first three days that I visited San Francisco I put in on my own time before I was willing to undertake the work. I did not undertake the work until I was fully satisfied that it was thoroughly meritorious and just and proper.

I have taken some pride in the work that I have had a share in doing. I am something of a nature lover myself. I have worked hand in hand with Frederick Law Olmstead[18] and some of the other noted landscape artists of the country. For many years I was consulting engineer to the Metropolitan Park Board of Boston, and I developed the plan for the Charles River basin in Boston and for the drainage of the Fresh Farm marshes in Cambridge. For many years I have been liberal of my time upon these public works, because I fully believed in them.

I came to this work in that same spirit, and I think if anyone will go through my report they can find everywhere the handiwork of a man who

Senator Thompson: William Howard Thompson (1871–1928) was a US senator from Kansas.

Henry L. Myers: Henry Lee Myers (1862–1943) was a US senator from Montana.

18 For more on Olmsted, see p. ooo.

tries not to tear down but to leave things more beautiful. That is one of the matters in which I take great pride. I was one of the original members of the Boston Metropolitan Water Board, and we have, more than any other board, beautified these reservoirs and made those reservoirs beauty spots for the recreation of the people of that city.

As I say, I approached this work in the same spirit. The scenic road which is shown in my report going around the lake was proposed by me with the idea of making the reservoir more beautiful and more available to the people of San Francisco and to the people who go up to escape the heat of the great valley. Long before I was connected with this Hetch Hetchy enterprise I have done engineering work in the Sierras all the way from the Los Angeles water supply in the southern part of California to the water supply of Seattle on the north, and even beyond that to the water supply of some of the cities of British Columbia. My first effort was to leave this valley more beautiful than we found it.

I explained the matter to **Mayor Rolph** and to Mr. Manson, and they at first thought I was rather extravagant in my plans, which will add to the cost to the city practically half a million dollars and which will add not a gallon of water to the supply. It was purely to make the valley more accessible to the people of California and to the people of the great valleys of California.

As that report now stands and as the works are proposed to be built the city will practically be spending a million dollars for purposes beyond those of a water supply. That expenditure is made for the purposes of making that valley available to a thousand people where only a dozen or fifteen can go in to-day and enjoy the solitude.

The Chairman. Well, now, it is nearly 6 o'clock, and I think a motion to take up this bill would be in order.

Senator Pittman. I move the committee report this bill out favorably.

The Chairman. It is moved that the committee make a favorable report to the Senate on this bill. Does any member of the committee wish to make any remarks?

Senator Pittman. I would just like to say one word in respect to this matter, and that is that I am a lover of nature just as much as any of the gentlemen who have spoken here to-day. I do not believe we can improve on God's handiwork in the Hetch Hetchy Valley. I do believe it is our duty to give to our children, God's children, throughout the country, who need it, that water. I want to say for myself that I would rather hear the laughing voice of a happy child, relieved of water famine and supplied with pure water, than

Mayor Rolph: James Rolph Jr. (1869–1934) remains the longest-serving mayor of San Francisco, holding office from 1912 until he became governor of California in 1931.

Senator Pittman: Key Denson Pittman (1872–1940) was a US senator from Nevada.

all the beautiful sounds of nature which have been described so eloquently here to-day.

The Chairman. The question is, gentlemen of the committee, whether we shall report this bill to the Senate. Is there anything else to be said by any member of the committee? If not, I will put the question.

(Thereupon the question was put to the committee, and the resolution offered by Senator Pittman was unanimously carried.)

The Chairman. The vote is unanimous, and it is therefore ordered that the committee favorably report the bill.

(Thereupon, at 5.25 p.m., the committee adjourned.)

DOCUMENT 36:

Extracts from the Statement of Hon. William Kent, Representative in Congress from California, to the Committee on Public Lands (1913)[19]

William Kent (1864–1928) represented California's 1st district in Congress from 1913 to 1917. A friend of John Muir's, he donated land in Marin County to form the Muir Woods National Monument but disagreed with Muir about Hetch Hetchy. In 1916, Kent was the lead sponsor of congressional legislation that created the National Park Service. Here he makes a case for San Francisco's pressing need for water and energy, which was also true for other parts of the country, a point he makes in reference to harnessing Niagara Falls if doing so would "lighten the burdens of the overworked"—a point about the Niagara Falls that John Muir disputed in Document 21.

ᘐ

Mr. Kent. I am rather inclined to resent the criticism that we who stand for this bill are opposed to conservation. I have tried to be an honest exponent of sane and sensible conservation, and to further the use of our national resources without unnecessary waste. But when an opportunity comes to give to a great community upward to 200,000 horsepower upon which not a cent of private profit shall ever be made; when it comes to the question of benefiting upward of a million people, then I believe that conservation demands that I do my duty and try to help rather than to hinder such a worthy project. I have heard it said right along—Mr. Whitman said in the hearings in the House, "you will find it is largely a question of water power."

I admit that. I want the people of the cities of California; I want the irrigationists and the people of the San Joaquin Valley to be forever free from any danger of being held up in the interest of private profit, if that can be done.

Mr. Johnson expressed great confidence in his knowledge of the purposes of the Creator in the matter of this valley. I do not know whether we can take it that he is absolutely sure of being right. He made the statement that those wonders were put there to be looked at. How are we going to tell what things are there to be looked at and what things are there to be used. It seems reasonable to me that we should use the useful things and look at the beautiful things; and that the highest use of the useful things is their use for the benefit of humanity.

I made the statement in the House that if Niagara Falls could be used to lighten the burdens of the overworked, I should be willing to see those Falls

Mr. Johnson: Robert Underwood Johnson (1853–1937), editor of the *Century Magazine* and a pivotal publisher and supporter of John Muir, fought with Muir for the creation of Yosemite National Park and to defeat the Hetch Hetchy project.

---

19 Virtual Museum of the City of San Francisco, accessed 19 September 2019.

harnessed. I would not be willing to see them harnessed for private profit, but if Niagara Falls could be utilized for the alleviation of overworked suffering humanity, I should like to see the Falls used for that purpose. That is the kind of a conservationist I am, and I put it in the rawest, baldest terms.

That is the purpose of the Almighty, it seems to me. I do not think people should be so sure of the purposes of the Almighty. I do not believe people should be so ready to asperse the methods of other people. I think it is time that the Members of Congress who have tentatively committed themselves to measures of this kind should ... talk back a little bit....

Union Calendar No. 11.

63D CONGRESS,
1ST SESSION.

H. R. 7207.

[Report No. 41.]

IN THE HOUSE OF REPRESENTATIVES.

AUGUST 1, 1913.

Mr. RAKER introduced the following bill; which was referred to the Committee on the Public Lands and ordered to be printed.

AUGUST 5, 1913.

Committed to the Committee of the Whole House on the state of the Union and ordered to be printed.

A BILL

Granting to the city and county of San Francisco certain rights of way in, over, and through certain public lands, the Yosemite National Park, and Stanislaus National Forest, and certain lands in the Yosemite National Park, the Stanislaus National Forest, and the public lands in the State of California, and for other purposes.

1   *Be it enacted by the Senate and House of Representa-*

2   *tives of the United States of America in Congress assembled,*

3   That there is hereby granted to the city and county of San

4   Francisco, a municipal corporation in the State of California,

5   all necessary rights of way along such locations and of such

6   width, not to exceed two hundred and fifty feet, as in the

i. HR 7207: A Bill Granting the City of San Francisco ...
Introduced by Congressman John Raker (D-CA), HR 7207, also known as the Raker Bill and the Hetch Hetchy Bill, granted San Francisco the right to dam the Hetch Hetchy Valley within Yosemite National Park. The House passed the bill with little debate. The Senate, however, debated the measure extensively before passing the legislation on December 6, 1913. President Woodrow Wilson signed the bill into law on December 19.

H.R. 7207, The Raker Bill, August 5, 1913; RG 233, Records of the US House of Representatives

Protest Against Diversion of Waters from Lands Requiring Irrigation

Adopted at Livingston, California, May 30, 1913

WHEREAS, A determined effort is being made by the city and county of San Francisco to secure the passage of a special act of congress granting to said city and county of San Francisco certain rights and titles to certain waters of the Tuolumne river; and

WHEREAS, The said city and county of San Francisco has declared its intention of diverting such waters to points outside of the San Joaquin Valley for uses other than those of irrigation and reclamation, if such rights and titles are granted; and

WHEREAS, Reports of United States army engineers show decidedly that the entire run-off supply of the watershed to the San Joaquin Valley is necessary for the Valley's proper agricultural and commercial development; and

WHEREAS, It has been clearly shown and proven through the medium of competent engineers that San Francisco can secure an adequate supply of water for its own use from other sources, where such water is not needed for the development of its contiguous territory; and

WHEREAS, The question of conserving all of the waters of the San Joaquin Valley watershed for use within said Valley is one of paramount importance to the very life of every county and community within said Valley; therefore, be it

RESOLVED, That the 2,000 citizens of Merced and Stanislaus counties assembled at Livingston bridge this 30th day of May, 1913, for the purpose of dedicating said bridge and the California State Highway to the use of the public, hereby take cognizance of this attempt on the part of San Francisco to divert certain waters of the Tuolumne river for other uses than those of irrigation and reclamation, and that we herewith protest strongly against such proposed diversion, and call upon the senators and representatives of the state of California in congress, and all other members of congress having the interest of conservation and irrigation at heart, to unite to protect the agricultural and commercial interests of the San Joaquin Valley, and thereby assure the proper development of the semi-arid lands of said valley, as well as make permanent the development of the natural resources of the state. Be it further

RESOLVED, That copies of these resolutions be sent to all senators and representatives of the state of California in congress, and that they be urged to use every legitimate means to enlist support in a movement directed against the passage of the Raker Hetch Hetchy bill, or any other measure that may be introduced into congress having for its purpose the granting to San Francisco, or any other city located outside of the San Joaquin Valley, any rights or titles to any waters of the Tuolumne river, or the waters of any other stream which forms a part of the San Joaquin watershed, wherein such rights or titles, if so granted, would give authority for the diversion of waters to any point outside of the San Joaquin Valley where they would be lost to the irrigation and commercial interests of said Valley. Be it further

RESOLVED, That this assemblage goes on record as favoring federal aid to the efforts of the citizens of the San Joaquin Valley to reclaim their semi-arid lands and make them fruitful, such aid to be given through the medium of scientific water conservation works and the storage of the flood waters of the streams of the San Joaquin watershed in reservoirs and basins along said streams as they come down into the San Joaquin Valley from the Sierra Nevada mountains; such waters so conserved and stored to be made available to the use of the people of the San Joaquin Valley in the irrigation and reclamation of 5,000,000 acres of valuable lands now laying in a semi-arid state, because of the insufficiency of the natural flow of the streams of said watershed.

Passed by a unanimous vote.

E. S. ELLIS,
President of the Day.

ii. Protest against Diversion of Water from Lands Requiring Irrigation

Committee on Public Land; Petitions and Memorials (SEN 63A-F26); Records of the US Senate, Record Group 46; NAID 7268067

Widows and Orphans and Mutual Aid Associations, Inc.,

OF THE

SAN FRANCISCO FIRE DEPARTMENT

San Francisco, November 24th, 1913

Hon. *Charles S. Thomas*
United States Senate, Washington, D. C.

We, the undersigned officers of the San Francisco Fire Department Widows and Orphans and Mutual Aid Associations, Inc., in behalf of said Associations most earnestly ask for your vote and support in favor of giving to our beloved City of San Francisco the right to use the much needed water supply, and the only supply adequate to meet its present as well as its future needs.

Gentlemen, we ask your favorable vote on this bill as a matter of justice, humanity and fair play, as the present supply is absolutely inadequate to meet even the present demands. We pray you therefore to grant us the use of the waters of the Hetch Hetchy Valley and the Tuolumne River.

Respectfully submitted,

CAPTAIN WILLIS E. GALLATIN, Jr.,
President.

Geo. F. Brown Secretary
Captain Engine Co., No. 39,
2136 Geary St., San Francisco, Cal.

iii. Petition from the Widows and Orphans and Mutual Aid Associations of the San Francisco Fire Department

The Widows and Orphans and Mutual Aid Associations of the San Francisco Fire Department submitted this letter requesting that Congress grant San Francisco the right to dam the Hetch Hetchy Valley. The letter came from members of the San Francisco Fire Department, including Captain Willis E. Gallatin, Jr. and Geo. F. Brown. Although the letter does not mention the 1906 San Francisco Earthquake, it is likely that the firemen remembered the destruction of the subsequent fires, which became an impetus of San Francisco to pressure the government for water rights.

Petitions and Related Documents That Were Presented, Read, or Tabled (SEN 63A-K8); Records of the US Senate, Record Group 46; NAID 7268071

SOCIETY FOR THE PRESERVATION OF NATIONAL PARKS

San Francisco, June 27, 1913.

Hon. George E. Chamberlain,
Senate Chamber,
Washington, D. C.

Dear Sir:-

The Yosemite National Park is not only the greatest and most wonderful national playground in California, but in many of its features it is without a rival in the whole world. It belongs to the American people and in world wide interest ranks with the Yellowstone and the Grand Canyon of the Colorado. It embraces the head waters of two rivers- the Merced and the Tuolumne. The Yosemite Valley is in the Merced basin; the Hetch Hetchy Valley, the Grand Canyon of the Tuolumne, and the Tuolumne Meadows are in the Tuolumne Basin. Excepting only the Yosemite Valley, the Tuolumne basin in its general features is the more wonderful and larger half of the Park.

The Hetch Hetchy Valley is a wonderfully exact counterpart of the great Yosemite, not only in its cliffs and waterfalls and peaceful river, but in the gardens, groves, meadows and camp grounds of its flowery park-like floor.

At a recent session of Congress a most determined attack was made by the City of San Francisco to get the right to use the Hetch Hetchy Valley as a reservoir site, thus depriving ninety millions of people of one of their most priceless possessions for the sake of saving San Francisco dollars.

As soon as this scheme became manifest, public-spirited citizens all over the country entered their protests, and before the session was over, the Park invaders saw that they were defeated, and permitted the bill to die without bringing it to a vote, so as to be able to try again.

Ever ready to take advantage of every political change, a bill having the same destructive purpose has been re-introduced at this session of Congress and is now pending before the Public Lands Committee, and its supporters are speciously urging that it should be rushed through at this special session as an emergency measure when in reality nothing like an emergency exists.

San Francisco may be in immediate need of an increased supply of water but her own engineers admit that the present supply can be more than doubled by adding to present nearby sources and that is the first and most economic plan of development before the city eventually goes to the Sierra for additional water.

-2-

The advisory Board of Army Engineers "is of the opinion that there are several sources of water supply that could be obtained and used by the city of San Francisco and adjacent communities to supplement the nearby supplies as the necessity develops. From any one of these sources the water is sufficient in quantity and is, or can be made, suitable in quality."

We are preparing data based on the reports of the Army Engineers which will demonstrate that San Francisco can obtain abundance of pure water from other sources than the Tuolumne Hetch Hetchy.

So important a bill should not be rushed through Congress without mature consideration and time allowed for its opponents to be heard. Anything less would be unjust to the American people, therefore in behalf of all who appreciate our mountain parks and believe that they should be preserved, we call on you to aid us in postponing consideration of this destructive bill until the regular session of Congress, for we have not even seen a copy of the bill now being considered. Ever since the establishment of the Yosemite National Park by Act of Congress, October 8th, 1890, constant strife has been going on around its boundaries and is likely to go on as part of the universal battle between good and evil however much its boundaries may be broken or wild beauty destroyed.

When this application was first made over ten years ago the Secretary of the Interior then holding office emphatically denied the right saying in part:

"Presumably the Yosemite National Park was created such by law because of the natural objects, of varying degrees of scenic importance, located within its boundaries, inclusive alike of its beautiful small lakes, like Eleanor, and its majestic wonders, like Hetch Hetchy and Yosemite Valley. It is the aggregation of such natural scenic features that makes the Yosemite Park a wonderland which the Congress of the United States sought by law to preserve for all coming time as nearly as practicable in the condition fashioned by the hand of the Creator - a worthy object of national pride and a source of healthful pleasure and rest for the thousands of people who may annually sojourn there during the heated months."

In behalf of all of the people of the nation we ask your aid in putting an end to these assaults on our great national parks and to prevent this measure from being rushed through before it can be brought to the attention of the ninety millions of people who own this park.

Faithfully yours,

John Muir

E. T. Parsons

Wm. F. Bade

R. M. Cosby

---

iv. Petition from the Society for the Preservation of National Parks against Granting San Francisco the Hetch Hetchy Valley

The Society for the Preservation of National Parks submitted this petition to Congress in order to urge them to defeat the Raker Bill, a bill to grant San Francisco the right to dam the Hetch Hetchy Valley. Led by John Muir, the Society believed that natural wonders should remain unspoiled. They connected their argument to issues of health. In this letter, the Society's leadership, including Muir, encouraged Congress to save the beautiful Valley so that the entire nation could enjoy the land for healthful pleasure and rest.

Committee on Public Lands; Petitions and Memorials (SEN 63A-F26); Records of the US Senate, Record Group 46; NAID 7268060

PETITION AGAINST THE SO-CALLED HETCH HETCHY BILL (H. R. 7207)

To the Senate of the United States:

The undersigned respectfully and earnestly petition your honorable body against the enactment of the bill now pending (November, 1913) granting to the city of San Francisco water and power rights in the Hetch Hetchy Valley and in other portions of the Yosemite National Park. In view of the opinion of the Army Board that there are several other sources of supply for the city and that the determining factor is one of cost, we believe the resulting destruction of the beauty of this valley and the commercial invasion of this great national park to be needless, and against enlightened public policy and the interest of the whole people.

NAME	OCCUPATION	ADDRESS
[Stratton D. Brooks]	President University of Oklahoma	Norman, Okla.
L. B. Nice	Prof. of Physiology	"
H. H. Lane	Prof. of Zoology	"
B. F. Tanner	Asst-Prof. of Path. Bact.	"
Fredrik Holmberg	Dean School of Fine Arts	"
W. P. Haseman	Prof. of Physics	"
G. H. Stocking	Dean School of Pharmacy	"
[F. Bizzell]	Director School of Electrical Engineering	"
John Alley	Prof. of Pol. Science	"
H. S. Browne	Asst Prof. of Pharmacy	"
R. T. House	Prof. of German	"
Roy Gittinger	Professor in History	"
S. R. Hadsell	Professor of English	"
S. W. Reaves	Professor of Mathematics	"
John Darling	Physical Director	"
Patricio Gimeno	Professor of Art	"
J. Dowd	" Sociology	"
J. W. Sturgis	" Latin	"
Lucile Dora	Prof. Romance Languages	"
A. C. Scott	Director Univ. Ext. Lectures	"
F. C. Keerl	Assoc. Prof. Math.	"
[Guy R. Ellison]	Professor Bacteriology	Norman
J. C. Parson	" Secondary Educa	Norman
J. S. Buchanan	Prof. History	
W. W. Phelan	Director School of Education	
Errett R. Newby	Secretary Registrar	

v. Petition from the University of Oklahoma Professors

In 1913, over a dozen professors from the University of Oklahoma signed this petition, which urged Congress to vote against the Raker Bill, a bill to grant San Francisco the right to dam the Hetch Hetchy Valley. These educators encouraged Congress to consider the interest of the whole country before unnecessarily invading the Valley. The University president, Stratton D. Brooks, was the first to sign the petition, followed by various professors and deans. Hundreds of university administrators and professors, from such schools as Harvard and Columbia, signed identical petitions that urged Congress to defeat the Raker Bill.

Petitions and Related Documents That Were Presented, Read, or Tabled (SEN 63A-K8); Records of the US Senate, Record Group 46; NAID 7268075

The Hetch Hetchy Valley

Resolutions unanimously adopted by the Massachusetts State Federation of Women's Clubs.

Whereas: The Hetch Hetchy Valley contains some of this country's most wonderful scenery and most stimulating resources for recreation; and

Whereas: This valley belongs to all the people and is used and enjoyed by the East as well as the West; and

Whereas: It is not, as has been asserted, "an inaccessible region of barren granite of no possible use to humanity except through the production of water and power", but it is on the contrary visited each summer by large parties of women as well as men who find health and inspiration as campers upon its fertile floor of matchless beauty; and

Whereas: Better transportation facilities with hotels and permanent camps which might readily be supplied by the Federal Government would give to far larger numbers the benefit of this sublime recreation ground; and

Whereas: The use of the Hetch Hetchy Valley as a municipal water supply for San Francisco would destroy its use and enjoyment by the whole people as a park and recreation ground; and

Whereas: With growing population the areas for public playgrounds are diminishing while the need for them is increasing; and

1st Vice-President, Mrs. Leila C. Pennock, 30 Boston Road, Somerville.
2d Vice-President, Mrs. Claude U. Gilson, Wellesley Hills.
3d Vice-President, Mrs. Royal Whiton, 36 Melville Avenue, Dorchester.
4th Vice-President, Mrs. Herbert J. Gurney, 125 Warren Avenue, Woollaston.
Clerk, Mrs. George R. Clark, 8 Boutwell Street, Dorchester.

1913 - 1914
MRS. GEORGE WINSLOW PERKINS, President.
130 BLUE HILL AVENUE, BOSTON

Assistant Clerk, Miss Jessie M. Fisher, 221 Church Street, Newton.
Corresponding Secretary, Mrs. Arthur A. Hibbard, 298 Eliot Street, Milton.
Treasurer, Mrs. Lena R. Wellington, 130 Highland Avenue, Winchester.
General Federation Secretary, Mrs. Darius Crocker, 28 Mechanic Street, Fitchburg.

Whereas: This proposed action by San Francisco would afford a precedent for handing over any or all of our National Parks and other public lands to private interests; and

Whereas: This action has been pronounced by eminent engineers as wholly unnecessary since San Francisco has other sources of abundant water supply, some even more available than Hetch Hetchy;

Now therefore be it Resolved:

That we, the Massachusetts State Federation of Women's Clubs assembled in the Town Hall of Whitman and representing 262 Clubs, earnestly oppose this needless and irrevocable sacrifice by the whole nation of an invaluable possession and we petition the President and urge our senators to defeat any bill which has for its object any such invasion of Hetch Hetchy or the cession of any public land whatever to any private or corporate enterprise unless such enterprise be shown without question by competent and impartial judges to be absolutely necessary to the public welfare.

Signed

President
Mrs. George W. Perkins

Corresponding Secretary
Wm Arthur A. Hibbard

25 November, 1913.

vi. Resolution of the Massachusetts State Federation of Women's Clubs

With this resolution, the Massachusetts State Federation of Women's Clubs urged Congress to defeat the Raker Bill, a bill to grant San Francisco the right to dam the Hetch Hetchy Valley. In 1913, women's clubs from across the country voiced their desire to protect nature and build a stronger National Park system for the sake of both moral and physical health. The Massachusetts State Federation of Women's Clubs here argued that both women and men found health and inspiration in the beauty of the Valley. Although not using strict preservationist arguments, the Federation stressed that with more hotels and better transportation, the Valley could be enjoyed by more citizens. According to their resolution, San Francisco had no need to dam the Hetch Hetchy Valley and its damming would be an irrevocable sacrifice by the whole nation.

Petitions and Related Documents That Were Presented, Read, or Tabled (SEN 63A-K8); Records of the US Senate, Record Group 46; NAID 7268076

WHEREAS, San Francisco has been, for twelve years, appealing to the Federal government for such rights in the high Sierras as will enable it to provide the people of the Bay counties with a pure and adequate supply of water, and

WHEREAS, the Hetch Hetchy region offers the only source to which San Francisco can look for such an uncontaminated supply as will provide for not only the immediate but the future needs of its people, and

WHEREAS, San Francisco already owns outright more than half the land in the floor of the Hetch Hetchy valley which will be flooded by the proposed reservoir, and has, in good faith, spent one and one-half million dollars in the development of its proposed municipal water system, and

WHEREAS, all that San Francisco asks of the Federal government is the right to construct a dam and the grant of the use, as a reservoir, of part of the Hetch Hetchy valley, which will, in no wise, be impaired in its natural beauty by the creation of a lake, and

WHEREAS, the natural beauties of the Hetch Hetchy region will be made more easily accessible to thousands of nature lovers by the building of roads and trains which San Francisco will construct into this entire region, and

WHEREAS, human consumption is the highest use to which the Hetch Hetchy water can be put, in that it will safeguard the health and supply the present needs of a community of 800,000 people, and the future needs of many times that number; **Therefore, be it**

RESOLVED, by the Augusta, Hallowell, & Gardner, Central Labor Union, that we most earnestly go on record as approving of San Francisco's petition to Congress for the grant of certain rights in the Hetch Hetchy region, and **be it**

FURTHER RESOLVED, that we declare our firm conviction that human needs are paramount to sentimental objection of so-called "nature lovers" who profess to see, in San Francisco's project, a desecration of nature, although the work of San Francisco in the high Sierras will, in reality, bring this wonder region closer to the real lovers of nature, and will in no wise impair the grandeur of the scenery there to be found. And, **be it**

FURTHER RESOLVED, That we regret the campaign of misrepresentation that has been made in the effort to prevent San Francisco from obtaining that pure and adequate supply of water to which every community should be entitled. And **be it**

FURTHER RESOLVED, That we petition the Senate of the United States to grant to San Francisco the rights for which it has so long appealed, and which are embodied in the Raker bill heretofore passed by the House of Representatives of the United States.

F. B. Tobey

....
President.

John H. Bunnell

Secretary.

vii. Resolution from the Augusta, Hallowell, and Gardner Central Labor Union of Maine in Favor of the Raker Bill

Labor unions from across the country submitted petitions to Congress in favor of the Raker Bill, a bill to grant San Francisco the right to dam the Hetch Hetchy Valley. The Augusta, Hallowell, and Gardner Central Labor Union of Maine submitted this resolution arguing that the Senate should pass the Raker Bill. The Union stressed that building a reservoir in Hetch Hetchy Valley would not only provide vital water to San Francisco, but would also add to the beauty of the entire Hetch Hetchy region. Dozens of other labor organization submitted identical petitions.

Petitions and Related Documents That Were Presented, Read, or Tabled (SEN 63A-K8); Records of the US Senate, Record Group 46; NAID 7268079

NIGHT LETTER

Form 2359 B

THE WESTERN UNION TELEGRAPH COMPANY

INCORPORATED

25,000 OFFICES IN AMERICA   CABLE SERVICE TO ALL THE WORLD

This Company TRANSMITS and DELIVERS messages only on conditions limiting its liability, which have been assented to by the sender of the following Night Letter. Errors can be guarded against only by repeating a message back to the sending station for comparison, and the Company will not hold itself liable for errors or delays in transmission or delivery of Unrepeated Night Letters, sent at reduced rates, beyond a sum equal to the amount paid for transmission; nor in any case beyond the sum of Fifty Dollars, at which unless otherwise stated below, this message has been valued by the sender hereof, nor in any case where the claim is not presented in writing within sixty days after the message is filed with the Company for transmission.

This is an UNREPEATED NIGHT LETTER, and is delivered by request of the sender, under the conditions named above.

THEO. N. VAIL, PRESIDENT   BELVIDERE BROOKS, GENERAL MANAGER

Office Senate P. O.
Phone Branch 87

RECEIVED AT

W MY.....110 NL. 5X EW

SANFRANCISCO CAL DEC 2-13

SEN GEO C PERKINS,WASHN,D.C.

SANFRANCISCO COUNCIL NO.615 KNIGHTS OF COLUMBUS COMPRISING 1500
MEMBERS IN REGULAR MEETING ASSEMBLED UNANIMOUSLY ENDORSE BILL PROVIDING
FOR A HETCHHETCHY WATER SUPPLY FOR SANFRANCISCO WE NEED PURE MOUNTAIN
WATER FOR OUR GREAT AND GROWING METROPOLIS OUR MEMBERS HAS SUMMERED
IN THE YOSEMITE AND KNOW THAT THE PASSAGE OF THE BILL WILL NOT DEPRE-
CIATE THE BEAUTY OF THE VALLEY BUT THE PLANS PROPOSED WILL XXXXXX
ENHANCE ITS NATURAL GRANDEUR THE PRIMARY OBJECT THAT WE AS
SANFRANCISCANS HAVE IS TO OBTAIN SUFFICIENT PURE DRINKING WATER FOR
OUR CITIZENS THE COMMERCIAL OBJECTIONS PUT FORWARD ARE BUT A SUBTERFUGE
RAISED BY MISGUIDED NATURE LOVERS

SANFRANCISCO COUNCIL KNIGHTS OF COLUMBUS
BY WARREN SHANNON,GRAND KNIGHT   832A 3

viii. Telegram from the San Francisco Council of Knights of Columbus 615

The San Francisco Council No. 615, Knights of Columbus, through its Grand Knight sent this telegram to Congress in which they unanimously endorsed the Raker Bill, a bill to grant San Francisco the right to dam the Hetch Hetchy Valley. The Knights argued that pure mountain water was necessary to support the healthy development of San Francisco. They further stressed that damming the Hetch Hetchy Valley would enhance the grandeur of the entire region.

Petitions and Related Documents That Were Presented, Read, or Tabled (SEN 63A-K8); Records of the US Senate, Record Group 46; NAID 7268080

San Francisco Examiner

PETITION

To the Senate of the United States:

WE, the undersigned, citizens of California, ask your favorable action on the bill giving San Francisco the right to use the water of the Hetch Hetchy reservoir site.

The Tuolumne river in the Hetch Hetchy valley furnishes the only available water supply not under private ownership. San Francisco owns three-fourths of the land in that valley in fee simple and it only requires your favorable action on this bill to let us utilize our ownership of that land so that it will procure for us a water supply without which the future of San Francisco is endangered.

San Francisco's need of this water supply is urgent and imperative. Without it the city is throttled; its health menaced; its development blocked.

The Government of the United States has completed the Panama canal. One of the principal benefits looked for from this magnificent enterprise was the development of the western edge of the United States, of which San Francisco is the metropolis. No benefit can accrue to San Francisco through the Panama canal if there is withheld from it a water supply capable of sustaining the health and life of the community.

Senators of the United States, San Francisco asks you for simple justice; for fair play. You have already granted to Seattle, to Portland and to Los Angeles the use of Federal reserves which gave those cities the water supplies they needed.

The need of no city ever has been so great as the need of San Francisco in this emergency. We ask your favorable vote on this bill, which will give San Francisco the only available water supply adequate for its present and future needs.

[handwritten signatures and addresses]

Mrs Amelia Barilla	835 A Union St.
Charles D Vincenzi	869 Union St
Thos M Mulla	814 Union St.
O Trussi	827 Union St.
L Vivincenzi	1926 Taylor St
L C Dowling	1686 Howard
J Devevenergi	1069 Union St
Elizabeth Ferroggiaro	847 Union St
Geo Ferroggiaro	847 Union St
F Ferroggiaro	847 Union St
Julie Lebaggi	810 Union St
F Mesita	1542 Mason St
S Pettoms	1352 Grant Ave

ix. *San Francisco Examiner* **Petition to the Senate of the United States**

In this petition, hundreds of California residents urged Congress to pass the Raker Bill, a bill to grant San Francisco the right to dam the Hetch Hetchy Valley. Written and distributed by the San Francisco Examiner, this petition stressed to Congress that San Francisco's need for water was urgent and that the Hetch Hetchy Valley was the only available water source not under private control. The paper, owned by William Randolph Hearst, published regular pieces in support of the Raker Bill.

Petitions and Related Documents That Were Presented, Read, or Tabled (SEN 63A-K8); Records of the US Senate, Record Group 46; NAID 7268086

PART 4

Hetch Hetchy Restored?

The construction of the O'Shaughnessy Dam, and the resultant flooding of Hetch Hetchy, was not a foregone conclusion. Neither has its concrete reality stopped the debate about its significance or purpose. A striking element of this continuing dialogue is that one of its late-twentieth-century instigators was Secretary of the Interior Donald Hodel. A life-long Republican, he served in President Ronald Reagan's administration; neither he nor the president were considered conservationists, quite the reverse. But in 1987, Hodel startled the Sierra Club and other liberal environmental organizations when he raised the question of whether the O'Shaughnessy Dam should be decommissioned. This would be the first step in a lengthy process, he believed, that would lead to the restoration of the Hetch Hetchy Valley. Whatever Hodel's motives—and at the time they sparked considerable speculation—his proposal has shaped the ensuing discussion about the possibility of reversing an earlier generation's legislative decision to approve the dam's construction. Ever since, the Sierra Club and its allies have pressed the City of San Francisco, the California state legislature, and the federal government to reconsider the history and legal status of the O'Shaughnessy Dam. They have also challenged public officials to assess whether there are other ways by which San Francisco and surrounding communities could secure sufficient water supplies without the Hetch Hetchy reservoir. This decades-long pressure led the state to publish, in 2006, the results of its thorough analysis of the costs and benefits of restoring the Hetch Hetchy Valley. A petition campaign in San Francisco led to a 2012 local ballot initiative that, had it been successful, would have compelled the city to develop a plan for draining the dam and restoring the valley. As Donald Hodel recognized at the outset, and as is clear from the subsequent debate and its shifting set of alliances and arguments, the Hetch Hetchy Valley remains a hot-button issue that will continue to roil US environmental politics for the foreseeable future.

DOCUMENT 37:

Carl Pope, "Undamming Hetch Hetchy," *Sierra Magazine*, November/December 1987, 34–38

When he wrote this article, Carl Pope (1946–) was the Sierra Club's deputy director of conservation. Later, he served as the executive director of the Sierra Club from 1992 to 2010. As with the next document, it offers some of the back story to the discussion between President Ronald Reagan's Secretary of the Interior Donald Hodel and the Sierra Club relative to the Hetch Hetchy Dam. Pope explores the complex dynamics of California's water and energy politics and casts doubt on the degree to which Secretary Hodel fully understood those dynamics. Yet he also recognizes that Hodel opened up a much needed "second debate" about the dam-and-reservoir complex.

ev

One Tuesday in August, Sierra Club Chairman Michael McCloskey received an astonishing telephone call from an old law-school classmate. On the line was Interior Secretary Donald Hodel, who has been on the opposite side of most political issues from McCloskey since those days.

"Hello, Mike—this is Don Hodel."

"Hello, Don," said McCloskey, who was frankly surprised by the call—and even more surprised by the time it was over. For during their conversation Hodel laid out an idea that he characterized as brand-new, yet one that from the Sierra Club's perspective was more than 70 years old: the restoration of Yosemite National Park's spectacular Hetch Hetchy Valley.

As most conservationists know, Hetch Hetchy was lost—presumably forever—in 1913, when Congress authorized the construction of O'Shaughnessy Dam to provide water and electrical power to the distant city of San Francisco. Ten years later the 430-foot-tall dam—then as now, the only major hydroelectric facility within a national park—was completed, and the waters of the Tuolumne River backed up to fill the narrow, eight-mile-long valley. The fight to save Hetch Hetchy was the last of John Muir's life, and its loss not only broke his heart but marked the first major defeat for the young Sierra Club, only then beginning to wage its battles on behalf of wilderness in the national arena.

Where had this bold idea come from? McCloskey asked Hodel. The Secretary said it had emerged from some discussions he'd been having with his staff, and that he was serious in proposing it. He told McCloskey that he had already outlined his proposal to **Mayor Dianne Feinstein** of San Francisco, the city that built O'Shaughnessy Dam and that not only derives its water supply from Hetch Hetchy reservoir but profits from the sale of

Mayor Dianne Feinstein: Feinstein (1933–) served on the San Francisco Board of Supervisors as its first woman president; became the first female mayor of the city following the assassination of George Moscone in 1978, was elected to the US Senate in 1992, and won her fifth term in 2018.

the electricity the massive dam generates. The conversation concluded with Hodel's indication that an extensive study would be conducted to see if the idea is workable, and how it might be best carried out. It would be an undeniably complex undertaking to tear down O'Shaughnessy Dam, locate alternative sources of water for San Francisco, and possibly compensate the city for lost revenues from the sale of power—but Hodel seemed determined to pursue the idea as far as practicable.

McCloskey hung up wondering why Hodel—whose previous enthusiasms seemed to be reserved for exploitative activities like offshore oil drilling the leasing of Alaska's Arctic National Wildlife Refuge for oil development—had suddenly turned into a conservationist on this issue. This is one of the two main questions that Hodel's intriguing initiative has raised—the other being, of course, whether the idea is in fact feasible.

No one except the Secretary of the Interior himself can say with certainty what caused him to support the idea of restoring Hetch Hetchy to its original splendor. Certainly the plan marks a sharp divergence from his other policies, which have favored development of the nation's natural resources over their preservation and protection. Some early press reports speculated that Hodel was really promoting the restoration of Hetch Hetchy as a way of building support for construction of the long-delayed, partially completed **Auburn Dam** on the American River in the Sierra foothills. There was certainly a basis for this speculation at one time: In a memorandum to Interior Department officials, Hodel suggested that if San Francisco were to require a new water source after the demolition of O'Shaughnessy Dam, Auburn might be it.

As much as anything else, this suggestion reflected Hodel's limited knowledge of the fine-grained complexities of California's water-delivery system. Hodel and his staff have since been made aware that environmentalists flatly oppose Auburn Dam, which would be far too expensive (at $2.1 billion) and environmentally damaging to complete, and in any case is not needed to provide San Francisco with its present level of water deliveries. Also, other cities have prior claim to water rights on the American River, while San Francisco's rights are to water from the Tuolumne River system. Hodel has subsequently withdrawn Auburn Dam as a possible alternative water source. He reportedly vowed at a late-summer meeting with environmental leaders, including the Sierra Club's McCloskey, that Auburn Dam "would not be built as a federal project in [his] lifetime."

Others have theorized that Hodel's proposal was motivated by a desire to split the alliance between conservationists and the Northern California politicians who have traditionally been sympathetic to their concerns. (For example, both groups have been actively opposing Hodel's plans for oil drilling off the California coast.) But this strategy, if such it be, is ill founded:

Auburn Dam: The Auburn Dam was never completed and was the subject of intense debate in California. It would have been the tallest concrete dam in California at a height of 680 feet (210 m) and would have stored 2,300,000 acre-feet (2.8 km³) of water. It was never completed due to geological hazards, high cost, and potential impact on local recreation along the American River.

While San Francisco and the Sierra Club have disagreed since 1906 on what to do with Hetch Hetchy Valley, these disagreements are certainly not going to disrupt their shared outrage at the idea of subjecting environmentally sensitive coastal areas to oil drilling and development.

It has also been suggested that Hodel, once James Watt's right-hand man at the Interior Department and a continuing supporter of his policies, has no desire to suffer a similar political fate. (Watt was drummed out of office by a flood tide of public indignation in 1983).[1] At the very least, his support for the restoration of Hetch Hetchy gives Hodel a response to use when newspaper editorial boards accuse him of being blindly, compulsively anticonservation.

More charitably, and without diminishing one's outrage at the rest of the Interior Secretary's policies, it must be noted that if Don Hodel were ever going to take a strongly proconservation stance, Hetch Hetchy would be a likely place to plant his feet. After all, his plan is nominally designed to promote the interests of national parks as recreation resources—and the concept of "parks for people" seems to be one of Hodel's soft spots.

The Secretary has made it clear that the mistakes that have so diminished the grandeur of Yosemite Valley must be avoided at Hetch Hetchy: There will be no lodges, no stores, no automobiles in the restored valley. That will make it possible for millions of people over the course of generations to enjoy Hetch Hetchy and still have a far more tranquil, natural experience than they can enjoy today at Yosemite Valley. And that idea, it appears, holds a very strong appeal for Hodel.

A drumbeat of opposition to the idea of restoring Hetch Hetchy has throbbed steadily in San Francisco's media since Hodel's announcement. "The Secretary's vision is terribly flawed," editorialized the San Francisco Chronicle, which went on to brag, in classic booster's rhetoric, that Hetch Hetchy "is a whirring core that produces water, energy, and capital for millions." (As if the dam were one of the wonders of the world, guaranteed to endure for centuries, or as if the generation of revenue for San Francisco were the legitimate function of a national park!)

For her part, Mayor [Dianne] Feinstein seems to want to strangle the very notion in its crib: "Crazy," "the height of folly," and "the worst idea ... since the sale of weapons to the Ayatollah" are among her public characterizations of the proposal. She has even called O'Shaughnessy Dam "beautiful" and the water it delivers to San Francisco the city's "birthright."

There are, of course, complexities that will have to be addressed, both in theory and in practice, before progress can be made toward realizing Hodel's plan. Critics of the plan often refer to the difficulty of replacing

1 *New York Times*, 10 October 1983, A1.

San Francisco's "lost" water supply. How, ask the local media, would San Francisco and the other cities to which it sells Hetch Hetchy water meet their needs?

The answer to that question is surprisingly simple: San Francisco would get its water from the same river it currently taps—the Tuolumne. Removing O'Shaughnessy Dam at Hetch Hetchy will not cause San Francisco to lose the water it now uses; the city will simply lose one of the many places where this water can be stored. (As David Brower has often said, you don't lose a drop of water when you tear down a dam. Rain and snow continue to fall on the watershed; all you lose is one place where the water stops, and where part of it evaporates.) There are other reservoirs on the Tuolumne system where it appears San Francisco can easily store the water that floods Hetch Hetchy today. In fact, the Tuolumne has more excess reservoir capacity than almost any other river in California.

Electrical power is a more difficult issue. With O'Shaughnessy Dam demolished, San Francisco would lose about half the power it generates on the Tuolumne. (About half comes from dams on the river that would not have to be touched in order for Hetch Hetchy to be restored.) Although there is enough surplus electrical-generating capacity in the region to replace this lost power, the city would lose the net revenue it derives from the sale of this power to other municipalities. (That sum—nearly $50 million in 1986—is expected to be reduced by half this year because of California's dry winter.) One may well ask why San Francisco's general fund should be enriched by a dam in a national park. Unfortunately, that question was answered by Congress in 1913 when it passed the Raker Act, which authorized the city to construct a dam at Hetch Hetchy. It will not be easy to work out the arrangements that will convince San Francisco to give up this jealously guarded source of revenue.

The power issue exemplifies one aspect of the thorniest problem of all: money. No one knows exactly how much the restoration of Hetch Hetchy Valley will cost, although San Francisco's immediate estimate of $6 billion is almost certainly excessive. In fact, the main purpose of the feasibility study that Hodel has proposed should be to identify the most cost-effective method for restoring Hetch Hetchy, and then to develop the means whereby that restoration may be financed.

The physical restoration of Hetch Hetchy Valley after it has been drained raises questions of its own. Some observers have speculated that the valley might be so damaged by silt that it would be decades, even centuries, before it could reattain the grandeur that visitors would seek. However, Alexander Horne, a professor of applied ecology at the University of California at Berkeley, believes that siltation will not present an insuperable problem, and that people could begin to visit the restored Hetch Hetchy Valley within two or three years.

A second objection raised by opponents of the reclamation proposal is that Hodel's noble intention to reduce congestion in overcrowded Yosemite Valley will be frustrated by a lack of sufficient flat land in Hetch Hetchy Valley. But this misses the point. True, there may not be enough flat land at Hetch Hetchy for banks, liquor stores, and hotel parking lots. But the fact that Hetch Hetchy is much narrower than Yosemite Valley, yet almost as long, means that the visitor's experience will be even more intense there, and that there would be even less justification for allowing motorized vehicles to enter the valley. Hetch Hetchy reclaimed can be Yosemite Valley as that treasure should have been allowed to remain.

It is important to understand that the restoration of Hetch Hetchy will be a long-term project. The Department of the Interior's study process will include the Sierra Club and other interested parties (among them the city of San Francisco). Such a study will determine the cost of restoring Hetch Hetchy; then the slow process of building public support for a specific plan will begin.

The first debate over Hetch Hetchy took a decade and mobilized public opinion across the country. The second debate may take even longer—but it has at least begun.

DOCUMENT 38:

"Interview with Secretary of the Interior Donald Hodel," *Environs: Environmental Law and Policy Journal*, 12:1, 1987–88, 15–16

Donald Hodel (1935–) served as President Ronald Reagan's secretary of energy (1982–85) and secretary of the interior (1985–89). This interview, part of an issue devoted to the debate over Hetch Hetchy that (re)emerged as a result of Secretary Hodel's proposal to tear down the O'Shaughnessy Dam, reveals some of the backstory to his public statement about the dam but also reveals his careful crafting of his answers so as not to be tied down.

e

1) The Solicitor General's Office is studying the newest San Francisco-Pacific Gas & Electric wheeling contracts. Has the Solicitor General given you any preliminary indication whether those contracts are in compliance with the Raker Act?

> The Interior Solicitor's office is presently reviewing all legal related aspects of my Hetch Hetchy proposal. It would be unwise for me to comment until that review is completed.

2) Have you personally given San Francisco's compliance with the Raker Act any consideration, and what are your conclusions?

> No, I have not, and until the Solicitor's office completes its review I am not going to comment.

3) If it is found that San Francisco is and has been violating the Raker Act, would you have any compunctions against initiating legal action to have the contracts reformed, voided or to take away San Francisco's rights to O'Shaughnessy Dam and the Hetch Hetchy system?

> It would also be unwise for me to speculate on this question.

4) Replacement of water and power resources for San Francisco have been the main focus of the Department of the Interior's public comments and studies so far. If San Francisco is determined to be in violation of the Raker Act, will water and power replacement still be a priority concern for the federal government?

Regardless of any legal questions, the City of San Francisco and the other Bay area communities that have been using Hetch Hetchy water and power still need to be assured a continuing water and power supply to meet their needs in the 21st Century. Therefore, any plan to eliminate the portion of the Hetch Hetchy system inside Yosemite National Park would need to provide water and power for the Bay area, at least in the amounts that would have been contributed by Hetch Hetchy.

5) Where did you get the idea to drain Hetch Hetchy Reservoir? How long had you been considering the idea before your August 1987 announcement?[2]

The idea came to me after I had signed off on a similar proposal to eliminate three dams in Rocky Mountain National Park in Colorado. These dams were owned by the City of Longmont, Colorado. They had deteriorated and were in need of major repairs. Rather than commit funds for repair, the city agreed to sell the dams to the National Park Service, which is now in the process of restoring those reservoir sites to a more natural condition. It occurred to me that while the parallels are not exact, the principal is the same and that this approach might assist us in our efforts to maintain superlative outdoor recreational opportunities at heavily used Yosemite.

6) Why did you announce your idea in August 1987?

I announced it then because I had contacted the Governor's office, then Mayor Feinstein, and certain members of Congress and told them we were planning to look at the feasibility of this idea.

7) Did your announcement have any relation at all to the then-pending negotiations between San Francisco and PG&E on the recently signed long-term contracts?

No, it did not. I was not aware of those negotiations.

8) What is the status of the $600,000 budget request you submitted for continued study of the Hetch Hetchy idea?

---

2   For a discussion of the immediate reactions to Hodel's 1987 announcement, see Dan Morain and Paul Houston, "Hodel Would Tear Down Dam in Hetch Hetchy," *Los Angeles Times*, 7 August 1987.

It has been considered in the committee hearings as part of President Reagan's budget, but, at this writing, no action has been taken.

9) Who do you count as opponents to the request both within and outside of the Congress, and why do they oppose the request?

People oppose this idea for several reasons, most of them obvious. Some would be inconvenienced to various degrees in switching to other water and power sources. Others have less philosophical aversion to dams in national parks. I suppose there might even be a few who oppose this idea because I suggested it. Overall, perhaps those who are opposed to even looking at the feasibility of such an idea are afraid that a feasibility study will show it can be done.

10) Who do you count as supporters of the request both within and outside the Congress, and why do they support the budget request?

Those who support this idea range from those who have always been upset by the presence of the dam in Yosemite to those who see this as a challenge of our stewardship of our great God-given treasures of natural beauty.

11) What do you think will happen to the budget request and the actual idea of restoring Hetch Hetchy Valley in January if a Republican administration is elected to succeed President Reagan? What if a Democratic administration is elected?

I would hope that whichever party occupies the White House in 1989 that this idea would be considered on its merits and not become a political issue. I am optimistic that it will get a fair hearing in any eventuality.

12) If the $600,000 budget request fails to get through Congress this year, what will be your next move as Secretary of the Interior?

I'll cross that bridge when I come to it.

13) Will you continue to work for and support this idea in January, after your term of office has expired?

Absolutely, with vigor and enthusiasm. Even under the best of circumstances, this idea will probably occupy several more Secretaries of the Interior before it is resolved.

14) If your Solicitor General concludes that San Francisco has violated the Raker Act, do you need Congressional approval to pursue action?

Again, until the Solicitor's office at Interior completes its review of all legal related aspects of my proposal, I am going to refrain from commenting.

15) If your idea proves to be feasible, to what extent would you contemplate removing San Francisco's power and water system—breach/removal of O'Shaughnessy Dam only or removal of any part of the system which lies within Yosemite National Park?

A decision of feasibility for this idea would carry with it some preliminary decisions but it would be premature to speculate on the details now. Obviously, getting water out of the reservoir is part of the basic idea but beyond that I wouldn't want to limit the range of alternatives now.

16) Do you think it is actually feasible to physically drain the reservoir and restore the valley?

Everything I have seen so far indicates that this would not be a major problem. The major consideration would be how much do you want to speed up the natural process with activities such as reseeding and replanting.

17) Has the January 19, 1988, Draft Report on Restoration Options for Hetch Hetchy Valley prepared by the National Park Service influenced your opinion on the feasibility or viability of your idea to restore the valley?

That report has encouraged me to continue my quest. All the factors aren't in yet, but I'm encouraged by the fact that what we are discovering now is positive as to the feasibility of this idea.

18) The January 19, 1988, Draft Report finds the idea eminently feasible, but attaches no cost estimates to any proposal. Have any preliminary cost estimates been made as to breach of the dam and restoration of the valley? If yes, what are those estimates?

There are any number of off-the-wall estimates, mostly from those opposed to this idea, but I am not aware of any estimates that are the product of thorough research. That process is still underway.

19) What is your reaction to the Department of Energy's report on the Hetch Hetchy idea?

Obviously, I don't agree with that report.

20) Why do you think that **Secretary Herrington** got involved in this issue?[3]

You will have to ask him that question.

Secretary Herrington: Energy Secretary John S. Herrington (1939–), who replaced Hodel at Energy (1985–89), served in various capacities in the Reagan Administration, was later chairman of Harcourt, Brace, Jovanovich publishers and chaired the California Republican Party.

---

3   Herrington blasted Hodel's proposal: see Robert A. Rosenblatt, "Herrington Cites Costs, Attacks Proposal to Drain Hetch Hetchy," Los Angeles Times, 5 November 1987 and George F. Will, "Dam-Busters," *Washington Post*, 3 December 1987; the two men's differences carried over to the next year and became personal: AP, 3 February 1988.

DOCUMENT 39:

Extracts from the Hetch Hetchy Restoration Study, The State of California, Department of Water Resources, 2006, 1, 24–25, 50–57

This report was written by the Department of Water Resources and the Department of Parks and Recreation in response to a legislative request. Its purpose was to review the many studies prepared over the preceding two decades on the potential for restoring the Hetch Hetchy Valley. Although this was the first cumulative assessment, the final report indicated that considerable more work would be needed, and that other stakeholders, including Indigenous peoples, the federal government, and the Public Utilities Commission of San Francisco, must be engaged to ensure a more complete analysis.

Foreword

The restoration of Hetch Hetchy Valley on the upper Tuolumne River has once again captured the public's imagination. In order to provide for an informed dialogue about this issue, the Resources Agency has objectively evaluated the many Hetch Hetchy Valley restoration studies produced during the past two decades. In so doing, the state also recognized the great value and benefit of providing a central clearinghouse of all Hetch Hetchy restoration work. Moreover, in conducting the study, the state provided a neutral, public forum to discuss issues related to Hetch Hetchy restoration, such as water supply and water quality, flood management, cultural resources, environmental impacts, energy generation, and recreation. In all, several hundred people participated in a July 2005 workshop in Sacramento and at other stakeholder meetings throughout the state. In addition, many interested Californians provided written comments for our consideration.

This final report is a comprehensive analysis of Hetch Hetchy Valley restoration studies. But even as a comprehensive analysis, we find, first and foremost, that much study remains to be done because there are major gaps in vital information. For example, objectives for replacing the water supply for the Bay Area, dam removal methods and impacts, and considerations of the public use and benefit of a restored Valley remain largely undefined. Another critical, missing element is a formal public involvement process to engage agencies, Native American tribes, stakeholders and other interested parties in this issue. While we offer no formal recommendation about next steps, it is clear that further investigations into Hetch Hetchy Valley restoration cannot be led by the State of California alone. Federal participation will be important to help shape future studies and to work with the San

Francisco Public Utilities Commission, tribes, and the public on any next steps in this process. Moving forward, the Resources Agency's role in studies and planning for Hetch Hetchy will be consistent with the state's approach to other significant natural resources such as the Sacramento-San Joaquin Delta or the Salton Sea—to protect the public trust by ensuring that these natural places are protected and utilized for the benefit of all Californians....

Cultural Resources

The draining of the reservoir and the restoration of Hetch Hetchy Valley will trigger compliance with various cultural resources laws and regulations regardless of the level of restoration. Because much of the valley is federally owned property, the most significant law that will apply is the **National Historic Preservation Act** (NHPA). Some data are currently available about archaeological sites present in the valley. Seven prehistoric archaeological sites were recorded around the edge of the reservoir by University of California, Berkeley, in 1951 (Montague and Mundy 1995:5). An additional 10 archaeological sites were recorded by National Park Service archaeologists in 1991 when the reservoir level fell to its lowest elevation since its original inundation (Montague and Mundy 1995). All of the sites contain prehistoric components, while three of the sites also include historic elements and one site reflects occupation by Native Americans during the historic era. Eleven isolated artifacts or features were also recorded during the National Park Service study; four were prehistoric isolates and seven were from the historic era.

Cultural resources, other than archaeological sites, also need recording and evaluation, including traditional cultural properties (TCP) and the dam and hydroelectric facilities. It is likely that the entire valley would be considered a TCP given the importance of the area to descendants of the Native Americans inhabiting the valley at the time of Euro-American contact. Furthermore, O'Shaughnessy Dam and the Hetch Hetchy system may be eligible for listing in the **National Register**.

January 2001 amendments to the NHPA implementing regulations require consultation with tribes during all phases of an undertaking from the identification and evaluation of cultural resources through decisions on mitigation efforts for National Register-eligible properties. Numerous federally recognized tribes and tribes without federal recognition have traditional ties to Hetch Hetchy Valley. These tribes reside on both sides of the Sierra Nevada and include the Tuolumne Band of Me-Wuk, the Southern Sierra Miwuk Nation (American Indian Council of Mariposa County), the North Fork Band of Mono Indians, the Bridgeport Paiute Indian Colony, and the Mono Lake Kutzadika Paiute Indian Community.

National Historic Preservation Act: The 1966 National Historic Preservation Act (NHPA; Public Law 89–665; 54 USC 300101 *et seq.*) is legislation intended to preserve historical and archaeological sites in the US. The act created the National Register of Historic Places, the list of National Historic Landmarks, and the State Historic Preservation Offices.

National Register: The National Register of Historic Places is the official list of the nation's historic places worthy of preservation. Authorized by the National Historic Preservation Act of 1966, the National Park Service's National Register of Historic Places is part of a national program to coordinate and support public and private efforts to identify, evaluate, and protect America's historic and archaeological resources.

To better understand Native American issues related to restoring Hetch Hetchy Valley, state officials met with approximately 20 Native American representatives on March 29, 2005, in Tuolumne, California. A wide variety of opinions were expressed by meeting participants. Should the reservoir be drained, participants were adamant about the need for the tribes to be thoroughly involved in the decision to drain and manage the land. Opinions ranged from returning full ownership of the land to the native tribes to maintaining the valley as a national wilderness area open to the public.

While the appropriate use of the valley would be determined by an intensive planning process involving all stakeholders, the tribes specifically considered several issues to be particularly important: 1) development in the valley should be very limited to avoid duplicating the level of development found in Yosemite Valley, 2) recreation should be restricted to low impact activities, 3) restoration of native plants, wildlife, and springs should be a priority, and 4) the tribes should be provided access to ceremonial grounds. The tribes want to participate fully in the management of any recreational development, including providing law enforcement and protection of resources.

Tribal participants called for a full inventory of cultural resources in the valley if Hetch Hetchy is drained, and for a full survey of cultural resources in any other areas to be inundated to compensate for the loss of Hetch Hetchy water....

Next Steps—Future Work

This study presents initial conceptual information for review and to promote discussion. It does appear technically feasible to restore the Hetch Hetchy Valley. However, it is premature to evaluate its financial feasibility. Based upon the low level of detail of information compiled during this state review, this chapter provides some guidance for others that may have continued interest in the restoration of Hetch Hetchy Valley.

The information from prior reports is not nearly detailed enough to make a decision on the financial feasibility of valley restoration. If a decision is ever to be made, policy makers and the public will need significantly more detailed quantitative information about costs, benefits, and tradeoffs associated with a specific proposal.

Role of the State

Further investigations into Hetch Hetchy valley restoration cannot be led by the State of California alone. Federal participation, specifically the active and direct participation of the U.S. Department of Interior, will be important to help shape future studies and to work with the San Francisco Public

Utilities Commission, Native American tribes, and the public on any next steps in this process. Federal authorization may be needed to initiate this federal role. A public/private partnership might be one mechanism to proceed with further evaluations. The Resources agency will participate in any future studies under its mission to manage California's natural resources with the goal of ensuring that future studies or plans adhere to principles of integrated regional water management, that they maximize public benefit, and that they protect the environment, as well as the public trust.

If more detailed information becomes available, the state will review it in light of potential impacts on California's natural resource management activities and responsibilities—including water, energy, environmental, and recreation—and how overall public benefits can be maximized. If the federal government continues the investigation of restoring Hetch Hetchy, the state will consider participating as an active member of a cooperative study.

More Dialogue Needed

More dialogue must occur among elected officials; federal, state, and local agencies; Native American tribes; environmental interest groups; and the public before a decision is made to continue with restoration studies. Together, these interests will need to grapple with questions such as:

- What specific processes and studies are needed to determine the feasibility of restoring Hetch Hetchy valley and replacing its current water and power benefits?
- Are water and power replacement options acceptable to the public?
- Can an adequate package of actions and mechanisms assure that a restoration and replacement program will be implemented and operated as intended?
- Who is willing to pay for a comprehensive Hetch Hetchy solution?

Prior to making a decision on whether or not to proceed with investigating the financial feasibility of restoring the Hetch Hetchy valley, future studies need to be committed to well-defined objectives and supported by a sound stakeholder process. Future studies should also be carried out to a consistent level of study.

Management Structure

The California Research Bureau (2005) discussed a number of major environmental restoration projects in California and around the country. The report identifies that these projects often utilize various management structures during different stages of their development. Described below are three general structures from the report:

- *Government-Run Study.* This approach relies on government expertise to direct and conduct the analysis. For a large, complex issue, this could be a multi-agency study like what is occurring in the Florida Everglades. These processes usually rely on public and stakeholder advisory bodies to provide advice and feedback.

- *Government-Appointed Task Force.* Projects around the country do not use the term "task force" in a consistent way. In some cases, it means a stakeholder group that will negotiate a result similarly satisfactory (or unsatisfactory) to all parties. In other cases it means a panel of experts or a distinguished leader that brings a neutral, unbiased approach to the problem. For the purposes of this report, the term is used in the spirit of a panel of experts or distinguished leaders. An example is the California's Marine Life Protection Act (MLPA) Blue Ribbon Task Force. Parties expect such a task force to conduct a transparent and unbiased study of the issues; listen to stakeholders, the public, and the experts; and then make recommendations to government. The credibility of the task force with stakeholders, government officials, and the public is key to its success.

- *Collaborative Stakeholder Process.* In the two models described above, stakeholders may be consulted or have a formal advisory role. In the third model, which we call a collaborative stakeholder process, they are directly involved in setting up and overseeing the investigation. Terms commonly used to describe this process are "collaborative analysis" and "joint fact-finding." The Sacramento area Water Forum is such a process.

It should also be noted that the management structure may not be the same throughout the study period, which could last up to 10 years.

Level of Study Detail

The level of detail in the previous Hetch Hetchy restoration studies is generally at the conceptual level or less. A next step in the studies could be elevating all the information to the same level of conceptual detail. Four specific areas could use more study to bring all information to the conceptual level of detail:

- public use
- valley restoration

- dam removal
- benefits

It is not essential for all the studies to occur at the same time. In fact, an analysis on public use and restoration early in the process would fill in important gaps and enhance efforts to quantify benefits, study dam removal, or define water and power replacement objectives.

Future studies of any subject areas related to Hetch Hetchy valley restoration will likely examine the issues identified to date through the following activities either under conceptual or appraisal level of study:

- development and analysis of alternatives
- public outreach
- alternatives assessment

More detailed feasibility studies should only be conducted if the proposal looks promising after these less detailed studies.

Formal Stakeholder Process

A formal stakeholder process engaging the city and county of San Francisco and the department of interior regarding objectives for water and power replacement is critical. As information becomes available, policy makers and the public will have the opportunity to continue, adjust, postpone, or stop the evaluation process.

Purpose and Need

None of the prior studies articulated project objectives for restoration, public use, and water and power replacement. The next step of study should be based on a well-defined purpose and need statement, accompanied by specific project objectives. This process should also establish performance measures for restoration, public use in Hetch Hetchy valley, and water and power replacement.

Develop and Evaluate Alternatives

Some of the studies looked at multiple concepts for their area of interest, but generally none evaluated alternatives for the entire project. The next step of studies needs to develop and evaluate a reasonable range of alternatives based on the purpose and needs and established objectives. The evaluation should identify benefits and costs for a range of public use and restoration alternatives, as well as the cost of replacing current water and power benefits.

Important Issues to Be Addressed

Through the public workshop and agency contacts to date, the study team has heard the issues and potential impacts identified by the stakeholders that should be addressed in future phases of study. Some of these issues are briefly summarized below....

Project Planning and Objectives

The acceptability of restoring Hetch Hetchy valley to interested parties around Yosemite National Park and to regional and statewide stakeholders needs to be considered. The planning and implementation issues include:

- project purpose and need
- objectives
- identification and development of a range of alternatives
- identification of potential project partners and financing
- required permits and agency consultation
- interrelationships with other projects and studies
- institutional arrangements
- agency and public education and participation

Restoration and Public Use

The potential beneficial and adverse effects of restoring Hetch Hetchy valley need evaluation. The alternatives evaluation should include analysis of the following factors:

- ambient water quality
- number, location, size, design, and impacts of new visitor use facilities
- impacts of removal or modification of O'Shaughnessy Dam
- disposal of material from dam demolition
- disturbance of valley floor by original construction
- restoration of valley walls
- sensitive terrestrial species and habitat
- natural recolonization by plants and animals

- cultural and other historic resources, including Native American issues[4]
- third party and environmental justice impacts
- National Park policies

System Operations, Conveyance Pipelines, and Facilities

Replacement water and power supplies from new facilities must be considered, including potential water quality and water supply reliability benefits and the institutional and operational agreements among potential participants. A key issue will be quantifying potential benefits of new facilities and identifying other water users who might be interested in obtaining those benefits. The conveyance, operation, and delivery issues include the following:

- delivered water quality
- delivered water amounts, timing, and reliability
- growth issues
- operational and institutional agreements among project participants
- location, size, and impacts of conveyance facilities
- risk management, including dam safety
- impacts to downstream users
- environmental impacts
- sensitive species and habitat
- reservoir and water supply security
- flood control
- operations during construction and coordination of operations with other projects
- statewide water management

Legal Issues

The legal issues raised by restoring Hetch Hetchy valley must necessarily be considered in a general way. They can only be fully and accurately described once a specific proposal is made on how the restoration is to be accomplished, and will obviously turn in great part on what facilities and by what institutional arrangements are proposed. Virtually all the alternatives for water and power supply replacement involve the use of potentially controversial water transfers in the Tuolumne River watershed (including Don Pedro Reservoir), the lower San Joaquin River, and the Sacramento-San Joaquin delta. The legal issues involved in restoration include:

---

4   See the full final document, "Cultural Resources," for an overview of this report's discussion with Indigenous representatives.

- reasonable use and public trust
- water quality and instream impacts
- environmental review, documentation, and mitigation
- safety
- flood control
- public use
- water transfers
- water rights
- organizational and contractual obligations
- Wilderness Act
- Wild and Scenic Rivers Act
- Raker Act, including dam removal authority

Cost, Financing, and Institutional Arrangements

The potential costs and financing for Hetch Hetchy valley restoration and water and power replacement, including allocation of costs among purposes and beneficiaries, must be determined. A method for determining the value of potential benefits is necessary to assist decision makers in allocating costs. The cost and financing areas of investigation include:

- methods for determining costs and benefits
- allocation of costs among project purposes
- funding and financing alternatives and associated institutional requirements
- institutional and operational arrangements among partner agencies
- operation and control of facilities
- mechanism for assuring commitments

Reports on dam removal by the Aspen Institute and the John Heinz III Center for Science, Economics, and the Environment stressed several issues important to dam removal:

- address the rights of dam owners and beneficiaries at the outset
- if new studies are necessary, take key steps up front
- revise permitting requirements to accommodate dam removal
- coordinate the applicable regulatory programs
- make dam removal activities eligible for funding from existing programs and seek private funds
- consider creative regulatory approaches

DOCUMENT 40:

San Francisco Proposition F Ballot Measure (2012): Shall the City prepare a two-phase plan that evaluates how to drain the Hetch Hetchy Reservoir so that it can be restored by the National Park Service and identifies replacement water and power sources?

Restore Hetch Hetchy and several other environmental groups placed Proposition F on the November 2012 ballot in San Francisco seeking to compel the city to begin planning for the tearing down of the O'Shaughnessy Dam, restoring the long-submerged Hetch Hetchy Valley, and securing new water and energy supplies. This document contains the For and Against position statements for the ballot measure, which lost at the polls.

The Way It Is Now: San Francisco owns the Hetch Hetchy Regional Water System (Water System), which provides water to about 2.5 million people in San Francisco and neighboring areas. Water System reservoirs collect water from the Tuolumne River and Bay Area watersheds. The Water System's largest reservoir is in Yosemite National Park's Hetch Hetchy Valley. The reservoir was created in 1923 by damming the Tuolumne River. The Hetch Hetchy Reservoir delivers 85% of the System's water. The water that flows from the reservoir also generates hydroelectric power for City services. In 2002, the voters of San Francisco authorized the San Francisco Public Utilities Commission to implement a $4.6 billion project to improve the Water System, including $334 million to develop additional groundwater, conservation, and recycled water supplies. The project is nearing completion.

The Proposal: Proposition F would require the City to prepare a two-phase plan to evaluate how to drain the Hetch Hetchy Reservoir and identify replacement water and power sources. The implementation of this plan would require voter approval.

The first phase would identify:

- New water supply and storage options;
- Additional water conservation opportunities;
- Expanded water filtration facilities; and
- Additional renewable energy sources to replace the reductions in hydroelectric power resulting from draining the Hetch Hetchy Reservoir.

The second phase would evaluate how to:

- Drain the Hetch Hetchy Valley and stop using it as a reservoir so that it can be restored by the National Park Service;
- Increase flows on the lower Tuolumne River; and
- Decrease storm water discharge into the bay and the ocean.

Proposition F would allocate $8 million to pay for the plan and create a five-member task force to develop it. Proposition F would require the task force to complete the plan by November 1, 2015, and require the Board of Supervisors to consider placing on the ballot a Charter Amendment to approve the plan.

A "YES" Vote Means: If you vote "yes," you want to require the City to prepare a two-phase plan that evaluates how to drain the Hetch Hetchy Reservoir and identifies replacement water and power sources.

A "NO" Vote Means: If you vote "no," you do not want the City to prepare this plan.

Controller's Statement on "F"

City Controller Ben Rosenfield has issued the following statement on the fiscal impact of Proposition F:

Should the proposed ordinance be adopted, in my opinion, there would be costs and benefits to the City and County. The costs would vary widely depending on how the City implements the ordinance, and on whether or not voters approve a Charter amendment that is specified in the ordinance. Planning costs over the next several years would be no more than $8 million. Future infrastructure costs could range from $3 billion to $10 billion if the voters approve a future Charter amendment specified in the ordinance. Benefits cannot be accurately determined at this time for the large-scale resource and environmental objectives in the ordinance. The ordinance specifies a planning process that would require the City to study and create; 1) an implementation plan for new water storage and treatment facilities and energy generation facilities sufficient to replace the capacity currently in the Hetch Hetchy reservoir and; 2) an implementation plan for removal of the Hetch Hetchy dam and environmental restoration of the affected areas and resources. The ordinance requires that the City draft a Charter amendment to allow a public vote in 2016 on these implementation plans. The ordinance specifies a wide variety of water, energy, and environmental goals that must be detailed in the plans, and requires studies of costs and financing methods for each. The water and energy plan would require implementation by 2025 and the plan for removal of the dam and related environmental restoration would require implementation by 2035.

There would be near-term costs under the ordinance of a maximum of $8 million under a provision requiring that the City appropriate funds for the planning effort. This amount is likely to be insufficient to complete the required work—in 2005, the State of California Resources Agency estimated the cost for a comparable planning and study process at $65 million.

The ordinance specifies that funds for the planning process and studies be appropriated from any legally available source and that other governmental or private sources could supplement City funding.

Significant long-term costs could occur as a result of the ordinance if a Charter amendment is eventually approved by the voters requiring development of new water and energy storage, transmission, and treatment facilities, removal of the Hetch Hetchy dam and reservoir, and implementation of environmental goals.

There are multiple possible methods for approximating these costs and estimates range widely. Under any method, the amounts are certainly substantial—in the billions of dollars. The State's compilation of estimates shows a range, in 2005 dollars, of not less than $3 billion, and up to $10 billion for these facilities and programs, depending on which elements of the water, energy and environmental resource issues are included. This estimate does not include increased operations and maintenance costs associated with the new infrastructure. In addition, the Public Utilities Commission estimates that the loss of hydroelectric energy and lost revenue from energy sales would cost the City an additional $41 million annually.

The ordinance states that funding sources for the water and energy facilities and the environmental programs that are called for could include federal, state and private sources. However, it should be noted that typically, water and energy facilities are funded by issuing 20 to 30 year bonds and the cost of this debt is recovered through charges to ratepayers. If ratepayer bonds were issued to replace Hetch Hetchy and build new water and energy facilities, customers of San Francisco's water and power utilities would experience rate increases. The Public Utilities Commission estimates that for every $1 billion in project costs, residential water users in San Francisco would pay between $60 and $170 more annually depending on how costs were distributed among local and regional users of the Hetch Hetchy system. As noted above, these large-scale costs would result not directly from the ordinance, but from voter approval of a future Charter amendment that is specified in the ordinance.

Proposition F: This measure requires 50%+1 affirmative votes to pass.

Proposition F: Vote Yes

San Francisco is an environmental leader. One great exception is when it comes to water:

- We rank *last* in California in water recycling—we recycle 0% of our water;
- We clean streets, wash cars and water parks with pristine Tuolumne River water rather than reclaimed water;
- We discard our 20 inches of annual rainfall through sewers into the Bay and ocean;
- We've virtually abandoned use of renewable local groundwater, using 75% less than we did in 1930;
- Our 100-year-old water system does daily environmental damage to Yosemite National Park;
- We're the only city in America to build a dam in a national park.

It's time to *plan* to do better.

Proposition F is a safe and reasonable measure that simply requires San Francisco to create a plan for our water future.

Prop F caps planning costs at $8 million. No outcome is pre-determined, and nothing can happen without future voter approval.

Prop F creates a public taskforce with environmental and city water experts who will **plan** how San Francisco can:

- Recycle 15% of our water by 2025;
- Increase renewable local groundwater use from 3% to 19%;
- Improve water quality by filtering all drinking water;
- Decrease storm water runoff into San Francisco Bay;
- By 2035, consolidate San Francisco's nine reservoirs into eight and restore Hetch Hetchy Valley to Yosemite National Park;
- Develop renewable energy, wind and solar to offset loss of hydropower.

If San Francisco leaders were truly doing everything possible for water conservation, we wouldn't be ranked last in California for recycling.

It's time for the voters to lead, and let our leaders follow. Vote YES on Prop F.

Yosemite Restoration Campaign
Restore Hetch Hetchy
Planning and Conservation League
Sierra Nevada Alliance
Foothill Conservancy
Earth Island Institute
Wild Equity Institute
Forests Forever
National Parks Conservation Association
Friends of the River

Proposition F: Vote No

We don't agree on everything, but we agree that Prop F would be a disaster for San Francisco.

Prop F is a veiled attempt to destroy Hetch Hetchy Reservoir, which supplies reliable, clean water to 2.6 million people in over 30 cities across the Bay Area. Hetch Hetchy is a cost-effective system that utilizes gravity to deliver water and generates clean, greenhouse-gasfree energy. This energy powers San Francisco's public schools, streetlights, **MUNI**, fire stations, hospitals and other vital city services.

MUNI: The San Francisco Municipal Transportation Agency (SFMTA), which is a department of the City and County of San Francisco responsible for the management of all ground transportation in the city.

Prop F would:

- Force the City to spend *millions of dollars* on a **PLAN** to destroy Hetch Hetchy Reservoir, which stores 85% of the San Francisco's water and generates clean, hydroelectric power.
- Pre-determine the outcome of the plan by coming back to voters in 2016 and asking them to destroy Hetch Hetchy—at a cost of as much as *$10 billion*.
- Jeopardize the water supply for 7% of California's population, as well our source of *publicly-owned hydroelectricity*.

This bad idea has already been studied at least *seven times* in the past 30 years. These studies have shown that not only would the cost be enormous, but San Francisco would experience water shortages *1 out of every 5 years*. It would also cost the City over $40 million annually to replace the clean power—and force municipal agencies to purchase expensive, dirty power.

The City is already pursuing the conservation goals that proponents are using to camouflage their true aim—draining Hetch Hetchy reservoir. We shouldn't waste millions on a plan that would be disastrous for San Francisco. Say no to this "Trojan Horse."

Mayor Ed Lee
Board President David Chiu
Supervisor Eric Mar
Supervisor Mark Farrell
Supervisor Carmen Chu
Supervisor Christina Olague
Supervisor Jane Kim
Supervisor Sean Elsbernd
Supervisor Scott Wiener
Supervisor David Campos
Supervisor Malia Cohen
Supervisor John Avalos

Tim Redmond, "Not Until We Have a Clean Energy System," *Earth Island Journal*, Summer 2012

Tim Redmond, at the time of this article, was executive editor of the *San Francisco Bay Guardian*. In the article he challenges "water dreamers" to recognize that the hydro power the O'Shaughnessy dam produces is a clean-energy supply that cannot easily be replaced, and must be before the dam can be dismantled.

ev

A few years before he died, I heard the legendary environmentalist **David Brower** talk about tearing down the O'Shaughnessy dam in Hetch Hetchy Valley. Oh, he said, it might take a while for nature to return, but slowly, inexorably, it would happen. "Every time a species returned, we'd have a drink," he said. "And in the end, we'd all be drunk and the valley would be restored."

How on Gaia's Green Planet could a booze-loving environmentalist like me possibly be opposed to that? Well, I'm not. I'm all in favor of tearing down the dam, bringing back the glory of John Muir's Holiest Temple and letting the Tuolumne River run wild and free. We just need a few things to happen first.

I'm not going to argue that all of the pristine water from the Hetch Hetchy reservoir is entirely irreplaceable. San Francisco's pretty good at water conservation, but we can get better—and the suburban communities that also use the city's water can do a whole lot better.

Water recycling, better use of rainwater, replacing lawns with native plants ... there are ways to cut water use. But if my friends at Restore Hetch Hetchy think they can tear down the dam and still keep my kids and my dog in drinking water without relying on the overstressed Sacramento-San Joaquin Delta, well, I don't believe it. The widely stated assertion that San Francisco can use other reservoir capacity doesn't stand up to factual scrutiny. There's no way to make this work without tapping into other water sources. A full 85 percent of the water delivered to Bay Area customers from the Hetch Hetchy system originates at O'Shaughnessy Dam.

But even if I give the water-dreamers the benefit of the doubt, there's a larger problem here—one that environmentalists all over the nation need to think about. The giant dam provides not only water but electric power: 1.7 billion kilowatt hours a year of electric power. That's enough to meet the needs of about 414,000 homes. And it does so without burning a single

David Brower: David Brower (1912–2000), a longtime member of the Sierra Club, and its executive director from 1952 to 1969. He founded Friends of the Earth (1969), co-founded the League of Conservation Voters (1969), and established the Earth Island Institute (1982). A prolific author and energetic activist, Brower was a creative and controversial force in the postwar environmental movement.

drop of oil or gas or a single grain of coal dust, or smashing a single atom in a nuclear reactor.

Damming rivers for power is a strategy whose time has passed, but existing large hydro is, by any environmental standard, better than nuclear or fossil fuels. And the sad reality is that no US city, including San Francisco, is in a position now to generate that much power from renewables.

Yes, some power could still be generated with downstream powerhouses— but the city would lose 42 percent of its generating capacity if the dam went away. If that power were replaced with natural-gas-generated electricity, the increased CO_2 emissions would total 387,000 metric tons a year.

There's more to the story, though. The dam was part of an historic compromise between conservationists, who didn't want a dam in a national park, and the public-power advocates, who believed that no private entity should control essential resources like water and electricity. The Raker Act, which allowed the construction of the dam, was supposed to be the Magna Carta of public power in the western United States, a guarantee that cheap hydroelectricity from Hetch Hetchy would prevent private utilities from ever controlling the grid.

That mission has been sidetracked for a century, mostly thanks to the political clout of Northern California utility Pacific Gas and Electric (PG&E). But the dam remains as the potential lynchpin of a new public power movement.

Why is that important? Because I believe the only real hope for a fully renewable energy future is the end of private utilities. No private company wants small, distributed solar; if every house in San Francisco generated its own renewable power, PG&E (which today can't even meet weak state standards for renewables) would be out of business. As the old saying goes, you can't put a meter on the sun. So as long as the private outfits call the shots, big power arrays, nuclear, and fossil fuels will be part of the picture.

I'm a hopeful environmentalist; that's how I keep from losing my mind. And I believe that sometime soon, the private utilities will be declining, cities will use public-power systems to build nonprofit distributed renewables and we won't need large-scale coal, gas, oil, nuclear—or hydro. When that happens—and California gets its water priorities in order—I'll be standing in line to push the button that blows up the Hetch Hetchy dam.

DOCUMENT 42:

Spreck Rosekrans, "Hetch Hetchy: A Century of Occupation in Yosemite National Park," *Maven's Notebook*, 19 December 2013

> Rosekrans is the executive director of Restore Hetch Hetchy, an organization devoted to the restoration of the Hetch Hetchy Valley. His piece recounts the century-long debate over the construction of the O'Shaughnessy Dam and indicates that Restore Hetch Hetchy, after the defeat of Proposition F in 2012, is lobbying Congress to rewrite the 1913 Raker Act to return the valley to Yosemite.

e

California's water wars date back to the Gold Rush, when miners established the right of *prior appropriation* (a legal doctrine known in schoolyards as "first dibs") for water as well as for veins of the precious ore. The wars continued into the early 20th century when a thirsty Los Angeles built aqueducts and pipelines that drained the Owens Valley in the eastern Sierra Nevada.

Controversy rages today over the Bay-Delta Conservation Plan, a proposal to divert water from mountain streams to California's largest cities and farms while bypassing the Sacramento–San Joaquin Delta. The BDCP is, of course, the successor to the 1982 peripheral canal campaign during which the *Los Angeles Times* not so subtly noted that the Hetch Hetchy Aqueduct was already a "peripheral canal."

It was not the pipeline but San Francisco's proposal to build a dam and flood the Hetch Hetchy Valley in Yosemite National Park that drew national attention in the early 20th century. National parks were new at the time, but they had already been widely embraced. More than 200 newspapers across the United States wrote editorials in opposition to building a dam in Yosemite. Despite this opposition San Francisco was successful and, when Pres. Woodrow Wilson signed the Raker Act on December 19, 1913, Hetch Hetchy's fate was sealed.

Three years later, however, Congress, reflecting on the rancorous debate over the Raker Act, passed the National Park Service Act—a law designed to manage our parks for all Americans and to prevent any more such intrusions. Subsequent proposals to build dams in national parks, including Yellowstone and the Grand Canyon, were defeated.

Over the course of the last 100 years, many have called for Yosemite's Hetch Hetchy Valley to be restored. In 1987 Donald Hodel, President Reagan's Secretary of the Interior, called for restoration. The National Sierra Club has repeatedly issued proclamations in favor of returning Hetch Hetchy

Valley to Yosemite National Park. And in 1999, Restore Hetch Hetchy was formed as a single issue organization dedicated to making it happen.

Studies by UC Davis, the Environmental Defense Fund and the California Department of Water Resources have confirmed that San Francisco's water and power needs could be met without the Hetch Hetchy Reservoir. The city would still rely primarily on Tuolumne River diversions, but San Francisco would make modest additional investments in surface and groundwater storage outside Yosemite, or could recycle and conserve water. Other California cities have successfully done far more to reduce the environmental impact of their water systems.

For more than a decade, Restore Hetch Hetchy has attempted to persuade San Francisco city officials to participate in constructive discussion on water system alternatives that would allow Yosemite's Hetch Hetchy Valley to be restored. In 2012, a well-financed and fact-challenged campaign convinced voters not to allow public consideration of alternatives. So Restore Hetch Hetchy is taking the decision-making process to others outside the city.

Restore Hetch Hetchy is pursuing a bipartisan effort in Congress to amend the Raker Act. An amended Raker Act would not affect San Francisco's other reservoirs in the Tuolumne River watershed, nor its pipelines and powerhouses. But an amended Raker Act would return Hetch Hetchy Valley to Yosemite National Park and the American people.

Restore Hetch Hetchy is also pursuing legal challenges to the ongoing operation of San Francisco's water system as a violation of both state and federal law.

One hundred years ago, Congress made a serious environmental mistake. Restore Hetch Hetchy invites our fellow citizens to join us, to correct that mistake, and to make Yosemite National Park whole again.

GLOSSARY OF KEY FIGURES AND TERMS

Conservation: During the Progressive Era (1890–1914), conservation was an umbrella term for the efficient and equitable management of natural resources. The conservation movement was the first in the United States to wrestle with the serious environmental problems that the industrial revolution generated. Many of those who argued for and against the Hetch Hetchy dam were conservationists.

Freeman, John: Freeman was a nationally known engineer who testified in support of the Hetch Hetchy project and designed the resulting water-conveyance system.

Hutchings, James Mason: Through his writings about Yosemite, Hutchings played a crucial role in identifying the Sierran landscape as a tourist haven and cultural landmark.

Muir, John: President of the Sierra Club, and a prolific writer, Muir was central to the framing, timing, and focus of the debate over Hetch Hetchy.

National Park Service: Founded in 1916, in the immediate aftermath of the decision to dam the Tuolumne River in Hetch Hetchy, the Park Service manages national parks, monuments, and historic and cultural sites.

O'Shaughnessy, Michael: An engineer, he designed the arch-gravity dam that inundated Hetch Hetchy, a dam that would be named for him.

Phelan, James: As mayor of San Francisco and later as a citizen, Phelan was an avid promoter of the Hetch Hetchy project.

Pinchot, Gifford: Chief of the US Forest Service, a leading conservationist, a confidant of President Theodore Roosevelt, and advocate for the Hetch Hetchy project.

Preservationism: The idea that the natural world should be protected from human depredation, one of the underlying arguments therefore in opposition to damming Hetch Hetchy.

Raker, John: California congressman whose district included Yosemite, he sponsored legislation that finally led to the construction of the O'Shaughnessy Dam.

Roosevelt, Theodore: Arguably the most environmentally minded president yet to serve in office, Roosevelt sympathized with John Muir's opposition to Hetch Hetchy but was also committed to providing San Francisco with a stable water supply.

Utilitarianism: The belief that the highest use of the natural world is for human benefit, whether for resources (such as the Hetch Hetchy Reservoir) or recreation (such as Yosemite tourism).

Yosemite Indians: Recent research by tribal historians, archaeologists, and anthropologists suggest that upwards of seven different groups managed, utilized, and competed for resources in the Yosemite region in the early nineteenth century. Miwok and Yokut occupied the eastern slope of the Sierra and the Paiute and Mono were established on the western slope. Each also asserted territorial claims to Yosemite and Hetch Hetchy, and each made considerable use of the trails that crisscrossed the Sierras for trade and to participate in ritual and social gatherings.

Yosemite National Park: Although formally established in 1890, its origins date back to President Lincoln's 1864 grant of Yosemite and the Mariposa Grove of Big Trees to the state of California to manage for tourism. The state returned the valley and grove in 1905, uniting these sites with the surrounding park.

SELECT BIBLIOGRAPHY

Brechin, Gray A. *Imperial San Francisco: Urban Power, Earthly Ruin*. Berkeley: U of California P, 1999.

Brinkley, Douglas. *The Wilderness Warrior: Theodore Roosevelt and the Crusade for America*. New York: HarperCollins, 2009.

Brower, Kenneth. *Hetch Hetchy: Undoing a Great American Mistake*. Berkeley: Heyday Books, 2013.

Bureau of Reclamation, Mid-Pacific Region. "Hetch Hetchy: A Survey of Water and Power Replacement Concepts." Prepared on behalf of the National Park Service, 1988

Clements, Kendrick A. "Politics and the Park: San Francisco's Fight for Hetch Hetchy, 1908–1913." *Pacific Historical Review* 48 (1979): 185–215.

Clements, Kendrick A. "Engineers and Conservationists in the Progressive Era." *California History* 58 (1979–80): 282–303.

Cohen, Michael P. *The History of the Sierra Club 1892–1970*. Berkeley: Sierra Club Books, 1988.

Hanson, Warren P. *San Francisco Water and Power: A History of the Municipal Water Department and Hetch Hetchy System*. San Francisco: City of San Francisco, 1985.

Hundley, Norris. *The Great Thirst: Californians and Water—a History*. Berkeley: U of California P, 2001.

Huntley, Jen A. *The Making of Yosemite: James Mason Hutchings and the Origins of America's Most Popular National Park*. Lawrence: UP of Kansas, 2011.

Jones, Holway. *John Muir and the Sierra Club: The Battle for Yosemite*. Berkeley: Sierra Club Books, 1965.

Long, David R. "Pipe Dreams: Hetch Hetchy, the Urban West, and the Hydraulic Society Revisited." *Journal of the West* 34 (July 1995): 19–31.

Madley, Benjamin. *American Genocide: The United States and the California Indian Catastrophe*. New Haven: Yale UP, 2016.

Miller, Char. *Gifford Pinchot and the Making of Modern Environmentalism*. Washington, DC: Island Press, 2001.

Muir, John. *The Yosemite*. Boston: Houghton Mifflin, 1914.

Nash, Roderick. *Wilderness and the American Mind*. 5th ed. New Haven: Yale UP, 2014.

Oravec, Christine. "Conservationism vs. Preservationism: The Public Interest in the Hetch Hetchy Controversy." *The Quarterly Journal of Speech* 70 (November 1984): 444–58.

O'Shaughnessy, Michael M. *Hetch Hetchy: Its Origins and History*. San Francisco: Recorder Publishing, 1934.

Richardson, Elmo. "The Struggle for the Valley: California's Hetch Hetchy Controversy, 1905–1913." *California Historical Society Quarterly* 38 (September 1959): 249–58.

Righter, Robert W. *The Battle Over Hetch Hetchy: America's Most Controversial Dam and the Birth of Modern Environmentalism*. New Haven: Yale UP, 2005.

"San Francisco—Water Supply" (collection of documents about San Francisco's water supply, including Hetch Hetchy). Virtual Museum of the City of San Francisco, www.sfmuseum.net.

Simpson, John W. *Dam! Water, Power, Politics, and Preservation in Hetch Hetchy and Yosemite National Park.* New York: Pantheon, 2005.

The Wilderness Idea: John Muir, Gifford Pinchot, and the First Great Battle for Wilderness. Directed by Lawrence Hott and Diane Garey. Direct Cinema, 1989.

Worster, Donald E. *A Passion for Nature: The Life of John Muir.* New York: Oxford UP, 2008.

PERMISSIONS ACKNOWLEDGEMENTS

California Departments of Water Resources and Parks and Recreation. "Hetch Hetchy Restoration Study," 2006.

Hodel, Donald. "Interview with Secretary of the Interior Donald Hodel," *ENVIRONS*, 1988. Copyright © The Regents of the University of California, Davis campus. Originally published in *ENVIRONS*. Reprinted with permission.

Pope, Carl. "Undamming Hetch Hetchy," *Sierra Magazine*, November/December 1987. Reprinted with permission.

Redmond, Tim. "Not Until We Have Clean Energy," *Earth Island Journal*, 2012. Reprinted with permission.

Rosekrans, Spreck. "Hetch Hetchy: A Century of Occupation in Yosemite National Park," *Maven's Notebook*, 2013. Reprinted with permission.

San Francisco Department of Elections. "Proposition F," November 6, 2012 California election.

From the Publisher

A name never says it all, but the word "Broadview" expresses a good deal
of the philosophy behind our company. We are open to a broad range of
academic approaches and political viewpoints. We pay attention to the
broad impact book publishing and book printing has in the wider world;
for some years now we have used 100% recycled paper for most titles.
Our publishing program is internationally oriented and broad-ranging.
Our individual titles often appeal to a broad readership too; many are
of interest as much to general readers as to academics and students.

Founded in 1985, Broadview remains a fully independent
company owned by its shareholders—not an imprint
or subsidiary of a larger multinational.

For the most accurate information on our books (including
information on pricing, editions, and formats) please
visit our website at www.broadviewpress.com. Our print
books and ebooks are available for sale on our site.

broadview press
www.broadviewpress.com

This book is made of paper from well-managed FSC® - certified forests, recycled materials, and other controlled sources.